LANGUAGES OF THE U.S.S.R.

LANGUAGES OF THE U.S.S.R.

BY

W. K. MATTHEWS

*Professor of Russian in the University of London
and Head of the Department of Language and Literature
at the School of Slavonic and East European Studies, London
Formerly Reader (Docent) in English Philology
in the University of Latvia*

CAMBRIDGE
AT THE UNIVERSITY PRESS
1951

PUBLISHED BY
THE SYNDICS OF THE CAMBRIDGE UNIVERSITY PRESS

London Office: Bentley House, N.W. 1
American Branch: New York

Agents for Canada, India, and Pakistan: Macmillan

Printed in Great Britain at the University Press, Cambridge
(Brooke Crutchley, University Printer)

CONTENTS

List of Illustrations		*page* vii
Preface		ix
Chapter I	The Linguistic Pattern	1
II	Palaeoasiatic Languages	3
III	Uralian Languages	14
IV	Altaic Languages	52
V	North Caucasian Languages	86
VI	South Caucasian Languages	97
VII	Indo-European Languages	102
Appendix I	Tabular Summary	122
II	Language Statistics	125
III	Bibliography	128
IV	Index of Languages and Dialects	156
V	Symbols and Phonetic Values	159
Index		161

LIST OF ILLUSTRATIONS

TEXT-FIGURES

Fig. 1	Diagram of the Soviet Language Stocks	page 2
Fig. 2	Diagram of the Palaeoasiatic Languages	12
Fig. 3	Diagram of the Samoyedic Dialects	20
Fig. 4	Diagram of the Uralian Languages	29
Fig. 5	Diagram of the West Finnic Languages	45
Fig. 6	The Uralian 'Family Tree'	49
Fig. 7	Diagram of the Manchurian (Tungusic) Languages	57
Fig. 8	Diagram of the Mongolian Languages	61
Fig. 9	Diagram of the Turkic Languages	74
Fig. 10	Diagram of the North Caucasian Languages	94
Fig. 11	Diagram of the South Caucasian Languages	98
Fig. 12	Diagram of the Pamiri Dialects	106
Fig. 13	Diagram of the Indo-European Languages	109

MAPS

Map 1	Language Stocks of the U.S.S.R.	xii
Map 2	Uralian and Indo-European Languages	15
Map 3	Palaeoasiatic and Altaic Languages	51
Map 4	North and South Caucasian Languages	85
Map 5	Administrative Divisions of the U.S.S.R.	121

PREFACE

A number of languages, including regional ones, are missing from this survey. The languages of the many national minorities, which constitute small colonies in town and countryside (see И. И. Зарубин, *Список народностей СССР*, Ленинград, 1927), do not strictly enter into our linguistic pattern and, even if admitted, would not alter its characteristic outlines. Among such languages are various Balkan types, Baluchi (Beluji) in Turkestan, the modified Indic of the Gypsies, and marginal languages like Asiatic Eskimo and Aleut, mainly on North-East Siberian islands, Kurdish in Transcaucasia, 'Moldavian' (a Rumanian dialect) in the Moldavian Federal Republic, Finnish in the Carelo-Finnish Republic, and Polish. These languages have their focus of characterisation outside the Soviet frontiers along with the two types of Germanic—German and Yiddish, both of which are used by a considerable body of speakers inside the revised frontiers of the U.S.S.R. and exhibit distinct regional associations, the first with the former German Republic on the lower Volga and the partitioned and annexed East Prussia, the second with White Russia and the Ukraine and the artificially created Birobijan (Jewish Autonomous Province), north of the middle Amur in Eastern Siberia.

For ease of recognition and reference I have yielded to the inertia of tradition and reluctantly abandoned the innovations in nomenclature which I advocated in the epitome of this book 'The Language Pattern of the U.S.S.R.' (*The Slavonic and East European Review*, xxv, 65, London, 1947) and necessarily the Confucian epigraph with which I pointed and emphasised them. My position in this matter remains unchanged. I am still persuaded that, for the sake of clarity, terms like 'Somian' (new to English) for 'Finnic', 'Turanian' for 'Turkic', 'Iverian' for 'South Caucasian', and, for the sake of brevity, terms like 'Aryan' (taken from Sweet by Jespersen) for the awkward and inanimate 'Indo-European' are eminently

PREFACE

desirable. Everyone acquainted with English books on languages, especially those of Eastern Europe and Northern Asia, will, I think, admit that our linguistic name-giving stands in serious need of revision.

In most cases I mechanically reproduce the Russian name and spelling of a particular language (e.g. 'Kirgiz' for 'Kirghiz', 'Uigur' for 'Uyghur', etc.) and leave the name in its radical form, i.e. without the Anglo-Latin ending *-ian* or the Anglo-Greek *-ic*. But I continue to write, e.g., 'Olonecian' for 'Olonets', 'Vepsian' for 'Veps', and 'Vodian' for 'Vote', because these latinised forms are, in my opinion, more appropriate to languages on the eastern perimeter of West European civilisation and because we have no adequate names for many of the West Finnic languages.

Names of places (e.g. Kiev, Verny) are written English fashion, but names of persons, being less general, appear in the more accurate international transcription (e.g. 'Stebnickij' instead of 'Stebnitsky'). The spelling of words in the various languages described is not uniform, and I have compiled a table of phonetic equivalents (see Appendix V) to assist the reader to pronounce them.

The illustrative material comprises sketches and sketch-maps, which I have deliberately made as simple and self-evident as possible by excluding everything but the bare essentials.

I wish to offer my sincere thanks to Professor N. B. Jopson for reading the summary of my book, to which I have referred in an earlier paragraph, to Sir Ellis H. Minns for his kindness and patience in going through a difficult MS. and for his stimulating and valuable suggestions, and especially to the Cambridge University Press for the great skill and scrupulous care with which they have reproduced both text and illustrations.

W. K. MATTHEWS

LONDON 1950

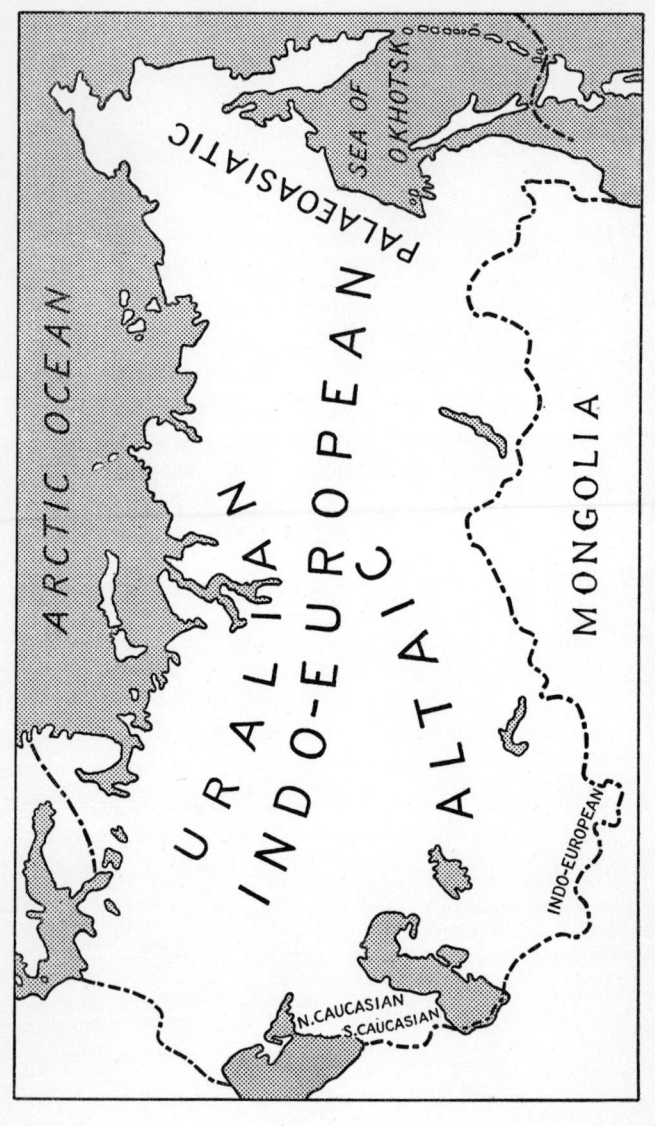

Map 1. Language stocks of the U.S.S.R.

CHAPTER I

THE LINGUISTIC PATTERN

As a linguistic mosaic the U.S.S.R. superficially resembles India. In either case we have a profusion of individual languages, several distinct groups or stocks distributed in a broadly similar fashion, a residue of isolated types, and an Indo-European (Aryan) *lingua franca*, whose lines of expansion run mainly eastwards and southwards. But apart from the ubiquitous Indo-European, none of the other stocks occurs in both countries: North Caucasian, for instance, is as typically Soviet as Dravidian is typically Indian. Bishop Robert Caldwell's correlation of Dravidian with Uralian (his 'Scythian') in 1856, still retained by J. L. Wyatt and T. R. Pillai in their revision of the third edition (1913) of his standard *Comparative Grammar of the Dravidian or South-Indian Family of Languages*, has rarely been taken seriously by competent linguists,[1] and the more recent hypothesis propounded by the Hungarian scholar W. Hevesy, that Uralian is ultimately cognate with Kolarian ('Muṇḍā-Sprachen'),[2] carries as little conviction as Father W. Schmidt's Austric theory,[3] connecting Austroasiatic (including Kolarian) with Austronesian, which it is designed to refute.

The U.S.S.R. has five language stocks—Uralian, Altaic, North Caucasian, South Caucasian, and Indo-European—each with a genetic basis, and a language complex tentatively called Palaeoasiatic,[4] which comprises related and evidently unrelated

[1] F. O. Schrader ('Dravidisch und Uralisch', *Zeitschrift für Indologie und Iranistik*, III, Berlin, 1925) accepts it, and quite recently T. Burrow has tried to substantiate it in a series of papers ('Dravidian Studies', IV–V, *Bulletin of the School of Oriental and African Studies*, London, 1944–5; 'Loanwords in Sanskrit', *Transactions of the Philological Society* (1946), London, 1947).

[2] *Finnisch-ugrisches aus Indien* (Vienna, 1932), whose challenging subtitles read: 'Es gibt keine austrische Sprachfamilie. Das vorarische Indien teilweise finnisch-ugrisch.'

[3] See *Die Sprachfamilien und Sprachenkreise der Erde* (Heidelberg, 1926) and his articles in *Anthropos*, XII–XIII (Salzburg, 1917–18).

[4] This term was first used by Leopold von Schrenck (*Reisen und Forschungen im Amur-Lande in den Jahren 1854–56*, I–IV, St Petersburg, 1856–1900) to cover

languages placed together on geographical grounds and because of a vague general resemblance in sound and structure. The linguistic pattern of the country may be represented geometric-

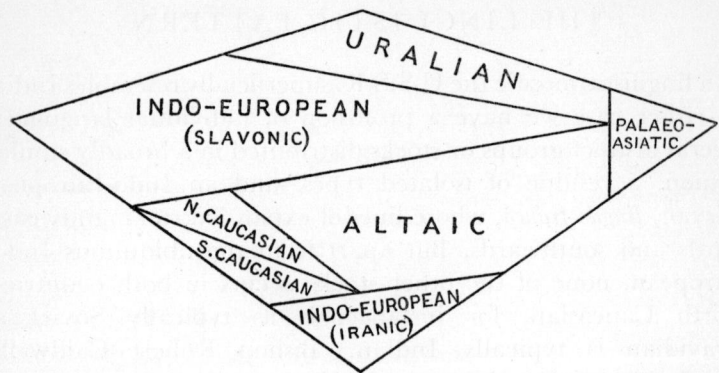

Fig. 1. Diagram of the Soviet language stocks.

ally as follows: a central wedge of Indo-European (Russian) divides a northern, Uralian zone from a southern, Altaic zone, and tapers off towards an eastern, Palaeoasiatic rim, while the mountainous isolation of the Caucasus in the south-west harbours two individual and territorially compact stocks—North Caucasian and South Caucasian—and, like the Pamirs farther east, preserves some ancient fragments of Indo-European.

the North-East Asiatic languages as well as Eskimo and Aleut (Aleutian). He believed these languages to be the remains of the aboriginal speech of Northern Asia.

CHAPTER II

PALAEOASIATIC LANGUAGES

I

The Palaeoasiatic languages are scattered over the Far Eastern littoral of the U.S.S.R., which reaches across more than twenty degrees of latitude from the intercontinental Bering Strait to Korea and includes the island of Sakhalin. They comprehend a knot of three languages—Chukcha (Luoravetlan), Koryak (Nymylan), and Kamchadal (Itel'men), constituting a single stock and spoken from Chukotka to Kamchatka; Yukagir (Odul), the mother-tongue of fewer than 500 persons in Northern Yakutia; Gilyak (Nivkh), used in North Sakhalin and on the lower Amur; Ainu, spoken in South Sakhalin, which was recently annexed from Japan; and the isolated language of the Yenisei Ostyaks (Kets) in Central Siberia.[1] Some of these languages are separated from one another by intruders of Altaic stock (Yakut and Tungus), and all of them have been variously modified by contact with Russian. Ethnic and linguistic idiosyncrasy have been partly recognised by the Soviet administration, which has subdivided the north-easterly (Anadyr') thrust of the Khabarovsk region (*kraj*), where the Palaeoasiatic languages are in use, into a Chukcha (northern) and a Koryak (southern) national area (*okrug*), extending from inner Kamchatka to the Arctic Ocean.

Whether related genealogically or geographically, the Palaeoasiatic languages have common traits, some of which they share with North American (North Amerindian), others with Korean and Japanese. Such considerations have led the Latvian orientalist P. Šmits (Schmidt) to include the last two

---

[1] 'Ostyak' occurs in three tribal names—Yenisei Ostyak, Ostyak Samoyed, and Ostyak proper. In the first two cases it is a misnomer. For Yenisei Ostyak see G. J. Ramstedt, 'Über den Ursprung der sogenannten Jenisejostjaken' (*JSFOu*, XXIV, Helsinki, 1907) and E. Lewy, 'Zum Jenissei-Ostjakischen' (*Ungarische Jahrbücher*, XIII, Berlin-Leipzig, 1933).

in his Palaeoasiatic group.[1] These languages, he observes, prefer initial voiceless consonants to voiced ones; final t tends to become r in Yenisei Ostyak, Gilyak, Ainu, and Korean; and there is no f in Chukcha, Koryak, and Yukagir, and perhaps it was missing in the older forms of the Sakhalin vernaculars, Gilyak and Ainu. Like Eskimo and the Indian languages of North America (e.g. Algonkin),[2] though not necessarily to the same extent, the Palaeoasiatic group shows a tendency to various degrees of incorporation, i.e. to crystallise the verb and its associates into a holophrase, or polysynthetic mass (cf. Chuk. *gelvulin* 'he got a wild reindeer' with Greenland Esk. *naakisarppaa^{i}t* 'they used to pity him').[3] Other peculiarities are: a pattern of vowel harmony, implying a classification of vowels into two contrasted series, the relative scarcity of words with initial voiced consonants, and a system of numeration based on finger and hand.

2

Leopold von Schrenck's purely territorial use of the term 'Palaeoasiatic' involved no attempt to discriminate among the constituent languages. To-day we know much more about them, but we have not yet reached the stage of comparative study, except in the case of the three cognate languages, which have been authoritatively dealt with by W. Bogoras (V. G. Bogoraz-'Tan').[4] The Chukoto-Kamchatkan[5] stock, as Chukcha, Koryak, and Kamchadal are still called by some Soviet

[1] *Ievads valodniecībā* (Riga, 1936).

[2] For linguistic analyses of North American language-types see F. Boas, *Handbook of American Indian Languages*, I–II (Washington, 1911–22) and H. Hoijer, *Linguistic Structures of Native America* (New York, 1946).

[3] See F. Boas, op. cit. Pertinent illustrations will also be found in И. И. Мещанинов, *Общее языкознание* (Ленинград, 1940) and ‚Палео-азиатские языки' (*Известия Академии Наук, отд. лит. и языка*, том VII, вып. 1, Москва-Ленинград, 1948). This author regards Gilyak as the most completely incorporative of the Palaeoasiatic languages and contrasts its systematic incorporation with the episodic incorporation of the rest.

[4] See 'Chukchee' in *Handbook of American Indian Languages*, II (Washington, 1922).

[5] 'Chukotian', a less awkward synonym, is also used.

investigators, following the outmoded fashion of compound epithets, also has a geographical designation, but it serves to describe a linguistic unity. The three languages, viewed structurally, combine a mainly verbal predicate with its subject and attributes, make plentiful use of prefixes, exhibit unequal developments in certain phonetic and grammatical categories (e.g. the marked preponderance of fricatives over plosives, the declinability of nouns and the indeclinability of adjectives, etc.), and have an abundant specialised vocabulary.

The northernmost member of the Chukoto-Kamchatkan or Chukotian stock, Chukcha (Luoravetlan), has a sound-system which emphasises velar articulation (note the prevalence of y, written ь, w, q, $ŋ$), opposes the vowel-series a-e-o and $æ$-i-u in a systematic vowel-harmony, and actively assimilates marginal sounds in syntactic context (e.g. *tot cáj* 'new tea' > *tor cáj*). It distinguishes noun cases (nine, including two comitatives) only in the singular and contrasts these with a solitary absolute-case form in the plural. Separation between adjective and verb is incomplete. The numeration is decimal, but the basic numeral is 'twenty'. Counting literally means 'fingering': 'five' is identical with 'hand', 'ten' with 'hands', 'twenty' with 'man', i.e. the possessor of twenty digits.[1] The transitive-intransitive dichotomy complicates the verbal system, which moreover distinguishes the customary three tenses and has a dual number, present also in the noun but not in the pronoun. Chukcha syntax is diversified by the presence of incorporative complexes[2] (e.g. *na-kьtgьnta-penrь-nat* 'they flung themselves at them at the double, lit. they-at the double-flung themselves-(at) them') and, unlike Koryak, by a variety of conjunctions. The literary

[1] Cf. the common Austronesian *lima* (*rima*), which means both 'hand' and 'five' and the colonial Dutch *vijf* in the sense of 'hand'. Kâte, a Papuan (non-Melanesian) language spoken in the Huon peninsula behind Finschhafen, New Guinea, has words for 'one' and 'two'; 'three' is expressed by 'one and two', 'four' by 'two and two', 'five' by the word for 'hand'; 'ten' is 'two hands', 'twenty'—'man', 'forty'—'two men'. See G. Pilhofer, 'Formenlehre der Kâte-Sprache' (*Zeitschrift für Eingeborenensprachen*, XVII, Berlin, 1927).

[2] Meščaninov (op. cit.) defines incorporation as a 'complex agglutination'.

language, for which a Latin-style alphabet has been devised, seems to be founded on a blend of the inland (Reindeer Chukcha) and maritime (Fishing Chukcha) dialects, which, owing to the nomadic life of the speakers, present no sharp divergences. Chukcha literature, like those of the other primitive North Asiatic peoples, is entirely post-revolutionary: the first book came out in 1932, and a small body of mainly political writing has been published since then.

Koryak (Nymylan), unlike the far more uniform Chukcha, is spoken in eight dialects by about 8000 persons (1936). Its phonetic system includes y (written ь), g (pronounced [γ]), and η, and excludes $š$, z, and f, the last found only in the Karagin dialect, and its vowel harmony, diverging from that of Chukcha, illustrates the opposition of *e-a-o* to *i-e-u*, with *e* present in both series. Morphologically the language is rich in affixes of derivation and has well-articulated systems of declension (with eight cases and three numbers) and conjugation. The pronoun has fewer case-forms than the noun and exhibits the plural only in the absolute case. The Koryak adjective is indeclinable, but distinguishes person, number, and degrees of comparison. As in Chukcha, the verbal paradigm is dominated by the polarity of a transitive and an intransitive conjugation. There are two past tenses, and the present tense functions also as a perfect. Besides the indicative, there are optative, conditional, and subjunctive moods. Syntactically the outstanding features of the language are an unstable word-order, the frequent omission of the subject, and the use of incorporation to create complex units, which are regarded as single words and, as such, are subject to the processes of declension and conjugation. A Latin alphabet, as in Chukcha, was introduced in the 1930's, to be supplanted later by the Cyrillic.[1] Till the Revolution picture-writing, similar to the kind known to Chukcha and Yukagir, was used in Koryak. Now there is a modest literature in its Chauchuven (Cawcuven) dialect.

[1] Cf. in this respect S. N. Stebnickij's manual of Koryak (1935), *Kalikal jejgucewyьkin kaleŋ cawcuvac'ajnaŋ*, 1, with G. M. Korsakov's (1940), which is listed in the Bibliography (Appendix III).

Kamchadal (Itel'men) was used in 1925 by hardly 800 speakers living in the Koryak National Area; the other Kamchadals (c. 3500) already spoke Russian as their mother-tongue. The language is also spoken in Shumshu, the northernmost island of the Kurile (Chishima) chain. Only two of the formerly numerous Kamchadal dialects now survive: Sedanka in the north and Khar'yuz in the south. Both have been influenced by Koryak and especially by Russian. Kamchadal is formally very like its congeners. Its phonetic system however is remarkable for consonantal complexes (e.g. *qtxz, txcz, ksx, ntxł*). It contains the typical Chukotian phonemes of the velar area, viz. *y* (written ь), *w*, *q*, and a velarised *l* of the Russian sort, written *ł*. Vowel harmony occurs in such contrasted pairs as *c'ooqtunuq* ('eight') and *c'aaqtanak* ('nine'). Kamchadal number and case are indicated by suffixes (e.g. *ьnc* 'fish', plur. *ьncen*; *qem-en* 'pits'; *azaz-en* 'ducks'; *qoz qem-enk* 'the reindeer (is) in the pit'; *qoz-an sasq* 'the reindeer's harness'; *inoq k'kexsknьn memanke* 'the ermine has got into the shed'). The numeral system is decimal with a quintal basis (e.g. *c'ooqtunuq* 'eight' < *c'ooq* 'three' and *qugum-tunuq* 'five'). A curiosity of Kamchadal syntax, according to S. N. Stebnickij,[1] is the use of the locative case for the subject, e.g. *isxenk nlalcen pexel* 'father will take (his) cap'; where *isxenk* is the locative case of *isx* (father), and *pexel* the absolute case of the word for 'cap'. Asyndeton is the general rule (e.g. *uxtenk nьnьł łxmen, c'salen, inoqen* 'there are sables, foxes, ermines in the birch spinney').

3

Of the isolated Palaeoasiatic languages, Yukagir is the most northerly. The native name for it is Odul, and, according to Teki Odulok (N. Spiridonov), it is not noticeably incorporative, though it manifests a tendency to form sentence complexes with prefixes and verbal forms. The earliest and still the best authority on the language, V. M. Jochelson, finds parallels

[1] ‚Ительменский (камчадальский) язык‘ (*Труды по лингвистике,* ч. ɪɪɪ, Инст. Народов Севера, Ленинград-Москва, 1934). For simple examples see also *Ntanselqzaalkicen!* 'Let's Learn!' (Leningrad, 1932).

between these features and North American (North Amerindian) speech-habits.[1] Generally speaking, Yukagir is agglutinative and has a 'nominative' syntax in contrast to the 'ergative construction' (*stroj*) of Chukotian. Its phonetic pattern comprises twelve vowels and nearly as many diphthongs balanced by twenty consonants. There is no gender, as in Chukotian and Samoyedic, the latter of which Yukagir resembles in both its nominal paradigm and its verbal system. The noun has eleven cases, the verb two tenses (perfect and imperfect). Only the indefinite and the imperative mood represent the Yukagir verb as finite; all the other modalities (e.g. the definite, the potential) can function as non-verbal parts of speech. Numeration is decimal, plainly superimposed on an earlier trial basis, as in Eskimo and some types of North American; there are words for 'one', 'two', 'three', 'five', and 'ten'; 'four' is 'three and one', 'six' is 'twice three', 'seven' is 'one above that' (i.e. 'six'), 'eight' is 'twice four', and 'nine' is 'one less than ten' (cf. the Roman figure IX, Finn. *yhdeksän* and Est. *üheksa*, both of which mean 'one from ten', i.e. 'nine',[2] and Malay *sĕmbilan* 'nine', lit. 'one taken'). Often there is no formal difference between noun and verb: nouns may be associated with tense and aspect, verbs used as attributes. Yukagir has two dialects—the Tundra dialect, with Lamut (Tungus) loanwords, and the Upper Kolyma dialect, which besides Lamut loans has others from Yakut. Characters resembling those of Chukcha, Koryak, Eskimo, and North American languages are found cut in birch bark: they are partly pure picture-writing, partly stylised. Before the Revolution Yukagir was proscribed in favour of Yakut and Russian; since then a 'culture base' (*kul'tbaza*) has been established and the Yukagir National Area delimited within Yakutia, and from 1930

---

[1] 'Über die Sprache und Schrift der Jukagiren' (*Sitzungsberichte der Geographischen Gesellschaft*, Berlin, 1899).

[2] Cf. also Hungarian *kilenc* 'nine', in which the second element -(n)c appears to represent the eroded form of a word meaning 'ten'. Dravidian illustrates the same phenomenon (e.g. Tamil *onbadu* 'nine' contains *pattu* 'ten').

onwards educational and other works in and on Yukagir have been prepared by the Northern Peoples' Institute (Институт Народов Севера) in Leningrad.

4

Gilyak (Nivkh), according to L. Sternberg,[1] who studied it *in situ* on the Amur and in Sakhalin, shows resemblance to North American and is not related to Ainu, as some investigators have alleged.[2] The language possesses phonetic idiosyncrasies, including aspirated consonants, voiceless *r*, palatalisation and other types of assimilation due to vowel influence, abnormally long vowels ending in a whisper (*ā, ē, ū*), and, apparently, vowel tone. Gilyak has no gender; distinguishes cases, like an agglutinative language (e.g. *mu* 'boat'; allative *mu-rox*; accusative *mu-ax*; ablative *mu-x*); indicates the plural, when needed, with the ending *-xun*;[3] has a verb with two conjugations, one flexional, the other uninflected; makes use of verbal infixes (e.g. *ni vind* 'I go'; *ni viind* 'I shall go'); couples verb and pronoun in the inflected verb (e.g. perfect tense sing. *ni vit* 'I went', *tši vir* 'you went', *hund vir* 'he went'; plur. *myzn vit* 'we went', *tšin vit* 'you went', *izn vit* 'they went'); distinguishes eight classes of tense; and, like the North American languages, forms compounds by the fragmentation of components (e.g. *tšaxr* 'three' and *rak* 'time' coalesce into *tšrak* 'three times').[4] To-day Gilyak is used in schools and at the culture base founded in 1929 on the Tyl in Sakhalin.

[1] 'Bemerkungen über die Beziehungen der Morphologie der giljakischen und amerikanischen Sprachen' (*Der Internazionale Amerikanisten-Kongress*, 1904).
[2] See F. N. Finck, *Die Sprachstämme des Erdkreises* (Leipzig, 1923³).
[3] This appears fragmentarily in the plural forms of personal pronouns: *myz-n* 'we', *tši-n* 'you', *iz-n* 'they'.
[4] S. Elisséèv, 'Langues hyperboréennes' in A. Meillet et M. Cohen, *Les langues du monde* (Paris, 1924), pp. 269–72. A fuller account of Gilyak will be found in Е. А. Крейнович, *Языки и письменность народов Севера*, III (Москва-Ленинград, 1934).

Ainu is spoken not only in South Sakhalin (Karafuto), but in Japan, where it appears to have been an earlier intruder than Japanese and not indigenous.[1] It occupies the southern and eastern peripheral area of the Sea of Okhotsk, including the Shikotan group of the Kuriles, which were annexed to the U.S.S.R. in 1945. Like Gilyak, Yukagir, Korean, and Japanese, it appears to be an isolated language. The phonetic structure of Ainu is simple and harmonious: there are no voiced plosives, no *l*, except dialectally as a modification of *r*, and the eight vowels include the basic ('alphabetic') five. The expiratory stress is not marked, but the length of the vowel is associated with modifying tones, and these may have semantic value ($\bar{e}$ 'to eat'; *e* 'to come'). Structurally Ainu resembles Korean and Japanese in being a loosely agglutinative language. It has no morphemes of gender and number, and syntactic relationships are indicated by word-order and by auxiliary words, which are mainly postpositional (e.g. *ainu kot tšisei* 'the man's house'; *seta otta kore* 'give it to the dog'). Personal pronouns are repeated for emphasis, as in Melanesian and Bantu (e.g. *kuani ku nukara* 'I see, lit. my being, I see'). Adjectives are mainly invariable, but may indicate the plural with the particle *pa* (e.g. *pirika* 'bonus', *pirikapa* 'boni'). The verb, in its turn, uses auxiliary particles to indicate time (e.g. *ku kik nisa* 'I shall beat'), mood, including the hypothetical, concessive, and potential, and voice, the last by using *an* 'to be' (e.g. *e kik an* 'thou art beaten'). In numeration the decimal and vigesimal systems coexist: the word *ašikne* 'five' is etymologically related to the word 'hand' (*aške*); from 'six' to 'ten' the subtractive method is used (e.g. *iwan* 'six' < *ine* 'four' and *wan* 'ten'); from 'ten' to 'twenty' the additive (e.g. *šine ikašima wan* 'eleven', i.e. $1+10$), and after 'twenty' (*hotne*), the multiplicative (e.g. *ine hotne* 'eighty'; cf. *quatre-vingts*), or the multiplicative and subtractive together (e.g. *wan e ašikne hotne* 'ninety', i.e. $5 \times 20 - 10$). The Ainu sentence

[1] Л. Я. Штернберг, „Айнская проблема" (*Гиляки, орочи, гольды, негидальцы, айны*, Хабаровск, 1933).

demands the subject at the beginning and the verb at the end, with the result that complements and subordinate clauses precede the verb.[1]

6

The agglutinative features of Yukagir rather than Ainu recall those of the most isolated and most westerly member of the Palaeoasiatic group, viz. Yenisei Ostyak, which along with the extinct Kot is represented by M. A. Castrén in his *Versuch einer jenissei-ostjakischen und kottischen Sprachlehre* (St Petersburg, 1858) as somewhat reminiscent of Uralian (q.v.). Yenisei Ostyak (Ket) has a phonetic structure like those of the more primitive Uralian types, the stress mostly on the first syllable, no gender, -*n*/-*ŋ* as the predominant plural suffix (e.g. Y.O. *fīg* 'man', plur. *fīgen*; Kot *iti* 'tooth', plur. *itaŋ*), and a set of eight nominal cases, including a prosecutive, a comitative, and a caritive in both numbers. Adjectives distinguish morphologically between definite (attributive) and indefinite (absolute) function (e.g. Y.O. def. *kuojäm* 'empty', indef. *kuojä*). The numerals show subtractive forms for 'eight' (Y.O. *ynä bēse xō*) and 'nine' (Y.O. *xusä bēse xō*), viz. $10-2$ and $10-1$ respectively. The present tense contains the future, as in West Finnic (q.v.), and very few verbs have personal indices. Yenisei Ostyak has been occasionally equated since Trombetti[2] with languages of Sinitic stock, notably Tibetan, but the available evidence is insufficient to make such a hypothesis tenable. This is yet another instance of linguistic fancy outstripping sober research.[3]

7

It is not improbable that in earlier, unchronicled times speakers of Palaeoasiatic languages occupied the greater part of Eastern Siberia, and that their habitat extended far enough south to

[1] For an account of Ainu see S. Elisséèv, 'La langue aïnou', in A. Meillet et M. Cohen, *Les langues du monde* (Paris, 1924), pp. 263–7.
[2] *Elementi di glottologia*, I–II (Bologna, 1922–3).
[3] See E. Lewy, 'Zum Jenissei-Ostjakischen' (*Ungarische Jahrbücher*, XIII, Berlin-Leipzig, 1933) and 'Languages of the Old Eurasian Region' (*Transactions of the Philological Society*, 1943, London, 1944).

include Manchuria and even the north-east of China, for Šmits (op. cit.) detects Palaeoasiatic features in Manchu and North Chinese (Mandarin) phonetics. The extinct Kots, who lived on the Agul, an affluent of the Yenisei, and whose language, as described by Castrén,[1] is more archaic than its congener Yenisei Ostyak (Ket), and, according to Šmits, the Bohais, who once occupied the Pacific coast of Siberia between the Amur estuary and

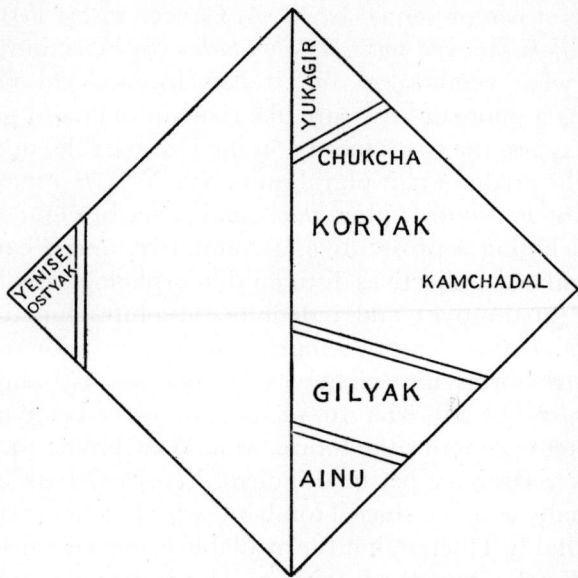

Fig. 2. Diagram of the Palaeoasiatic languages.

Korea, and the ancient 'I-chia', known till the Christian era in the north-east corner of China, were Palaeoasiatics. At the present time however linguistic geography finds the Palaeoasiatic languages, except Yenisei Ostyak, confined to a remote and marginal eastern zone, already penetrated by alien speech (Altaic and Indo-European), and in spite of encouragement given by the Soviet authorities, they are probably doomed to extinction in a not too distant future.

[1] Op. cit. and *Nordiska resor och forskningar* (Helsinki, 1852–8).

PALAEOASIATIC LANGUAGES

Whether the Palaeoasiatic peoples of prehistory possessed a higher culture than the hunting, fishing, and reindeer-keeping tribes of to-day is not known. But one thing seems clear: the common word for 'mother', found even in Korean and Japanese, points to an original matriarchate. Gilyak is particularly instructive here: the aboriginal *ömök* means 'mother', whereas 'father' (*ötik*) appears to be a later loan-word (cf. Khalkha Mongolian *ecege*).

CHAPTER III

URALIAN LANGUAGES

I

Against the Palaeoasiatic zone, which follows the Pacific littoral, two genetic stocks abut in broad, horizontal bands, viz. the Uralian, stretching across tundra and taiga from the Baltic Sea to Yakutia, and the Altaic, stretching across steppe and sand from the Crimea to the relatively recent Tungus (Lamut) lands of the Sea of Okhotsk.

Since the earlier half of the nineteenth century, when Castrén, Hunfalvy, and Böhtlingk accepted W. Schott's[1] 'Uralo-Altaic' hypothesis, correlating Uralian and Altaic genetically in virtue of shared vowel harmony, and since the later and more considered views of H. Winkler, who extended the linguistic limits of the complex to include Korean and Japanese,[2] attempts have not been lacking (e.g. A. Sauvageot's)[3] to establish a Uralo-Altaic unity, in spite of O. Donner's insistence on the obvious need for a preliminary detailed study of individual languages.[4] Unfortunately, and notwithstanding the recent valuable work of Soviet scholars, the absence of an adequate comparative grammar of the two stocks, especially of Altaic,[5] makes it impossible to go beyond superficial speculations, and the existing dichotomy of Uralian and Altaic must be allowed to remain. Centuries of geographical proximity have no doubt contributed something to the undeniable, if vague,

[1] *Versuch über die tatarischen Sprachen* (Berlin, 1836).
[2] *Uralaltaische Völker und Sprachen* (Berlin, 1884); *Der uralaltaische Sprachstamm, das Finnische und das Japanische* (Berlin, 1909); and *Die altaische Völker- und Sprachenwelt* (Breslau, 1921). Incidentally, in 1928, G. J. Ramstedt ('Remarks on the Korean Language', *MSFOu*, LVI, Helsinki) adduced proof of the relationship of Korean and Altaic.
[3] *Recherches sur le vocabulaire des langues ouralo-altaïques* (Paris, 1930).
[4] 'Die uralaltaischen Sprachen' (*FUF*, Helsinki, 1902).
[5] J. Grunzel's *Entwurf einer vergleichenden Grammatik der altaischen Sprachen* (Leipzig, 1895) is only a sketch.

Map 2. Uralian and Indo-European languages.

likeness between them. Vowel harmony (synharmonism) characterises most languages of both stocks; there are widespread traces of the Uralian type of consonantal alternation (*Stufenwechsel*, Finn. *astevaihtelu*, Hung. *fokváltakozás*) discovered by E. N. Setälä; the phonetic systems exhibit points of resemblance (e.g. the occurrence of rounded front vowels and the avoidance of initial consonant-groups); the morphological features include agglutination in various stages of development; there are similar personal pronouns; and some investigators have even collected a skeleton common vocabulary of words expressing rudimentary nominal and verbal notions, but excluding the numerals.

2

The Uralian languages of the U.S.S.R. separate into three branches—Samoyedic, Ugrian, and Finnic (Somian[1]). The essential unity of the Samoyedic dialects or languages with Ugrian and Finnic was confirmed in epitome a generation ago by E. N. Setälä.[2] It is obvious not only in structure but in vocabulary (cf. Yur. Sam. *sawa* 'good', *jaha* 'river', *maṇ* 'I', *lъ* 'bone', *jileş* 'to live', *tu* 'fire', *haḷa* 'fish', *pa* 'tree', *ne* 'woman', *jaBeş* 'to drink', Tav. Sam. *ṇim* 'name', Ost. Sam. *pelæk* 'half', with the corresponding words in Finnish, viz. *hyvä, joki, minä, luu, elää, tuli, kala, puu, nainen, juoda, nimi, puoli*), which however does not include more than two doubtfully shared numerals, namely 'one' and 'seven' (cf. Ost. Sam. *okkʏr* 'one' with Finn. *yksi*, Yur. Sam. *sibiw* 'seven' with Finn. *seitsemän*). A trend towards vowel harmony and a consonantal alternation of Finnish type exist as phonetic peculiarities beside notable morphological resemblances in noun cases, the pronouns, especially interrogative and possessive, and verbal forms (preterite, imperative, subjunctive). Samoyedic is distinctly

[1] The designation used in East Baltic scholarship. I suggest it here seriously to obviate the use of the invariably confounded 'Finnic' and 'Finnish', the stock and the member.
[2] 'Zur Frage nach der Verwandtschaft der finnisch-ugrischen und samojedischen Sprachen' (*JSFOu*, xxx, Helsinki, 1913–18).

agglutinative, but with palpable marks of flexion and even traces of amorphism.

The five extant types of Samoyedic are spoken by a small nomadic community (c. 21,000) scattered over a wide expanse of cold desert, which extends from the Khatanga Gulf, east of the Taimyr peninsula, to the White Sea, where the Lappish world begins, as well as over the islands of Novaya Zemlya. Yurak (Nenets), of which there are two dialects (Taiga and Tundra), is spoken from the Kanin peninsula to the estuary of the Yenisei river, Yenisei (Enets) along its lower course, Tavgi (Nganasan) in Taimyr, Ostyak Samoyed (Sel'kup) in the basin of the upper Ob', and Kamass by a tiny remnant of a mostly turkicised tribe living in the Turkic-speaking country north of the Altai range. According to P. J. von Strahlenberg[1] and P. S. Pallas[2] other languages belonged to this stock in the eighteenth century, viz. Sagai, Kacha, Koibal, Motor (Madur), Karagass, and Soyot (Tuva), all of which are now members of a branch of Altaic.[3] The resemblances between the Samoyedic languages may be illustrated by the following transitive (objective) verbal forms: Tav. *matabama* 'I cut it' (past tense), *matabara* 'you cut it', *matabatu* 'he cut it'; Yur. *madaw, madar, madada*; Yen. *mota, motaro, motada*. But on the whole the discrepancies between individual languages in forms and vocabulary are appreciable.

Taken separately the four principal types of Samoyedic exhibit the following features. Yurak (Nenets), the best-known member, has the usual five letter-vowels of the Latin alphabet, all of which may be long or short, besides long and short *ə* and *y* (written ь). The consonantal system shows a preponderance of plosives, which include the glottal *h*, known to the I.P.A. as [?]. Palatalisation, indicated, as in Latvian, by a subliteral comma (e.g. *l̦*), is frequent in sounds of the labial, dental, and alveolar

---

[1] *Das Nord- und Ostliche Theil von Europa und Asia* (Stockholm, 1730).

[2] *Reise durch die verschiedenen Provinzen des russischen Reichs*, I–III (St Petersburg, 1776–1801).

[3] The Yakut-speaking Dolgans on the Kheta and Khatanga rivers, in the Taimyr or Dolgan-Nenets National area, also appear to have once used a Samoyedic language.

areas. Yurak stress is unstable and not well marked. Assimilation and apophony (Ablaut) of both vowels and consonants occur, the former representing a kind of vowel harmony (e.g. nom. sing. *ŋuda* 'hand', loc. sing. *ŋudahana*; nom. sing. *ŋano* 'boat', loc. sing. *ŋanohona*). Noun and verb are not clearly distinguished from each other, and the former is capable of combining with suffixes of the intransitive verb (e.g. *pьdar ŋuḍan* 'thou art small', *pьdar ŋuḍanaş* 'thou wast small'; cf. *pьdar ton* 'thou hast come', *pьdar tonaş* 'thou camest'). The noun has six oblique cases, including a lative, and there are three numbers. The system of declension is complicated by the presence of possessive suffixes (e.g. nom. sing. *nişa* 'father', *nişami* 'my father', gen. *nişani*, dat. *nişahani*), which are also used predicatively for sentence-building (e.g. *maŋ hasawam* 'I am a man', *pьda hasawa* 'he is a man'). Yurak numeration is decimal, with etymological traces of earlier systems (e.g. *sidntet* 'eight' means 2 × 4). Conjugation represents the intersection of mood (hypothetical, conditional, auditive, etc.), tense (aorist and preterite), person, and threefold number. The verb distinguishes an objective (transitive) form, which incorporates the object (e.g. 1st sing. aorist *madaw* 'I cut it'), from a subjective (intransitive) form. The subject of the sentence usually stands at the beginning, the verb in most cases at the very end; the qualifier precedes the qualified; the object and adverbs precede the verb.

Tavgi (Nganasan), Yenisei (Enets), and Ostyak Samoyed (Sel′kup) have similar phonetic systems to Yurak. In all three cases the vowel pattern shows the presence of centralised types (i, $ə$), and Ostyak Samoyed has ø (written *ө*), æ, and *y*. The consonants too are the most chequered in this language and include several part-voiced phonematic variants absent in the other Samoyedic types. The grammatical structure is much the same in the various representatives of Samoyedic, though characteristic differences of detail are numerous enough (e.g. the Ostyak Samoyed adverbial ending *-k* in *somak* 'well'; cf. *tat somak mesal* 'you have done well' with *soma gup* 'good man'). The principal differences are mainly lexical (e.g. Yur. *nişa* 'father', Tav. *jase*; Yen. *yōb* 'one', Ost. Sam. *okkьr*).

Speakers of Samoyedic languages are racially Mongoloid and leiotrichous, and some scholars incline to the view that they learnt their present language from Uralian conquerors in the Stone Age prior to 3000 B.C. This would imply that their ancestry lived much farther south. And if, as seems likely, the present-day Turkic-speaking Dolgans, Koibals, Kamasses, Motors, Karagasses, and Soyots were formerly Samoyedic in speech, the earlier domain of the Samoyeds must certainly have been more hospitable than the one they now inhabit.

According to Kai Donner,[1] the dissolution of Uralian unity took place several millennia before our era, for Samoyedic has no Indo-European loan-words. These are found only in Ugrian and Finnic, and go back to c. 2000–3000 B.C. The study of West Siberian place-names reveals that the Ugrian Ostyaks wrested part of their present habitat on the Irtysh tributaries Vakh and Vasyugan from the Ostyak Samoyeds (Sel'kups). The Samoyeds were the first Uralians to enter Siberia, and their first contacts were with the Turkic representatives of the Altaic-speaking peoples, whose point of dispersion is thought to have lain to the east of Lake Baikal. Uralian culture was that of food-gathering, hunting, and fishing tribes in the Stone Age. The Uralians appear to have known a metal (copper), tamed the dog and perhaps the reindeer, bartered furs, been organised in clans, and possessed elementary numeration and the rudiments of religion (e.g. the conception of the soul). All these assumptions are founded on the comparative study of lexical material.[2] This also gives an adequate notion of the foreign contacts of each Samoyed tribe. The Yuraks seem to have been the first to name the Russian, viz. 'Lūtsa', which is presumably derived from the Varangian 'Roþs' (cf. Finn. *ruotsa-lainen* 'Swede'). The Ostyak Samoyed (Sel'kup) name 'Rus' is a later loan-word, borrowed after the change of *r* into *l*, and 'Kazak' ('bandit') is a loan from Turkic. The same Ostyak Samoyeds call the Tungus, an Altaic people, 'Pombak', and appear to have borrowed this

[1] *Siperia* (Helsinki, 1933).
[2] See E. N. Setälä, 'Suomensukuisten kansojen esihistoria' (in the symposium *Suomen suku*, I, Helsinki, 1926).

designation from the Yenisei Samoyeds. The Yuraks have loans from Zyryan (Komi), a Finnic language, partly through Ugrian. The Ugrians learnt reindeer-keeping from the Samoyeds, and the Samoyeds stock-breeding from the Turkic peoples, whose influence in a different sphere may be seen in some structural features of Samoyedic (cf. the Ost. Sam. comparative suffix -*la(qь)* with Turk. -*rak*, and the infinitive ending -*qo* with Turk. -*k*).

To-day the territories occupied by the Samoyeds have been divided into three national areas—one in Europe and two in

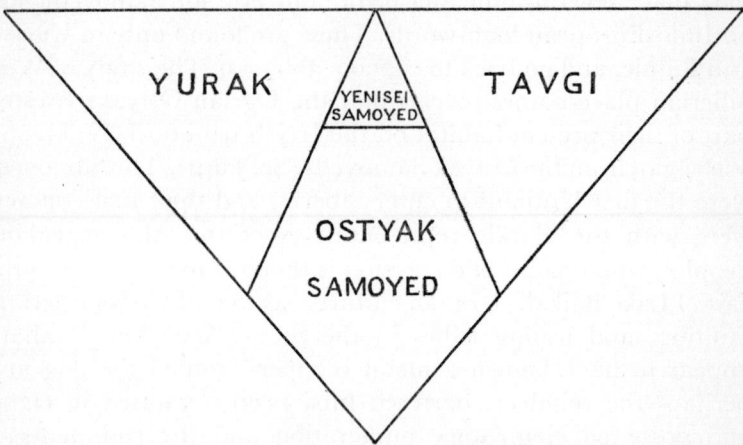

Fig. 3. Diagram of the Samoyedic dialects.

Siberia—viz. the Nenets (Nenecia) from the Kanin peninsula to the Kara river, with the administrative centre at Naryan-Mar (formerly Pustozersk), the Yamal, taking in the Yamal peninsula and the entire Ob' estuary (capital Salekhard, formerly Obdorsk), and the extensive Taimyr National Area between the mouth of the Yenisei and the lower Khatanga basin (capital Dudinka).

3

Ugrian and Finnic are often hyphenated as Finno-Ugrian. The Ugrian languages are in many ways the more conservative, and the more primitive of them, Ostyak and Vogul, both spoken in an autonomous enclave (the Khanty-Mansi National Area) of the Omsk province in Western Siberia (i.e. the lower basins of the Ob' and the Irtysh below Tobol'sk), still cling to approximately those parts from which the original dispersion of the Uralians is supposed to have taken place. To-day the westernmost and entirely isolated Ugrian outpost is in Hungary, where for over a millennium the numerically and culturally most important Uralian language was moulded into its present shape under Slavo-German and Turkish influences. But Hungarian has developed outside the U.S.S.R., as indeed have the other two cultivated Uralian languages, Finnish and Estonian.

The 'primitive' or East Ugrian languages, Ostyak and Vogul, are referred to, along with Hungarian, by the name (Yugra)[1] which was used to designate their territory in medieval Arabic records and Russian annals. One Arab author of the ninth century mentions bartering Bolgar swords with the Yura(!) tribes for furs.[2] At that time Yugra appears to have meant the sources of the river Pechora. Later the Ugrians moved across the Urals into Siberia as the bearers of a Bronze Age (chalcolithic) culture, for place-names testify to their cis-Uralian origin. Their first contacts with the Russians took place c. 1000 as a result of Novgorodian forays. In the thirteenth century Yugra became a Novgorodian province (*volost'*), but from that time till the early seventeenth century there was strong Ugrian opposition to the Russians (e.g. the Vogul prince Asyka harried Komia in 1455).[3] The long resistance of the Ugrians to Russian encroachment proves that they once had a much higher culture than they have to-day. Christian mission-work was done among them under Peter the Great, but incompletely, and there are adherents of the older religion even at the present time. Racially the Siberian Ugrians are not pure: Samoyed strains

[1] Setälä (op. cit.) derives 'Ugri' from Ονογουροί, explaining this name as compounded of Turk. *on* 'ten' and *ogur*, the latter a development of O.Turk. *oguz*. The change of *z* into *r* is peculiar to Bolgar-Chuvash. See also M. Zsirai, *Finnugor népnevek*, 1. *Jugria* (Budapest, 1930).

[2] See I. Manninen, *Soome-sugu rahvad* (Tartu, 1929).

[3] See A. Kannisto, 'Der Wogulenfürst Asyka in Chroniken und Volkstradition' (*FUF*, XIV, Helsinki, 1914).

are noticeable in the north, Russo-Tartar in the south. It has been conjectured that, like the Samoyeds and the Lapps, the Ugrians were not originally Uralian in speech.

Of the two Siberian Ugrian peoples, the Ostyaks are to-day the more vigorous numerically: there are 23,000 of them as against about 6000 Voguls. They call themselves 'Hanti-hə' or 'Hanty' (Russ. Khanty), not 'Ostyak', a name perhaps derived from Ost. *As jah* ('Ob' people'), and the Voguls call themselves 'Mansi', which Setälä (op. cit.), following up an idea of Reguly's, equates with the first syllable of 'Magyar', and V. N. Černecov[1] with Finn. *mies* 'man'. Ostyak (Khanty) is spoken in seven dialects and has a complex vowel-system, comprising full and reduced, long and short phonemes, and a notable variety of consonants, including voiceless nasals (in the Middle Ob' dialect), unvoiced plosives, labialised velars, palatalised *s*, *n*, *l*, and several other types of the 'liquid'. The stress is usually final. Like all the other Uralian languages, Ostyak has no gender and makes no formal difference between noun and adjective. It retains the dual number, has a paradigm of six cases (three formal), extended by postpositions (e.g. *jeŋk əhtinь* 'on the ice') and suffixed pronouns, uses a typically Finno-Ugrian system of numeration, is limited in mood and tense, and, like Samoyedic, Mordvin (q.v.), and Hungarian, isolates an 'objective conjugation' (Hung. *tárgyas igeragozás*).[2] Ostyak secular literature began in 1931 with the help of a latinised alphabet. In 1937 Cyrillic was substituted for this as in many other instances.

Vogul (Mansi) closely resembles both Ostyak and Hungarian. Its phonetic structure is like that of Ostyak, except that the 'suprasegmental' length phoneme is not exploited semantically to the same extent, and the *o*-phoneme has an open and a close variant. The system of declension is as simple, and there is also the familiar set of possessive suffixes, which, like the paradigm

[1] See Г. М. Прокофьев, *Языки и письменность народов Севера*, I (Москва-Ленинград, 1937).

[2] J. Pápay, 'Über die Objektivkonjugation im Nordostjakischen' (*FUF*, XIII, Helsinki, 1913); D. Fokos, 'A vogul-osztják tárgyas igeragozásról' (*NyK*, XL, Budapest, 1911).

of cases, is complicated by a dual. In the verb we have the transitive-intransitive antithesis, and this, as in Ostyak and Hungarian, is marked off by special morphemes (e.g. *varmum* 'I do', *varumlum* 'I do it', *varum* 'he does', *varumte* 'he does it'). Syntactically Vogul displays the Samoyedic rigidity by using subject and verb as the initial and final members of the sentence respectively (e.g. *ne vit toti* 'the woman carries water, lit. woman water carries'). Like Ostyak, but not the more developed Hungarian, Vogul remains mostly within the limits of the simple sentence. The lexical affinities of the three Ugrian languages may be illustrated here with a few parallels, viz. Vog. *sem*, Ost. *sem*, Hung. *szem* 'eye'; Vog. *min-*, Ost. *man-*, Hung. *men-* 'to go'; Vog. *hot*, Ost. *hət*, Hung. *hat* 'six'; Vog. *man*, Ost. *muŋ*, Hung. *mi* 'we'; Vog. *jole*, Ost. *ił(i)*, Hung. *alá* 'down'. Consider also the following morphological equations:

	Vogul	Ostyak	Hungarian
Sing.			
1	*hapum* 'my boat'	*hopem* 'my boat'	*kezem* 'my hand'
2	*hapun*	*hopen*	*kezed*
3	*hape*	*hopbł* (*hopł*)	*keze*
Plur.			
1	*hapuw*	*hopev*	*kezünk*
2	*hapan*	*hopbn*	*kezetek*
3	*hapanbl*	*hopeł*	*kezük*
Sing.			
1	*varmum* 'I do' (intrans.)	*małbm* 'I give' (intrans.)	*nyelek* 'I swallow' (intrans.)
2	*varmbn*	*małbn*	*nyelsz*
3	*varum*	*mał*	*nyel*
Plur.			
1	*varmuv*	*małuv*	*nyelünk*
2	*varmen*	*małti*	*nyeltek*
3	*varmbt*	*małbt*	*nyelnek*

The relations between Vogul and Ostyak are naturally closer than those of either with Hungarian, and this applies to both structure and vocabulary. Like Ostyak, Vogul, for instance, has a dual number, and both share loans from Samoyedic, Zyryan, Tartar, and Russian. Though spoken by only some

6000 persons, it has seven dialects, the northern and the eastern being the predominant ones. The first Vogul book—two Gospels in Latin script—was published in 1868, the first primer in 1903. Vogul research in the U.S.S.R. began in earnest with the foundation of the Northern Department at the Leningrad Oriental Institute in 1926. This developed into an independent institution—the Northern Peoples' Institute—and has had the services of V. N. Černecov and his wife, who have published Vogul readers and collections of Vogul folk-tales.[1] The Černecovs' work now takes its place beside the classical folk-song collections of the Hungarians Reguly and Munkácsi.[2] Conditions among the Voguls have improved with the establishment of a 'culture base' and are favouring the growth of the language.

4

The Uralians in closest contact with the Ugrians, apart from the 'aboriginal' Samoyeds, are the Zyryans (Komi). These and the remaining Uralians belong to the Finnic (Somian) branch, which distinguishes three separate and conspicuous types of language—the Permian, the East Finnic (Volgan), and the West Finnic (Baltic).

The Permian branch, which comprises two languages, Zyryan and Votyak (Udmurt), is in some respects a link between Ugrian and Finnic, and it is important both linguistically and historically. Its linguistic importance derives from the distinction that Zyryan, after Hungarian, whose oldest document, a funeral oration (*A Halotti Beszéd és Könyörgés*), goes back to c. 1200, is the earliest recorded Uralian language, St Stefan of Perm' having devised an alphabet for it in the second half of the fourteenth century, and its historical importance is due to the mention of the Beormas in King Alfred's

---

[1] E.g. V. Černecov, *Iļpi ļonh̥h* 'The New Trail' (Leningrad, 1933); I. Černecova, *Mansi mojt* 'Vogul Tales' (Leningrad, 1936). For the work of the Černecovs see the article by Alo Raun, 'Mõnda soome-ugri hõimust—vogulitest' (*Päevaleht*, Tallinn, 1936).

[2] See P. Hunfalvy, *A vogul föld és nép* (Budapest, 1864) and B. Munkácsi, *Vogul népköltési gyüjtemény*, I–IV (Budapest, 1892–6).

record of the voyages of the Norwegian navigator Óttarr or Ohthere (ninth century) and of the Bjarmar in Snorri Sturluson's *Heimskringla* (c. 1220–30). The first appears to be an original interpolation in King Alfred's version of the early fifth-century *Historiae adversus paganos* by Paulus Orosius. Alfred says that his informant thought the Beormas to be a numerous people, who spoke the same language as the Finnas (Lapps). This would lend colour to the hypothesis that the Beormas were West Finnic.[1] Alfred however adduces no linguistic material, and there are only two significant names in the Icelandic source. In that part of Snorri's work which contains the biography of King Óláfr Haraldsson (St Olav), we read of an expedition to Bjarmeland (1206) made by Karl and Gunsteinn, both of Hálogaland, like Óttarr, and how these with Þórir Hundr desecrated the image of Jomala, the deity of the Bjarmar, in spite of Þórir Hundr's warning: 'Let none be so presumptuous as to rob him.' The name of the idol suggests the West Finnic word for 'God' (cf. Finn. *Jumala*, Lapp. *Jupmel*, originally perhaps 'heaven'). On the other hand, 'Beormas' and 'Bjarmar' may be variants of the name which is recorded in the Old Russian chronicles as 'Perm'' and survives to this day in the Russian designation of the southern Zyryans as Permyaks.

Separating from their Votyak kinsmen, with whom till the eighth century they were the bearers of the Iron-Age Permian culture, the Zyryans began to migrate in the ninth towards the north and west, into the 'Ugrian' valley of the Pechora. They made contact with the Carelians on the Northern Dvina (Finn. Viena) in the tenth century and probably absorbed their Carelian loans then, but the contact was of relatively short duration, because the two peoples were divided at an early date by a wedge of Russian intruders. The First Novgorod Chronicle (a fourteenth-century MS.) mentions the levying of tribute on Zyryans and Ugrians alike in the eleventh century, but Russian colonisation did not seriously begin till the thirteenth. In the next century this was intensified as the result of the missionary activities of St Stefan. Zyryan resistance

[1] A. S. C. Ross, *The Terfinnas and Beormas of Ohthere* (Leeds, 1940).

to the Russians was less dogged and implacable than Ugrian, and Moscow ultimately completed without undue effort the conquest that Novgorod had begun.

To-day Zyryan is the language of over 400,000 speakers. It has several dialects, including the Vychegda-Pechora (Zyryan proper) and the Kama (Permyak). The modern literature is based on the former in the Komi Autonomous Republic (capital Syktyvkar, formerly Us'tsysol'sk) and on the latter in the Sverdlovsk province, which contains the Komi-Permyak National Area (capital Kudymkar). The Komi-Permyak territory comprises part of the Kama river basin, and this perhaps gives the Komi people their name, unless, as some incline to think, 'Komi' is cognate with the Indo-European root for 'man' (cf. Lat. *homo*, Goth. and O.E. *guma*).

Permyak, described in detail by I. I. Maišev,[1] may be taken as representative of Permian. The phonetic system of this language contains seven vowels, among them *ö* and *y* (written ы) and is typically triangular. Its varied consonants, which include voiced and voiceless correlatives lacking in West Finnic, present a Russian-style palatal series of dentals and alveolars. Initial syllables are generally stressed. The Permyak noun declension numbers seventeen oblique cases, including a possessive (*bośtan*), genitive (*asalan*), conjunctive (*ötlaötan*), privative (*emtömtan*), comparative (*ordčalan*), finitive (*loktan*), inceptive (*pyran*), approximative (*sibötan*), disjunctive (*ylyntan*), translative (*vudžan*), and limitative (*dortan*). This complex system becomes still more involved by the intrusion of numerous postpositions and of a well-articulated paradigm of possessive suffixes (e.g. *kiyt* 'thy hand', gen. *kiytlön*, poss. *kiytliś*, etc.). The adjective is indeclinable, but the pronoun has a complete set of cases. In contrast to the complexity of the noun and pronoun, we have the relative simplicity of the verb, which, unlike its West Finnic counterpart, has a future and two past tenses, but only two effective moods—the indicative and the imperative. The system of tenses is modified, as often in

[1] И. И. Майшев, *Грамматика коми-пермяцкого языка* (Москва-Ленинград, 1940).

Uralian, by aspective suffixes, and the *verbum finitum* is contrasted with various forms of the *verbum infinitum*, and the affirmative with a negative conjugation. The Permyak, like the Zyryan, vocabulary contains Iranic, Chuvash, and Russian loans.

The closely related Votyak (Udmurt) is the language of a population of more than half a million settled between the Vyatka and Kama rivers and concentrated chiefly in the Udmurt Autonomous Republic (capital Izhevsk). 'Udmurt'[1] reads 'Votud' in Zyryan and may be identical in origin with the Βουδῖνοι (Budini) of Herodotus.[2] All these names appear to contain the root from which 'Votyak' and perhaps the West Finnic name 'Vodian' (Vadja, O.Russ. Vod') are derived. W. Tomaschek[3] conjectures that Herodotus's Βουδῖνοι were the ancestors of the Permians, who are known to later history as a trading people with some culture. Permian unity, as we have seen, lasted till the eighth century. In prehistoric times the Permians, to judge from loan-words, must have been neighbours of the Iranians and accordingly must have lived to the south of their present habitat. They appear to have been cut off from direct intercourse with the Iranians by the irruption of the Turkic Bolgars (the ancestors of the present-day Chuvash people), who founded Bolgar the Great on the Kama in the eighth century. This state flourished for some hundreds of years till it was destroyed by the Tartars in the thirteenth century. The Tartars established their hegemony *inter alia* over the Votyaks, for Votyak loans from Tartar show the relationship of master and serf. About the same time Russians from Novgorod began to colonise Vyatka, and, after the destruction of Tartar power by the Russian capture of Kazan' in 1552, the Votyaks came under Russian tutelage. They took part in the Pugačov rising as late as the eighteenth century. Repeated

[1] Cf. Zyr. *mort* 'man', with which we may equate Pers. and Urdu *mard*, Arm. *mart'*, all of them with the same meaning.

[2] *Historiarum libri*, IX (c. 443–425 B.C.), IV, 21–7, 103–9.

[3] 'Kritik der ältesten Nachrichten über den skythischen Norden' (*Sitzungsberichte der Kaiserlichen Akademie der Wissenschaften*, Phil.-hist. Classe, CXVII, Vienna, 1889).

failure has humbled them. Their proverb says: 'The Tartar is a wolf, the Russian a bear, the Votyak a hazel-grouse'.[1]

At present the Votyaks use two dialects corresponding to their subdivision into two tribes—Vatka (the northern) and Kalmez (the southern). There is little difference between them. The structural peculiarities of the language are on the whole similar to those of the cognate Zyryan. In its phonetic system back vowels predominate; *ü*, defined [y] by Munkácsi,[2] has been lost, except in the southern (Kalmez) dialect, but is known to have existed in the northern some sixty years ago; there is no vowel harmony; and, as in Zyryan, the voice-voiceless correlation gives a balanced set of plosives. Morphologically and syntactically parallels between the two forms of Permian are as close. Word-formation in Votyak is characteristically agglutinative, and there is a well-defined tendency to treat syntagmas and sentence-complexes as single words and to subject them to morphological modification by case suffixes.[3] The basic form of the imperative is formally identical with the nominal base (e.g. *iz* 'to grind: millstone'; *ym* 'to gorge: mouth'; *tyr* 'to fill: full'). The latter figures in a system of declension which comprises both abstract and local cases, the local distinguishing the contrasted notional categories of rest and motion (cf. the adessive with the allative, the inessive with the illative or elative). Twelve oblique cases constitute the nominal paradigm in both singular and plural, and the singular has the remains of a lative case. Possessive suffixes are added to the inflected noun-forms and help to complicate the relatively straightforward, genderless system of declension (e.g. nom. sing. *tired* 'thy axe' < *tir*; adess. *tiredlen*; abl. *tiredleś*). Personal pronouns and allied forms, including the reflexive and the interrogative, are declined in both numbers, and the interrogative pronoun recognises the antithesis of animate and inanimate (e.g. *kin* 'who?'; *ma(r)* 'what?'). The Votyak verb expresses the future tense by means

---

[1] '*Biger kijon, d'jüs gondyr, udmort śala.*'
[2] *A votják nyelv szótára* (Budapest, 1890–6).
[3] А. И. Емельянов, *Грамматика вотяцкого языка* (Ленинград, 1927).

of a special form (cf. *veralo* 'I shall speak' with *veraśko* 'I speak'), has optative and conditional moods, and uses auxiliaries to construct compound tenses (e.g. *veraśko val* 'I have seen'; *baśtem val* 'he had seen'). The first Votyak grammar appeared in 1775, the first ABC in 1847. The Cyrillic character with diacritic marks, which was introduced in 1905, is still current, though investigators, from time to time, have preferred a more involved Latin-style transcription. The earliest Votyak literary efforts came in the wake of the 1905 revolution (e.g. Michail

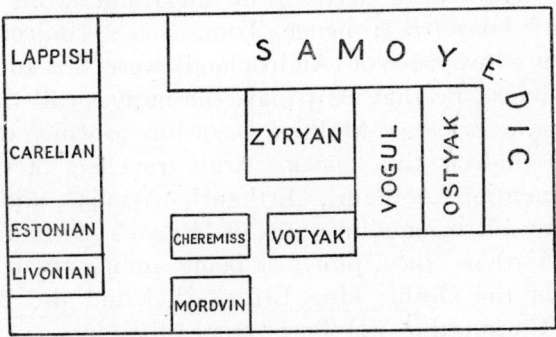

Fig. 4. Diagram of the Uralian languages.

Možgin's poem *Begloj* ('The Refugee'); the newspaper *Vojna yś Ivor* ('News of the War') started to appear in 1916, followed by others the year after. Since then a considerable literary output has made Votyak one of the richest languages in the Union.

5

The East Finnic peoples comprise the Cheremiss (Mari) of the Mari Autonomous Republic (capital Yoshkar-Ola, formerly Tsarevokokshaisk), north of the middle Volga, and the Mordvins (Russ. Mordva), who live interspersed with Russians partly inside and partly outside the grudgingly drawn boundaries of the Mordva Autonomous Republic (capital Saransk) within the Volga bend. The native designation 'Mari', meaning 'men' (cf. Votyak 'murt'), may be the modern representative of

'Merja',[1] which occurs in the Old Russian annals, as well as of the 'Merens' (acc. plur. form) of Jordanes (Jornandes), the historian of the Goths. The alien name 'Cheremiss' derives from the Chuvash (Turkic) and is translated 'defender'. The 'Imniscaris', not 'Sremniscans', as this was formerly read, in Jordanes's *De origine actibusque Getarum* (551), are now identified not with the Cheremiss but with the once Finnic-speaking Meshchera. Tomaschek (op. cit.) equates the Cheremiss with the Μελάγχλαινοι (Melanchlaeni) of Herodotus. Mordvin, on the other hand, is supposed to derive from an Iranic word meaning 'cannibal' (*mardxvā*); hence Tomaschek's conjecture that Herodotus's Ἀνδροφάγοι (Androphagi) were the ancestors of the Mordvins. Be that as it may, the natives call themselves either Erzya (Erz'ä) or Moksha, according to which of the two divergent dialects they speak. Arab travellers of the ninth century mention 'Arthani', 'Erthani', 'Arsaija', and 'Arisu', which may all be modifications of 'Erzya'. Jordanes speaks of the 'Mordens' (acc. plur.) as being among the conquered subjects of the Gothic king Ermanaric,[2] and the Byzantine emperor Constantine VII Porphyrogenitus (905–59) writes in his *De administrando imperio* (c. 952) of a Mordia (Μορδία) lying ten days' journey beyond Pechenegia (Πατζινακία). The extinct Muroma tribe, from which the Russian folk-hero Il'ja Muromec derives his cognomen, was probably West Mordvin and perhaps in immediate contact, on the Oka river, with Baltic (Aestic)[3] tribes, whose language has contributed loan-words to Mordvin and through Mordvin to Cheremiss (cf. Erz. *mukaro* 'buttocks' with Latv. *mugura* 'back' and Mok. *sora* with Lith. *sóra* 'millet').

As Cheremiss seems to link East Finnic with Permian geographically and linguistically, so Mordvin seems to link it with

[1] See M. Zsirai, 'Merja. Adalékok egy kihalt finnugor nép ismeretéhez', (*Berzeviczy-Emlékkönyv*, Budapest, 1934).

[2] See J. J. Mikkola, 'Die Namen der Völker Hermanarichs' (*FUF*, xv, Helsinki, 1915).

[3] K. Būga, following K. Jaunius, consistently applied the term 'Aestic', culled from Tacitus, to the Baltic-speaking peoples. It was used by some of his pupils for a time, but is now obsolete.

West Finnic. There are on the whole more points of affinity between Mordvin and, say, Finnish than between Cheremiss and Finnish.

Cheremiss, which was the mother-tongue of nearly half a million persons in 1939, has two dialects—the Lower (*kožla mari* 'Forest Cheremiss', Russ. *lugovo-marijskij*) and the Upper (*kuruk mari* 'Hill Cheremiss', Russ. *gorno-marijskij*), so-named because one is spoken on the low northern, the other on the high southern bank of the Volga, which flows partly through Cheremiss territory.[1] Both have a literary form. Till the Revolution Cheremiss literature was mainly missionary and ethnographic; now a substantial body of socio-political, economic, educational, and imaginative literature exists in Cyrillic script. Phonetically Cheremiss illustrates the progressive assimilation of vowels, tending towards vowel harmony in Upper Cheremiss. Lower Cheremiss has a triangular grouping of vowels, including *y* and rounded front *ü* and *ö*, and its consonantal system contains the fricatives [β], [ð], [ɣ].[2] Word stress is not well marked and gives the impression of instability, but seems to be affected by vowel quality when it is not final.[3] Cheremiss declension, with its ten cases, distinguishes abstract from local (spatial) relations, like Mordvin and West Finnic. There are six possessive declension series (cf. nom. sing. *kit* 'hand', gen. sing. *kìðən*; acc. sing. *kìðəm* with the possessive forms: nom. sing. *kiðem̥* 'my hand', gen. sing. *kiðem̥ən*, acc. sing. *kiðem̥əm*) and two asemantic conjugations; the apparatus of derivation is well developed; and although agglutination predominates, there are traces of amorphism and flexion. In

---

[1] The Estonian authority on Cheremiss, M. Veske („Исследование о наречиях черемисского языка', *Изв. общ. арх., ист. и этнографии*, VII, Казань, 1889), substitutes 'Eastern' for 'Lower' and 'Western' for 'Upper' on geographical grounds and subdivides each into a northern and a southern variety. The dialect of the capital Yoshkar-Ola is classified as a southern variety of Eastern (Lower) Cheremiss.

[2] See В. А. Богородицкий, „Характеристика звуковой системы марийского (черемисского) языка' (*ИАН, отд. лит. и яз.*, т. III, вып. 6, Москва, 1944).

[3] See E. Lewy, *Tscheremissische Grammatik* (Leipzig, 1922).

syntax qualifier precedes qualified, as in cognate languages, and the predicate is generally final.[1] The Cheremiss vocabulary shows an abundance of Chuvash[2] and Tartar, as well as of Russian loans.

Of the two dialects of Mordvin, used by a total of 1,450,000 speakers in 1939, Moksha is spoken in the south and west, Erzya in the north and east of the Mordva Republic, the second by a slight majority. There are notable differences between them, as there are between the individual Samoyedic dialects, and some scholars, for instance the Mordvin M. E. Jevsev′jev,[3] prefer to call them the 'Mordvin languages'. In phonetic structure Mordvin, especially the Erzya type, closely resembles Russian,[4] as may be seen in its widespread use of palatalised consonants (cf. the phonetic resemblances between unrelated North American stocks). In Moksha the stress falls typically on the first syllable for the most part; in Erzya it is freer. Mordvin morphology is complex and recalls certain types of Palaeoasiatic. Its system of declension, which extends to adjective as well as to noun, has ten cases in Moksha, eleven in Erzya, and two sets of declensional forms—the definite and the indefinite, the former being 'articulate' like the definite noun in Armenian, Scandinavian, and some Balkan languages (e.g. Erz. nom. sing. indef. *moda* 'soil, earth', def. *modaś*; nom. plur. indef. *modat*, def. *modat′n′e*). Mordvin conjugation exhibits few tenses, but many moods, including the subjunctive, desiderative, and conditional, and, like Ugrian and Samoyedic, discriminates formally between an objective (inclusive) and a non-objective (exclusive) series, i.e. between forms which incorporate the direct object and those which do not (e.g. 2nd sing. pres. *palat*

---

[1] See examples in Y. Wichmann, *Tscheremissische Texte mit Wörterverzeichnis und grammatikalischem Abriss* (Helsinki, 1923).

[2] M. Räsänen, 'Die tschuwassischen Lehnwörter im Tscheremissischen' (*MSFOu*, XLVIII, Helsinki, 1920).

[3] Основы мордовской грамматики (Москва, 1931²).

[4] E. Lewy, 'Der Bau der europäischen Sprachen' (*Proceedings of the Royal Irish Academy*, XLVIII, Sect. C, No. 2, Dublin, 1942); N. Trubetzkoy, 'Das mordwinische phonologische System verglichen mit dem russischen' (*Charisteria G. Mathesio*, Prague, 1932).

'you kiss', *palaśamak* 'you kiss me'; 1st sing. pres. *palan* 'I kiss', *palatan* 'I kiss you'). It shares with Cheremiss a well-articulated system of word-formation and blends its predominantly agglutinative tendency with features of other structural types, including rudimentary incorporation. Word-order is free, but the qualifier nevertheless tends to precede the qualified as elsewhere in this language-class. The Mordvin vocabulary has become perceptibly larger since the Revolution by both borrowing and derivation: Tartar and Russian loans are prominent. The earliest Mordvin (Erzya) newspaper *Tśiń Stjamo* ('Sunrise') came out at Ul'yanovsk in 1920, to be followed the next year by *Jakstere Teśte* ('Red Star'), which was originally published in both dialects. The first independent Moksha newspaper was *Od Vele* ('The New Village'), printed at Penza in 1924. Literary work first appears in the daily press and in almanacs. Mordvin literature has developed considerably during the last generation and now possesses many imaginative as well as technical items. As in Cheremiss, the Cyrillic alphabet is used, with small modifications only in Moksha (e.g. я for *ä* and рх, лх, йх for voiceless *r, l, j*).

6

West Finnic as represented in the U.S.S.R. to-day comprises two linguistic groups, viz. one made up of the languages of recently annexed territories and the other of languages with the Soviet tradition. The first group contains Estonian, the official language of the former Estonian Republic (Eesti Vabariik), and Livonian, spoken by a small and declining fishing community on the north-west coast of Latvian Curonia (Kurzeme), which became part of the U.S.S.R. towards the end of the Second World War. These languages lack the Soviet historical and ideological background, and their evolution, like that of the Baltic group (q.v.), pursued characteristic individual ways during two full decades of political independence (1918–40). There is record that both languages were used in their present habitat in the ninth century and, according to a recent hypothesis of East Baltic archaeology,[1] their speakers are aboriginal in the East Baltic area. In opposition to this hypothesis the older, still widely accepted view regards the ancestors of the Estonians, Livonians, and their West Finnic kindred as having reached the Baltic coasts in the first centuries of the Christian era from a focus of dispersion located in the middle Urals.[2]

The name 'Estonian', as used, for instance, by the Anglo-Saxon voyager Wulfstān[3] and by Snorri Sturluson in his saga of King Óláfr Tryggvason,[4] probably meant a member of the diverse peoples inhabiting the East Baltic littoral. This is the sense too in which Tacitus must have used 'Aestii' in his *Germania*.[5] As applied to the Finnic-speaking people south of the Gulf of Finland to-day it represents a national specialisation of a vague collective term. The natives call themselves by it (*eestlased*), and the Livonians and Lithuanians apply it to them, but their immediate neighbours, the Finns and the Latvians, know them by narrow tribal names—the former as 'virolaiset' (Vironians), i.e. the inhabitants of the north-eastern Estonian province (*maakond*) Viru (cf. Finn. Viro 'Estonia'), the latter as 'igauņi' ('Igaunians'), earlier 'ugauņi', i.e. the inhabitants of the south-eastern tribal area Ugandi (Oandi).

To-day Estonian is spoken by over a million persons in the Estonian S.S. Republic (capital Tallinn), the successor of the independent Estonian Republic, and by c. 200,000 colonists in other parts of the U.S.S.R. It distinguishes two principal dialectal forms—the Northern or Tallinn dialect and the Southern or Tartu-Setu dialect. The first is the more important numerically and in literary culture, and is spoken in the islands (e.g. Hiiumaa 'Dagö', Saaremaa 'Ösel', and others), and on

---

[1] H. Kruus, *Eesti ajalugu*, 1 (Tartu, 1936); R. Indreko, 'Eesti rahva asumisest oma kodumaale' (*Kodukolle*, No. 6, Stockholm, 1946).

[2] See my article 'Nationality and Language in the East Baltic Area' (*The American Slavic and East European Review*, VI, 16–17, Menasha, 1947).

[3] H. Sweet, *Extracts from Alfred's Orosius* (Oxford, 1893).

[4] F. Jónsson, *Heimskringla. Nórégs konunga sǫgur* (Copenhagen, 1936); P. E. Ólason, *Heimskringla Snorra Sturlusonar*, 1 (Reykjavík, 1946).

[5] 'Aestii' appears as 'Aesti' in Cassiodorus and Jordanes. See my article 'Baltic Origins' (*Revue des études slaves*, XXIV, Paris, 1948).

the mainland north of a line curving from the Latvian frontier to Viljandi (Fellin) and from there north-eastwards to Lake Peipsi (Peipus), which it abuts on well to the north of the Ema (Embach) estuary. The southern dialect, which has its own early literature and modern poets, is current in the southern parts of the Viljandi and Tartu provinces and in Valga, Võru, and Petseri.

Phonetically Estonian differs from its congener Finnish in having two characteristic back vowels, both represented in the spelling by *õ*, the diphthong *õu*, and—in the standard speech—undiphthongised long *e* and *o*, as well as semi-palatalised consonants. Vowel harmony exists only in the Southern dialect (e.g. *lövväsi* 'they found'; cf. the literary *leidsid*). Quantitative differences in both vowels and consonants and their systematic alternation[1] are subtle and more numerous than in Finnish (e.g. the three degrees of *n* in *lina* 'flax' and in the gen. sing. *linna* and allat. sing. *linna* < *linn* 'town'). Stress falls on the first syllable, as in the other West Finnic languages and in Latvian (q.v.). The sixteen cases include the instructive plural, which Johannes Aavik's language reforms have tried to 'resuscitate'. The genitive case has lost its original ending -*n*, except in *maantee* 'highroad' (< *maa* 'country' and *tee* 'road'), and some of the other cases their final vowel, whose existence is inferred from a comparison with Finnish (e.g. ablat. -*lt* < *-lta*, adess. -*l* < *-lla*, iness. -*s* < *-ssa*). A new comitative case, unknown to Finnish, ends in -*ga*. The plural case-endings are morphologically identical with those of the singular, except that they are associated with plural indices (-*d*, -*t*, -*i*-). The newer or reformed literary language, which owes so much of its pliancy and energy to the enthusiasm and linguistic genius of Johannes Aavik and his followers, is far more complicated than, say, the language described last century by F. J. Wiedemann.[2] Among its many innovations is a new *i*-infixed super-

---

[1] Estonian grammar (see O. Loorits, *Eesti keele grammatika*, Tartu, 1923) distinguishes between *aste* ('grade'), which is qualitative, and *välde* ('length'), which is quantitative.

[2] *Grammatik der estnischen Sprache* (St Petersburg, 1875).

lative, derived from Finnish (e.g. *suur, suurem, suurim* 'big, bigger, biggest'). The personal pronouns are the same as in Finnish, except the 3rd person singular *tema* (*ta*) and the 3rd person plural *nemad* (*nad*), which, as Finnish parallels suggest, appear to be personalised demonstratives and are found in their new capacity in Livonian and Vodian, but not in Vepsian (q.v.). Estonian has no pronominal suffixes like those of Finnish (cf. *minu isa* 'my father' with Finn. *isäni*); the 3rd person present of the verb ends in *-b* (cf. the Finnish suffix *-pi*); there is a past tense in *-si-* (sometimes *-i-*), a relative mood (reported speech) morpheme *-vat*, passive forms for both present (*-akse, -dakse, -takse*) and past (*-di, -ti*) not to be found in Finnish, and a generalised negative particle *ei*, instead of the conjugated Finnish negative verb. Present and future are not distinguished, as in West Finnic generally. The Estonian vocabulary shows considerable indebtedness to Low German (cf. Latvian), and there are numerous earlier loans, unevenly shared with its congeners, from Baltic, Germanic, and Slavonic in that chronological order.

Whether the Livonians, the southern kindred of the Estonians, were indigenous or intruders in their now almost denationalised country, where their language is confined to a few fishing villages along the Latvian littoral north of Ventspils (Windau), is a matter of conjecture. History names them in the Old Russian Primary Chronicle (*Povĕst' vremennych lĕt*) in the eleventh century, and they are known to have occupied the estuary of the Western Dvina (Väina, Latv. Daugava, Germ. Düna), where Riga now stands, when the Hanseatic merchants arrived there in the early twelfth century. The German crusaders and their ally, the Roman Church, established a hegemony over the Livonians in the twelfth and thirteenth centuries, after a bloody conflict which so reduced their numbers that it was possible for their Latvian neighbours to absorb the majority of them in the course of the seven centuries that followed. To-day only some 2000 speakers, if that, use Livonian as their mother tongue. But even this remnant, primed and assisted by Finnish and Estonian scholars (e.g.

L. Kettunen, O. Loorits, and others) has created for itself a literary language and has published newspapers and a small imaginative literature. This language is nearer to Estonian than to Finnish in phonetics, structure, and vocabulary, and has been considerably influenced by Latvian, from which it has acquired its verbal prefixes, unknown in the other West Finnic languages (e.g. *ne sa-rękkandist*, Latv. *tie sa-runājās* 'they agreed'), and through which it has lost its rounded close *ü*[1] (cf. Liv. *ni* with Finn. *nyt* 'now'; Liv. *kila* with Finn. *kylä* 'village') and retained its spontaneously evolved hush-sibilants and affricates (cf. Liv. *ikš* 'one' with Finn. *yksi*; Liv. *vīž* 'five' with Finn. *viisi*) and its glottal plosive (e.g. gen. sing. *mje'r* 'of the sea'). Like Estonian, it tends to discard final short vowels, is well supplied with diphthongs, and has, curiously enough, developed a new comitative case, though with a different (the Finnish-Estonian translative) ending (e.g. *saksadəks* 'with the Germans'; cf. Est. *sakslastega*). Among its idiosyncrasies are a considerable loss of case-endings, the use of the Estonian 3rd sing. index *-b* for the other persons of the present tense, the negative particle *äb* (cf. O.Est. *ep*), the initial *v-* before vowels (e.g. *vo'l'* 'was'; cf. Est. and Finn. *oli*), two characteristic vowels *ę* and *ə* (i.e. [ɤ] and [ə]), the use of voiced plosives (*b, d, g*) initially, the rounding of *a* to open *ǫ* (e.g. *mō* 'land', *louldə* 'to sing'; cf. Est. *maa, laulda*), and the use of the German conjunction *un* (cf. Latvian) for the West Finnic Gothic-style *ja*.

7

The second and purely Soviet group of West Finnic languages is represented first and foremost by Carelian, spoken in the Carelo-Finnish S.S. Republic (capital Petrozavodsk), a large forested area bordering on Finland in the east and known to the Finns as Eastern Carelia (Itä-Karjala), the home of the epic *Kalevala* and the ethnic *Finlandia irredenta*. Olonecian (Aunus), spoken along the eastern shores of Lake Ladoga (Finn. Laatokka), and the Ingrian, or Isurian (Russ. *ižorskij*), of Ingria (Ingermannland),

[1] This vowel appears in the now extinct East Livonian described by J. A. Sjögren (see *Livische Grammatik nebst Sprachproben*, St Petersburg, 1861).

the maritime area between Estonia and Leningrad, are dialectal varieties of Carelian, which is also the language of compact bodies of settlers in the Novgorod and the eastern part of the Kalinin (formerly Tver') province, where their forebears emigrated in the seventeenth century. There are two types of Carelian proper[1]—a Northern and a Southern dialect, and these, together with the other varieties already referred to, give a total of six, viz. Carelian proper, Northern and Southern, Olonecian, Ingrian, and the two expatriate or colonial types spoken in the Russian provinces. The number of Carelian speakers to-day apparently far exceeds a quarter of a million; which makes this language numerically the principal West Finnic type in the U.S.S.R. after Estonian. Carelian seems to have occupied even more extensive tracts in North-Eastern Europe a millennium or more ago. Scandinavian annals tell of an expedition made by the Swedish King Ívar Vídfamne against the King of Garðaríki (Russia) through 'Kyrjalabotn' about A.D. 700, i.e. probably before the Carelians had reached the White Sea. Óttarr (King Alfred's Ohthere) mentions the Bjarmar (Carelians, if not Permians) at the estuary of the Northern Dvina (Finn. Viena) in 875. The Bjarmar were celebrated for their wealth and attracted Viking traders and adventurers. The best known of the many trading expeditions was the one in which Þórir Hundr of Hálogaland and his companions desecrated the image of the god Jomala (see supra). The name Carelia (Russ. Korela, or Karela) first appears in Russian chronicles in 1143. Till the seventeenth century the White Sea coast was known as the Carelian Shore (*karel'skij bereg*), and J. A. Sjögren and A. Ahlquist have discovered numerous Carelian place-names in the vicinity of the Northern Dvina.

Phonetically Carelian differs from the related Finnish, especially from the eastern (Savo) dialect of that language, in

---

[1] The Finnish scholar Lauri Kettunen (see *Suomen heimon kirja*, Porvoo, 1931) regards Carelian as a variety of Eastern Finnish, artificially separated from Finnish since the time of the Treaty of Oreshek or Pähkinäsaari (1323) by several centuries of divergent religio-political development. In this view Olonecian is South Carelian.

having hush for hiss sibilants (š and tš for s and ts), e.g. *šelkä* 'back' for *selkä*, *šormi* 'finger' for *sormi*, *itše* 'self' for *itse*. It palatalises its consonants before *i* (e.g. *män'i* 'went', *ol'i* 'was'), like Russian; tends to drop final *n*, and often has final *h* for *s*, especially in the infinitive and in the illative case; assimilates adjacent sounds in juxtaposed words, like certain Finnish dialects and Italian; diphthongises *aa* into *au* and *oo* into *ou* (e.g. *ottau* 'takes', *šanou* 'says' for Finnish *ottaa, sanoo*); has weak medial *b*, *g*, *z*, especially in its Southern dialect, for their voiceless equivalents (e.g. *otti leibeä* 'took bread', *jälgi* 'footprint' for Finnish *otti leipää, jälki*); changes *j* into palatal *d'* (e.g. *d'äi* 'remained' for *jäi*),[1] and, like the other West Finnic languages in the U.S.S.R., except Estonian and Livonian, prefers velar to alveolar *l*, where this is not palatalised (e.g. *kołmas* 'third'). Lexically Carelian shows notable Russian influence even to the extent of retaining initial voiced plosives in Russian loans, which include the conjunction *i* 'and' for Finno-Estonian *ja*. The Ingrian dialect, owing to its proximity to Estonian, shows Estonian features in phonetics and vocabulary.

The other three West Finnic languages of the U.S.S.R. are Vepsian, Vodian (Votish), and a Lappish dialect (Saam), in the order of their historical importance. Vepsian is spoken by about 20,000 persons now living on either side of the Svir' (Finn. Syväri) and on the Oyat', and by Ludians (who call their language *l'üdin* and even *livvin kieli*) on the south-west shores of Lake Onega (Finn. Äänis). The Russians call them 'Kajvany' or, less kindly, 'Čuchari' ('foreigners') and 'Čud'' (idem). They have been known to history since the sixth century, when Jordanes mentions the 'Vasina-broncas', their conquered ancestry, as subject to Ermanaric. The medieval records of Arab travellers refer to a tribe called 'Visu',[2] and in 1075 Adam van Bremen writes: 'Ibi (i.e. in Ruzzia) sunt etiam qui

---

[1] Cf. Finn. *jalka* and Est. *jalg* 'leg' with the Hungarian *gyalog* 'on foot', which illustrates the same change, viz. [j] into [ɟ].

[2] Saxo Grammaticus (see *Gesta danorum*, c. 1200), the original narrator of the Hamlet story, has a Visinnus (cf. the Saga name 'Visinn') as the hero of one of his stories.

dicuntur Alani vel Albani qui lingua eorum Wizzi dicuntur.'[1] It is difficult to decide whether his 'Albani' (from Lat. *albus*) or 'Wizzi' (cf. Germ. *weiss*) were actually Vepsians. These names, for an obvious reason, have been connected with Belo-ozero ('White Lake'). The Ves', according to medieval Russian annals, were one of the peoples which participated in the founding of the Varangian state in Russia, and one of the Varangian (Swedish) princes is said to have settled in Belo-ozero among them. This was the Sineus of Russian history text-books. Whether such a person ever existed has been disputed, and one interpretation suggests[2] that the name was mistakenly extracted from Old Swedish words meaning 'his (i.e. Prince Ryurik's) household', as the name of the third brother Truvor was from words meaning 'loyal forces'. The original expression seems to have read not 'Ryurik, Sineus, and Truvor', as the chronicles misinterpreted, but 'Ryurik, his household, and loyal forces'. There was only one Varangian prince, according to this view, and *he* settled in Novgorod the Great (Hólmgarðr).

The purer, southern type of Vepsian, like the Carelian-modified Ludian (North Vepsian) has an even more russianised phonetic structure (with its *b, d, g, l, z, š, ž, tš*) than Carelian (e.g. *ištūbad* 'they sit', Finn. *istuvat*; *män'bad* 'they went', Finn. *menivät*). The vocabulary is predominantly Finnic, but Russian loan-words and even turns of phrase are common (e.g. *ī joudnud i n'ägehtada* 'they did not even see', Finn. *ei joutunut katsomaan-kaan*, where the second—Russian—*i* corresponds to the Finnish suffix -*kaan* 'even'), and there are numerous parallels with Estonian and Livonian (e.g. *rebāne* 'fox' and *n'eiz'n'e* 'girl', where Finnish has *kettu* and *tyttönen* respectively). Among the individual features of South Vepsian are such words as *mor'z'ä*[3] 'wife' (cf. Finn. *vaimo*, Est. *naine*) and *an'i* 'very' for Finnish

[1] *Gesta Hammaburgensis ecclesiae pontificum sive Bremensium praesulum historia* (1075).
[2] See Н. Т. Беляев, *Начало Руси* (Лондон-Прага, 1925); N. de Baumgarten, *Aux origines de la Russie* (Rome, 1939).
[3] Est. *mõrsja* and Finn. *morsiamen* both mean 'bride'.

hyvin and Estonian *väga*, the comitative case in *-mu* (e.g. *tütärdmu* 'with the daughter'; cf. Est. *tütrega*), a reinforced demonstrative *n'etse* 'this' (cf. the constitution of Fr. *voici*), and *u* for preconsonantal *l* (e.g. *koume* 'three'; cf. Finn. *kolme*). Vepsian diminutives (e.g. *lehmān'e* 'little cow'; cf. Finn. *lehmänen*) and vowel harmony recall Finnish and Carelian equivalents, but the harmony is not complete. The conjunction which helps to vary the usual asyndetic constructions is the Russo-Turkic *da* 'and'.

Vodian (vadja, Finn. vatja, Germ. Wotisch) is an almost extinct type of West Finnic, like Livonian, and it is confined to some 500 speakers living in small fishing villages near the Luga (Est. Luuga) estuary in the north-western part of the Leningrad province. It appears however to have been the ancient vernacular of Ingria (then Vodia). Some conjecture that Pseudo-Nestor's Čud' were Vodians. In any case the name 'Vod'' occurs in the Old Russian chronicles as a Russian version of the national, or tribal name. Like the Vepsians, its bearers seem to have taken part in the creation of Varangian Rus'. The Vodian name first definitely appears in the eleventh century in Prince Yaroslav's *Ustav o mostěch* ('Highway Code'), where *vočkaja oblast'* ('Vodian Province') is mentioned.[1] Of the five provinces of the Grand Duke (Prince Paramount) of Novgorod, one was called *votskaja pjatina* (i.e. 'the Vodian Fifth').[2] Vodians were known to Medieval Rome as 'pagani Vatlandie' (cf. Germ. Watland). By that time this strong and numerous people had begun to be decimated by war and famine. After the annexation of Ingria to Sweden by the Treaty of Stolbovo in 1617, large numbers of Vodians emigrated to Russia, and Ingria was repopulated from Finnish Carelia by the ancestors of the present-day Savakot and Äyrämöiset (*-t* is the plur. ending). In modern times Ingrians have far outnumbered Vodians in the Leningrad province, but they are not to be regarded as exclusively the descendants of the seventeenth-century immigrants. Ingrians

---

[1] 'Vočkaja' for 'votskaja' is a *č*-dialect form peculiar to North-West Russia.

[2] Cf. the English administrative unit 'riding', i.e. 'third part'.

(Isurians) were known in Ingria in the Middle Ages. In papal bulls of the twelfth and thirteenth centuries Ingrians and Vodians are mentioned separately (e.g. 'crudeles pagani Carelie, Ingrie, Lappie et Vatlandie'). The Ingrians probably occupied the east, the Vodians the west of Ingria.

Vodian, like its Soviet congeners, has a Russian-looking phonetic system (e.g. *b, d, g, z, tš, ł*) and many Russian loans (e.g. *sługalę i juttęb* 'and says to the servant'; cf. Finn. *ja palvelijalle sanoo*). Other Vodian loans derive normally from Finnish and Estonian. Some dialects of Vodian, especially those within the territory of the Estonian S.S.R., show marked Estonian affinities, among them *-b/-p* in the 3rd person sing. of the present tense (e.g. *tuęb* 'comes', Est. *tuleb*; *viskap koiręlę* 'throws to the dog', Est. *viskab koerale*), an unrounded back vowel of the *o*-series, written *ę* (Est. *õ*, Liv. *ę*), and the dropping of original final vowels. All have individual features, which include vowel harmony, as in Setu Estonian and Vepsian, the negative particle *ep/eb* (cf. the older Est. *ep*, Liv. *äb*), the Russian-style conjunction *i* 'and', and—most characteristic of all—the change of *k* into *tš* before a front vowel (e.g. *tšüsümä* 'to ask' for Est. *küsima*).[1] Like Vepsian, Vodian represents a transition from Finnish and Carelian typology to Estonian and Livonian.

Lappish, as a Soviet language, is limited to a small body of speakers (c. 1800 in 1926) out of a total of over 30,000, found mainly in the northern parts of Scandinavia and Finland. These are thought to have acquired their Uralian speech without completely absorbing West Finnic culture. The Russian Lapps live a semi-nomadic existence in the tundra of the Kola peninsula, hunting, fishing, and pasturing reindeer. Since the Revolution elementary schools have been started for them, but on the whole the Kola Lapps (Saams) are the most backward, as they are the minutest of the Lappish communities. Unlike their kin in Scandinavia and Finland, they still have only a small literature, apart from old missionary versions of the Scriptures (e.g. St Matthew's Gospel, 1878). They call themselves

---

[1] L. Posti, 'Vatjan kielen *k > tš* äänteenmuutoksen iästä' (*Kalevalaseuran Vuosikirja*, Helsinki, 1934).

'Saam'. Compare with this the Scandinavian Lappish self-designation 'Sabme(laš)' or 'Same', which Setälä, following Sjögren and Genetz, derives from an archaic *s*-form of the Finnish name 'Hämäläinen', current in South-West Finland. They are first mentioned in the *Germania* (A.D. 98–9) of Tacitus, who calls them by the Germanic name 'Fenni' (perhaps 'nomads').[1] In many other historical documents, both Latin and vernacular, 'Fenni' is synonymous with 'Lapps', and to this day 'Finn' means 'Lapp' in Norwegian (cf. O.N. sing. Finnr, plur. Finnar). Procopius of Caesarea (sixth century)[2] distinguishes the Lapps as Σκριθίφινοι, and the first part of the name probably represents the Old Norse word *skríða* ('to run').[3] This name is repeated by later authors, for instance the Lombard historian Paul Varnefrid, as 'Scritovinni'. The name 'Lapp'[4] occurs in Russian sources from the thirteenth to the fifteenth century and is first located in Olonecia, with which it is associated even to-day. Lapps were found in Southern Finland as late as the sixteenth century. The connections of their language with Finnish and West Finnic generally are to be seen in a common vocabulary, which includes a great many Germanic and even Baltic loans. The former are in some cases direct, the latter entirely borrowed through Finnish. The Lapps have been subject to Germanic influences from Old Nordic times (A.D. 400–800), as their six dialects, including three spoken in Sweden, show.

Kola Lappish (Saam) displays the characteristic features of the extra-Soviet varieties, except that it has been exposed to Russian influence (e.g. the existence of palatalised consonants, and *i* 'and' for the *ja* of other Lappish dialects) and derives part

---

[1] Cf. the meaning of the Germanic tribal name 'Vandal'. O. Schrader (*Reallexikon der indogermanischen Altertumskunde*, I, Berlin-Leipzig, 1917–23, p. 312) suggests that the stem *Finn*- is neither Finno-Ugrian nor Indo-European.

[2] See οἱ ὑπὲρ τῶν πολέμων λόγοι (VI, XV, 16–25).

[3] The basic element is at least as old as Ptolemy's Φίννοι.

[4] The first appearance of this name is in the saga *Fundinn Norégr*, c. 1200. Etymology connects it with a Germanic root meaning 'to run' (cf. Engl. *leap*, Germ. *laufen*, Swed. *löpa*).

of its culture words from there. Like Lappish as a whole, it is nearest related to West Finnic, and must be classified as a solitary and aberrant member of that branch. The West Finnic affinities of Lappish are more evident in morphology than in phonetics, which reveals unusual complexity. The language possesses a quadrangular system of vowel phonemes, based on the opposition of *a* and *å* [ɔ], and palatalised correlatives of a normally full system of consonants. Its morphological resemblances may be seen in such parallels as:

	Kola Lappish	Finnish
Singular		
Nominative	*murr* 'tree'	*puu* 'tree'
Genitive	*mur*	*puun*
Accusative	*mur*	*puun*
Essive	*murrəŋ*	*puuna*
Locative-elative	*murəşt*	*puussa* (iness.)
		puusta (elat.)
Dative-allative	*muɤɤe*	*puulle* (allat.)
Comitative	*murəŋ* (plur. *murəguim*)	*puine* (comit. plur.)
Abessive	*murha*	*puutta*

As in Estonian, the genitive and accusative cases (cf. Est. nom.-gen.-acc. *puu* 'tree') have lost the distinctive endings which Finnish has preserved. In the plural the oblique cases insert *-ə-/-e-* (cf. Finn. *-i-*), and in some instances there is an accompanying vowel-mutation in the root syllable (e.g. Kola Lapp. acc. and dat. plur. *voaɤeɤ* 'to the woods' and the abess. plur. *vaɤeha*). The system of possessive suffixes is well developed in a complex paradigm (e.g. 1st person sing. nom. *puaza(m)* 'my reindeer', 2nd sing. *puazat*, 3rd sing. *puazəš*, 1st plur. *puaza(m)*, 2nd plur. *puazant*, 3rd plur. *puazədəş*). The adjective is declined when not attributive, and its paradigm is identical with that of the noun (cf. *nurr* 'young' with *murr* above). Kola Lappish numeration is characteristically Finnic, with subtractive forms for 8–9 (e.g. *kahc* 'eight', *ahc* 'nine'; cf. *əht* 'one', *kuht* 'two'). The personal pronouns are formally almost identical with the Mordvin types (cf. Kola Lapp. 1st to 3rd sing. *monn, tonn, sonn*, and 1st to 3rd plur. *mıj, tıj, sıj* with Erz. Mord. *mon,* *ton, son, min', tyn', syn'*). The Kola Lappish verb distinguishes moods, tenses—a present-future and a past—and, apparently, aspects (e.g. the iterative and semelfactive). As in West Finnic generally, the past tense index is a vowel of the front series, and there is a negative conjugation. Syntactically Kola Lappish is flexible: the predicate usually follows the subject, and the object the verb (e.g. *tall porr nuərjeṭ* 'the bear eats seals'). Notwithstanding its present geographical position, Lappish in all its dialectal variety seems to be in some sort, by a curious freak of geography, the modern representative of the original link between West Finnic and Mordvin: its personal pronouns, as we have observed, recall Mordvin, and its general structure resembles Finnish.

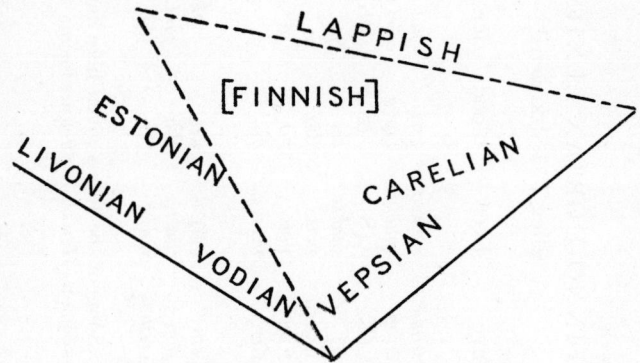

Fig. 5. Diagram of the West Finnic languages.

8

Characteristic of the Uralian languages, whose numerous representatives have now been named and examined, is a 'family likeness' which places the genetic unity of the three branches—Samoyedic, Ugrian, and Finnic—beyond effective dispute. The common features and bonds are not only phonetic (e.g. vowel harmony), but structural and lexical as well.

Naturally each branch, even each language, exhibits idiosyncrasies. Ostyak and Vogul, like Samoyedic and Lappish, have a dual number, missing elsewhere, and, like Samoyedic

TABLE OF FINNO-UGRIAN LEXICAL PARALLELS
(after T. I. Itkonen)[1]

Meaning	hand	ear	eye	liver	blood	ice	stone	winter	we	six
I. Finnic										
Finnish	käsi	pieli	silmä	maksa	veri	jää	kivi	talvi	me	kuusi
Lappish	kit	pel	čalm	muökse	varra	jeekŋa	—	talv	mīj	kuht
	(K)		(K)	(S)	(S)	(S)		(K)	(K)	(K)
Mordvin (Erzya)	kedʹ	pile	selʹme	maksa	ver	jej	kev	tele	mīnʹ	koto
Cheremiss	kit	polaš	šindzä	mokš	βür	i	kü	tel	me	kut
Votyak	ki	pelʹ	sʹim	mus	vir	jö	kö	tol	mi	kwatʹ
Zyryan	ki	pelʹ	sʹin	mus(k)	vir	ji	-ki	tẹl	mi	kvait
II. Ugrian										
Ostyak	ket	pol	sem	mūɣǝt	jǝr	jeŋk	keu	tal	muŋ	hat
Vogul	kāt	piļ	säm	mait	βūr	jāṅG	käβ	tal	man	hot
Hungarian	kéz	fül	szem	máj	vér	jég	kő	tél	mi	hat

[1] *Suomensukuiset kansat* (Helsinki, 1921). Some of the forms given here have been taken from J. Szinnyei, *Magyar nyelvhasonlítás* (Budapest, 1927⁷) and Г. Н. Прокофьев, *Языки и письменность народов Севера*, I (Москва–Ленинград, 1937)

and Hungarian, they incorporate the pronominal object. The more conservative types of Finnic have a complicated case-system (15–18 cases), only inferior to that of Hungarian (21–24 cases), and with local cases, as opposed to abstract, in evidence; there is also a special negative conjugation; and Mordvin has, exceptionally, an objective conjugation, like the Samoyedic and Ugrian languages. The plural suffixes are *-t* and *-k* and their voiced counterparts and substitutes, one of which (*-b*) serves as the dual index in Vogul. Another plural suffix—*i*—is also found in West Finnic as well as in Ugrian representatives. The Permian languages, typologically, are more agglutinative than the other forms of Finnic, whose flexion shows Indo-European irregularities, and their vocabulary has affinities with Ugrian (e.g. the numerals). Of the East Finnic (Volga) languages, Mordvin seems to have detached itself from West Finnic at a comparatively late period (consider here the Finnish-looking pronominal suffix of the 3rd sing. *-zo*, e.g. Erz. *kudonzo* 'his houses', the participle in *-vt-*, the infinitive ending *-ms*, and the past tense sign *-y-/-i-*). Cheremiss, which incorporates its negative particle, like Turkic, has points of resemblance with both Permian and Mordvin: it resembles Zyryan, for instance, in its case morphemes, its tendency to form compounds (cf. Samoyedic, Finnish, and Estonian), and its numerals. The West Finnic languages form a more compact group than either the East Finnic or the Permian, but, in common with these, they have submitted to Russian influence, which is especially noticeable in the disturbed vowel harmony and in the vocabulary of some of the types spoken in the interior of the Union.

All three branches of Uralian exhibit a tendency to differentiate verb and noun, and this culminates in the West Finnic noun-verb dichotomy. Uralian moods and tenses are simple. The indicative has mainly two tenses—a progressive (which includes present and future time) and a perfect (which expresses past time). The remaining moods are the potential (concessive), conditional, imperative, optative, and conjunctive. In West Finnic there is a thematic *-i-* (*-si-*) in the past tense;

East Finnic (e.g. Mordvin), East Ugrian, and Samoyedic have -*s*- (-*š*-). The concessive shows the theme -*n*- (e.g. Kola Lappish potential *kūskŋem* 'I may touch' from *kūske*- 'to touch'). Conjugations with this element, representing a diversity of moods, occur in most types of West Finnic, in Cheremiss, and in Ugrian. The imperative and optative suffixes (-*ka*, -*ko*) are obviously related. The suffix -*l*- is frequentative in Uralian generally (e.g. Ost. *man-ł-* 'to go', Votyak *mыnыl-* 'to go', Mord. *nev't'le-* 'to show'). Negation is nearly always expressed by a negative verb, which is often freely conjugated. Infinitives and participial constructions recall Turkic. The system of numeration appears to have 'seven' as its base:[1] the words up to 'seven' are identical, except in Samoyedic; the words for 'eight', 'nine', and 'ten' are different. West Finnic 'ten' is *kymmenen* in Finnish, *kemen'* in Erzya Mordvin, *loģḳ* (*lȧģḳ*) in Kola Lappish, *lu* in Cheremiss, and *lou* in Vogul. The last three correspond to Finnish *luku* 'number'. Ostyak has *jaŋ* for 'ten' (cf. Turk. *on* 'ten', Yak. *u̯on*); Zyryan and Votyak have the Indo-European *das*. 'Eight' and 'nine' are expressed by 'two' and 'one' from 'ten' respectively (e.g. Kola Lapp. *kahc* 'eight', *ahc* 'nine', Erz. Mord. *kavkso*, *veikse*, Cher. *kandakse*, *əndekše*, Est. *kaheksa*, *üheksa*, Finn. *kahdeksan, yhdeksän*). The word for 'hundred' is *satəm*-style Indo-European and the same in all the languages (e.g. Ost. *sot*, Erz. Mord. *śado*, Finn. *sata*), and that for 'thousand' represents loans from various members of the same stock (e.g. Ost. *şorыs*, Votyak *śurs*, Erz. Mord. *t'ožom*, Finn. *tuhat*).

Three systems of transcription have been used to symbolise Uralian sounds, viz. the Finnish, devised by A. Genetz and H. Paasonen and perfected by E. N. Setälä for the *Finnisch-Ugrische Forschungen*;[2] the Hungarian of J. Budenz, developed by B. Munkácsi and I. Kunos for the *Keleti Szemle* ('Oriental

[1] The word for 'seven' looks Indo-European. See A. S. C. Ross, 'Some Remarks on the Numerals of Finno-Ugrian' (*Transactions of the Philological Society*, 1941, London, 1943). He suggests a sextal numeration as basic on etymological grounds.

[2] See E. N. Setälä, 'Über Transkription der finnisch-ugrischen Sprachen. Historik und Vorschläge' (*FUF*, I, Helsinki, 1901).

Review'); and the Russian Cyrillic, which has served mainly practical purposes. The last has also been used by scholars like Lytkin and Rogov for Zyryan, which, it will be remembered, had an original alphabet (St Stefan's) dating from the fourteenth century. The Cyrillic orthographies adapted to the Finnic languages of the U.S.S.R. to-day are not only sound phonetically, but, being free from diacritic excrescences, are simple and convenient to use.

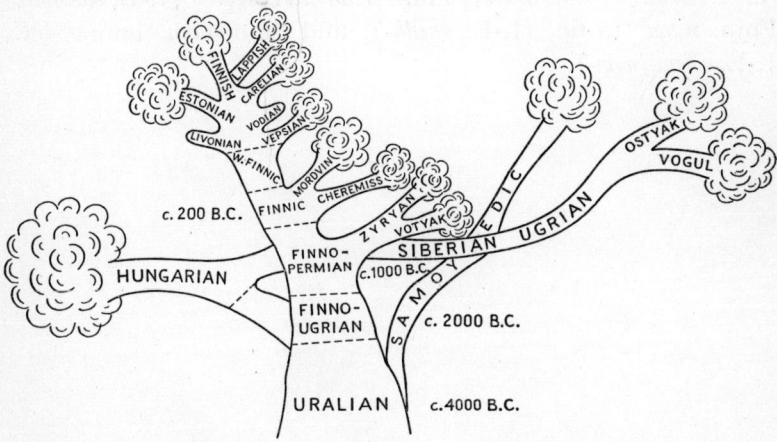

Fig. 6. The Uralian 'Family Tree' (after Lauri Kettunen[1]).

Of all the non-Indo-European stocks, Uralian, like Semitic, shows certain morphological (e.g. personal endings of the finite verb) and lexical resemblances, which have been held by some investigators[2] to point to an original Indo-European-Uralian unity. The lexical resemblances are apparently not the outcome of borrowing, but primordial parallel forms, which may or may not imply relationship. E. N. Setälä[3] lists several, including some which were published by N. Anderson as early as 1879.[4] Here

[1] *Suomen heimon kirja* (Porvoo, 1931).
[2] B. Collinder, *Indo-uralisches Sprachgut* (Uppsala, 1934).
[3] *Suomen suku*, 1 (Helsinki, 1926), pp. 121–2.
[4] 'Studien zur Vergleichung der ugrofinnischen und indogermanischen Sprachen' (*Verhandlungen der Gelehrten Estnischen Gesellschaft*, Tartu, 1879).

follow a few from Setälä's list, which has been slightly modified:
Finn. *vesi* 'water' (cf. I.-E. **ṷed-*); Vog. *hum*, Votyak *-kum*, Ost.
Sam. *qum/qup* 'man' (cf. Lat. *homo*, A.S. *guma*, I.-E. **g'hm-*);
Finn. *kave* 'creature; woman' (cf. I.-E. **skab-* 'to create');
Finn. *kaarne* 'crow' (cf. Lat. *cornix*); Finn. *asema* 'station'
(I.-E. **es-*, Lat. *esse*); Finn. *purra* 'to bore' (cf. I.-E. **bher-*,
Lat. *forare*); Finn. *tehdä, teke-* 'to make' (cf. I.-E. **dhe-k-*);
Finn. *viedä* 'to carry' (cf. I.-E. **ṷeg'h-*); Finn. *ajaa* 'to drive'
(cf. I.-E. **ag'-*, Lat. *agere*); Finn. *vetää* 'to convey' (I.-E. **ṷedh-*);
Finn. *nitoa* 'to tie' (I.-E. **nedh-*); and Finn. *nimi* 'name' (cf.
I.-E. **nem-/nom-*).

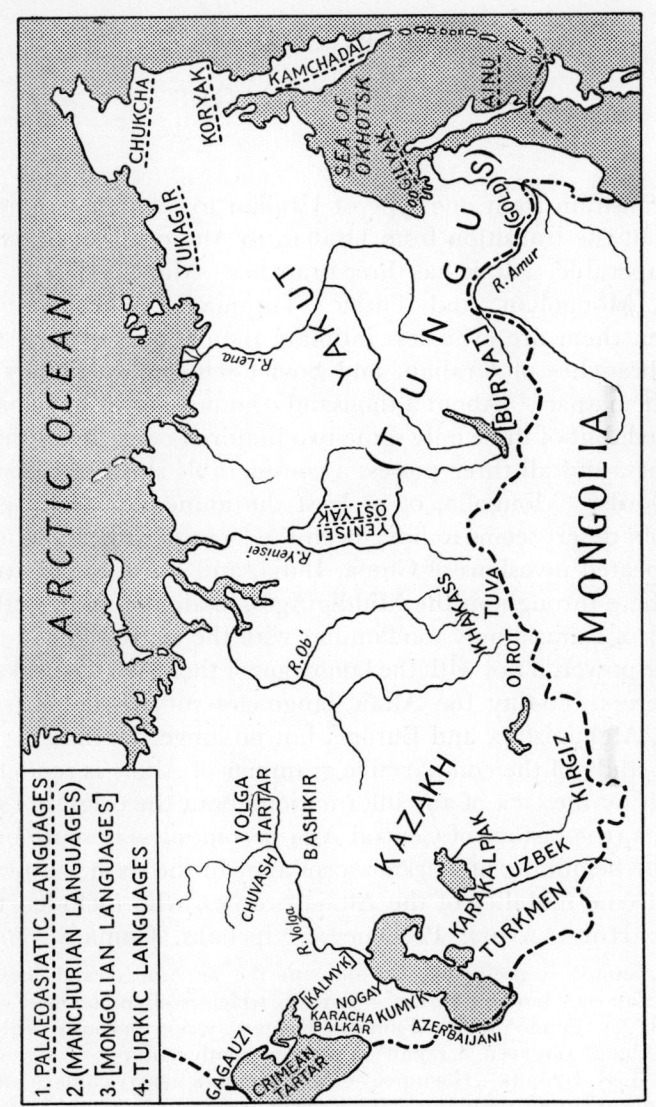

Map 3. Palaeoasiatic and Altaic languages.

CHAPTER IV

ALTAIC LANGUAGES

I

The transition from one type of Uralian to another is hardly easy, but the transition from Uralian to Altaic still appears to be insuperable. Altaic has three branches—Manchurian (Tungusic), Mongolian, and Turkic (Turanian).[1] The relations between them are even less intimate than those between the three branches of Uralian, and Soviet scholarship prefers to keep them apart.[2] About a thousand common words have been collected, but of these only some two hundred occur in all three branches, and all three possess a considerable stock of Chinese loan-words.[3] Mongolia, or at least the immediate vicinity of the Gobi desert seems to have been the focus of dispersion, and the repeated invasions of China, India, and Europe, radiating from there throughout the Middle Ages, made the more settled peoples of Eurasia only too familiar with the aggressive vitality and the power, if not with the languages of their Altaic-speaking conquerors. To-day the Altaic languages survive in parts of China, Afghanistan, and Europe, but no longer in India.

The study of the comparative grammar of Altaic is rendered difficult by the lack of any information about the origins of the speakers (the history of Central Asia becomes less obscure only after the beginning of Turkic ascendancy in the sixth century); the extreme mobility of the Altaic peoples, who included the Turkic Huns, Avars, Pechenegs, Kipchaks, Cumans (Polo-

[1] 'Turanian' is preferable not only to the antiquated and inexact 'Turco-Tataric', but to 'Turkic' ('Turki'), which is often confused with 'Turkish', as 'Finnic' is with 'Finnish'. The term was erroneously used for 'Uralo-Altaic' and even 'Uralian' in the nineteenth century.

[2] See Д. В. Бубрих, ‚К вопросу об отношениях между самоедскими и финноугорскими языками‘ (*ИАН, отд. лит. и яз.*, т. VII, вып. 6, (Москва-Ленинград, 1948).

[3] See A. Velics, *A kinai nyelv szerepe az ural-altáji, indo-európái és sémi nyelvekben* (Budapest, 1899).

vecians, Russ. Polovcy), and Khazars, and the Mongolian Tartars (more properly Tatars); the numerous recorded changes of language (e.g. the Kirgiz, according to Chinese sources, were located between the Ob' and the Yenisei in the first century B.C. and were not originally Turkic);[1] the relatively close resemblance existing between the constituent members of individual branches (e.g. among Turkic languages, only Yakut and Chuvash are markedly aberrant); and the slowness of evolution of recorded languages, viz. Turkic from the eighth, Mongolian from the thirteenth century. The affinities between Turkic and Mongolian are more obvious than those between either and Manchurian. The phonetic features which all three have in common are—vowel harmony at various stages, a double series of velar plosives flowing out of the vowel harmony, the tendency to eschew initial voiced constrictives (continuants), the clarity and stability of vowels and the instability of final n/η, the absence of consonantal grouping initially and finally, the nonexistence of long or geminated consonants, and proneness to open syllables. Among morphological characteristics the most outstanding are—the presence of possessive suffixes, the absence of gender and the dual number, the use of plain or unaugmented stems (bases) verbally as imperatives and substantivally as nominatives, agglutination of suffixes, both lexical and grammatical, a rudimentary tendency towards flexion in Manchurian and Mongolian, and an almost total lack of syndetic particles. Syntactically Altaic follows the rule of subordinating, in this case preposing, secondary to principal categories, and so the determinant precedes the determinate, the governed the governing word, the subject the predicate, and the adverb the verb, which has final place and emphasis in the sentence.[2]

[1] See W. Radloff, *Altaische Inschriften*, p. 425. The Meshcheryaks (Mishars), Tepters, and Soyots are thought to have originally spoken Uralian. The bulk of the Kamass people, formerly Samoyedic in speech, adopted Turkic in 1840 and Russian in 1890, but preserved part of their Samoyedic vocabulary in the process.

[2] See J. Deny, 'Langues turques, mongoles et toungouzes' in the symposium *Les langues du monde* (Paris, 1924), pp. 185–93.

2

Of the three branches of Altaic the easternmost and least significant numerically is the Manchurian or Tungusic. This comprises two subdivisions, viz. the declining Manchu of Northern Manchuria (Manchukuo), with the related languages of the Golds, Oroches, Shibos, Dahurs (Daurs), and Solons (the last two now partly mongolised) on the one hand, and the more primitive and vigorous Tungus (Evenki) and its cognates—Orochon, Manegir, Birar, Kile, Olcha or Mangun (on the Amur), Negidal (Negda), Samagir, Orok (in Sakhalin), Inkagir, Lalegir, Lamut (Even), Uchur, Maya, Bital, Kangalass, and Chapogir—on the other. This south-north division is based on L. von Schrenck (op. cit.), to whose analysis Sternberg's criticism (op. cit.) opposes a purely geographical classification, viz. Manchurian (comprising Manchu, Gold, Solon, etc.), East Siberian (with Oroch, Olcha, Lamut, Negda, Orok, etc.), Yeniseian, and Ilian (this in the Russo-Chinese riverine frontier-zone). Schrenck's classification was taken over and modified by P. Šmits (Schmidt),[1] who recognised the same two groups, but constituted as follows: Manchurian (Manchu, Gold, Oroch) and Tungusic (Tungus proper, Orochon, Manegir, Solon, Lamut, Negidal, Samagir). In 1930 Ja. P. Al'kor (Koškin) altered Šmits's classification by including Samagir with Gold and recognising three varieties of each principal type. His own takes the following form: (1) Tungusic, consisting of (a) Tungus proper, or Evenki (with Orochon, Manegir, Birar, Solon, Onkor), (b) Lamut, or Even (with the Orochel of Kamchatka and the Okhotsk littoral), (c) Negidal, or Elkenbeye; and (2) Manchurian, consisting of (a) Manchu, (b) Gold, or Nanai (with Olcha, Orok, Samagir, Kile), and (c) Ude, or Udekhe (with Oroch and Kyakar). This classification prevails in Soviet scholarship.[2]

[1] П. Шмидт, *Этнография Дальнего востока* (СПБ, Владивосток, 1915), p. 30.
[2] See В. И. Цинциус, ‚Проблемы сравнительной грамматики тунгусо-маньчжурских языков' (*ИАН, отд. лит. и яз.*, т. VII, вып. 6,

The Manchus apply the name 'Orochon' (reindeer-hunter) to the Tungus in general. Some distinguish between the Orochons (i.e. the mainly inland Tungus) and the Lamuts (maritime Tungus), for the mobile and enterprising Tungus tribes have extended their world from the Arctic Ocean to the Pacific. They have reached the Arctic in the Taimyr peninsula, west of the Khatanga, and at the mouth of the Yana, east of the Lena estuary in Yakutia, and the Pacific coast, as the Lamuts ('sea folk'), or Evens of the extensive area between the Laptev and the Okhotsk Sea. The principal seats of the Tungus (cf. Chinese 'Tung-hu', which is doubtfully derived from Manchu *tonki* 'people'), who call themselves Evenki and numbered c. 60,000 in 1931, are however the three Tunguska affluents of the Yenisei, largely included in the Evenki National Area (*okrug*) of the Krasnoyarsk Region (*kraj*), where they are known to the Samoyeds as 'aiya' ('younger brother'), a name whose meaning calls to mind a Chinese designation of the Japanese (Cant. *ai džai* 'little fellow'). The Amur too is still mainly a Tungus river, and Tungus tribes are found along its tributaries Shilka, Sungari, and Ussuri.

Only the Manchus, under Mongolian influence and as the result of conquest which placed a Manchu dynasty on the throne of China in the seventeenth century, succeeded in giving themselves a literary language, written with characters adapted from the Mongolian alphabet, itself an adaptation of the Turkic Uigur (Uyghur). The other forms of Manchurian, including the Tungusic languages, have been transcribed more or less accurately by scholars.[1] They all share common traits. Vowel harmony is not so strictly adhered to as in the other branches of Altaic (cf. Manch. *miŋgan* 'thousand' with Tung. *mənən* 'money'), the vowel *i* (close front) induces the change of *k/g* into *ts/dz* and *s* into *š*, and crases of vowel-flanked words (e.g.

Москва-Ленинград, 1948). This author adds Solon to the Nanai (Gold) group and distinguishes between literary Tungusic (Evenki, Even, Nanai, Ude) and its non-literary varieties (Negidal, Orok, Oroch, Olcha).

[1] See Г. М. Василевич, *Учебник эвенкийского (тунгусского) языка* (Ленинград, 1934) and В. И. Левин, *Самоучитель эвенского языка* (Москва-Ленинград, 1935).

memama 'foster-father', from *meme* and *ama*) are commoner than in Mongolian and Turkic. Postpositions are handled as in the former, but there are fewer declensional cases in Manchu and its congeners (5–8) and more in Tungusic, which besides two accusatives, a definite (*-wa*) and an indefinite (*-ja*), a genitive (*-ni*), a dative-locative (*-du*), and an ablative (*-duk*), has a prolative (*-duli*), an illative (*-tiki*), a comitative (*-nun*), and an instrumental (*-t*), as well as others, making a total of fourteen oblique cases. Three of these, viz. the nominative, accusative, and dative, are basic to all Manchurian languages. The plural suffix is attached to a limited number of mostly personal nouns in Manchu, but is more widespread in Tungusic (e.g. *bira* 'river', *biral* 'rivers'), and Manchu has borrowed a number of numeral coefficients (numeratives) from Chinese (e.g. *fali* for inanimate objects). Possession can be indicated by mere juxtaposition, as in Welsh and the Semitic 'construct state', but also—in Tungusic only—by possessive suffixes of the first two persons derived from personal pronouns (e.g. Tung. *bi* 'I', *-m* 'my'; *bu* 'we', *-p/-w* 'our'). The verb, as in Mongolian and Chinese, disregards distinctions of number and person in Manchu, but the Tungusic verb has personal predicative suffixes of pronominal origin. The tenses, by Indo-European standards, are imperfect; which implies that the burden of verbal expression is imposed on adverb and participle. Like Mongolian, the Manchurian languages use affixes to express modality in the verb (e.g. the Manchu causative *ara-bu* 'to cause to write' and the reflexive *wa-ja* 'to kill oneself'), and masculinity coupled with the notion of strength on the one hand and femininity coupled with that of weakness on the other are rendered by vowel alternation, *a* being the masculine index, *e* the feminine (e.g. Manchu *haha* 'man', *hehe* 'woman'; *ama* 'father', *eme* 'mother'; *amila* 'cock bird', *emile* 'hen bird'; *gaŋgan* 'strong', *geŋgen* 'weak'). This process has been carried into loan-words: *garudai* 'male phoenix', from the name of the Sanskrit man-eagle Garuḍa, is contrasted with a female *gerudei*, and the Turkic *arsalan* 'lion' has a counterpart in *erselen* 'lioness'.

ALTAIC LANGUAGES

As a representative of Tungusic spoken in the U.S.S.R. we may examine literary Evenki, which is founded on a southern dialect, viz. that of the Katong, formerly Kireng National Area, described by G. M. Vasilevič (op. cit.). The Evenki vowels distinguish long and short correlatives and include the central vowel ə (ə̄), whose incidence is frequent and colours the entire, rather monotonous system. The consonant g is pronounced with friction as [ɣ], ӡ is the voiced palatal plosive [ɟ], w and ɲ have their I.P.A. values, c is [tʃ], and ṇ the palatal nasal. Vowel harmony involves the subtle interplay of a rather small set of vowels:

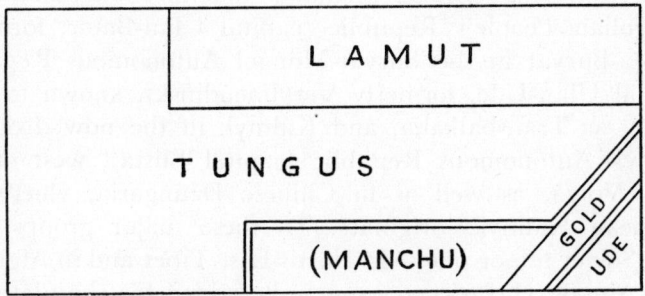

Fig. 7. Diagram of the Manchurian (Tungusic) languages.

thus radical a, ō, ē, u, i, are followed by a in the suffix, o by o, and ə, ə̄, u, i by ə and ə̄ (e.g. acc. sing. mo-wa 'the tree'; gen. sing. oron-mo 'of the deer'). Evenki morphology is typically agglutinative. The case-system expresses both abstract and spatial concepts. There is a plural suffix -l (e.g. mo-l 'trees'), and this is retained in the possessive series (e.g. nom. plur. mo-l-in 'his trees'). The already noticed Manchu vowel-alternation to express sex-gender may be paralleled by Evenki examples (e.g. amin 'father', əmin 'mother'; akin 'elder brother', əkin 'elder sister'). The Evenki verb has an abundance of moods and tenses, the former distinguishing a hypothetical and a necessitative, the latter a future. Syntactically Evenki presents the Altaic characteristic of the finite verb in final position, where the sentence is purely narrative (e.g. nuɲan həgdidu tatkittu alaguwӡaran, literally 'he in a big school is learning').

A Tungus literature arose in the U.S.S.R. after the Revolution, when an alphabet was framed and readers and primers issued.[1] As there are several forms of Tungusic, these have had to be taken into consideration: thus the Evens (Lamuts) as well as the Golds of the lower Amur, who call themselves Nanai and numbered c. 5300 in 1926, received their alphabet at about the same time.

3

The Mongolian branch of Altaic consists of four large dialect-groups, viz. Mongolian proper, spoken outside the U.S.S.R. in Inner Mongolia (Ordoss, Chahar), Khalkha Mongolian in the Mongolian People's Republic (capital Ulan-Bator, formerly Urga), Buryat in the Buryat-Mongol Autonomous Republic (capital Ulan-Ude, formerly Verkhneudinsk), known to geography as Transbaikalia, and Kalmyk in the now dissolved Kalmyk Autonomous Republic (capital Elista), west of the lower Volga, as well as in Chinese Dzungaria, where the European Kalmyks originate. To these major groups, two extra-Soviet minor ones—in North-East Tibet and in Afghanistan (Aimak, Hazara, etc.)—may be added for completeness. The above grouping, suggested by A. D. Rudnev,[2] is primarily geographical.

The U.S.S.R. has representatives of two of the Mongolian language-groups—Buryat, the most northerly type of Mongolian, spoken by nearly a quarter of a million persons in 1926, and Kalmyk, the most westerly, spoken by c. 130,000. Both these, though wide apart, are closely interrelated as well as closely related to Khalkha Mongolian, with which they share recent Russian loans. Of the three, Khalkha Mongolian is the most conservative.[3] The differences, in any case, are compara-

[1] Я. П. Алькор, *Проект эвенкийского алфавита* (Ленинград, 1930); G. M. Wasilevic, *ðləkəsipti əwədi dukuwun* ('First Tungus Book', Moscow, 1931); P. N. Zulew, *Dukuwun taɟin ʒarin*, 1 ('Reading Book', Leningrad, 1933).

[2] „Опыт классификации монголов" in Г. И. Рамстедт (Ramstedt), *Сравнительная фонетика монгольского письменного языка и халхаско-ургинского говора* (СПБ, 1908).

[3] See Р. Ринчинэ и Г. Д. Санжеев, *Краткий монгольско-русский словарь* (Москва, 1947).

tively small and appear to be chiefly phonetic. Buryat, which has three sub-dialects, one of them spoken in Manchuria, is naturally nearer to Khalkha Mongolian than to Kalmyk.

The common literary language of the Mongols has differed from the colloquial ever since it was inaugurated in the thirteenth century, after the foundation of the first ephemeral Mongolian empire by Jenghiz Khan. Its perpendicular, left-to-right alphabet was adapted from the Turkic Uigur, itself borrowed from Sogdian. This alphabet represents an earlier pronunciation (cf. *dologan* 'seven' with Kal. *dolān*; *ulagan* 'red' with Kal. *ulān*; *jagon* 'what?' with Kal. *jūn*). Before the Uigur alphabet was adopted, Chinese ideograms had been used, and from 1269 to about 1350, following the example of Kublai Khan, official use was made of the 'square' (*dürbäldžin*) script of forty-one characters based on Tibetan models and invented by the lama 'Phagspa.[1] The Kalmyks, under Manchu influence, perfected the Mongolian alphabet in 1648 (Zaya Paṇḍita's reform) by diacritically modifying seven characters, so as to bring them more in harmony with colloquial distinctions; the angularity of the letters too was replaced by more rounded outlines. The use of this perfected alphabet however was coupled with that of Literary Mongolian, which the Kalmyks abandoned for their own dialect only in 1931. Buryat literature, which began in the eighteenth century with translations of Buddhist books from the Tibetan, was also based on Literary Mongolian till recent times (1928), when colloquial Buryat, first introduced in the periodical *Manja Keln* ('Our Language'), took its place. Since then both Buryat and Kalmyk have acquired a modern literature, both imaginative and practical, newspapers, and school books. But the most attractive part of their literature still remains their very abundant folklore, which comprises both folk-tales and epic verse (e.g. *Xa Ošir*).[2]

The Buryat dialects, including Bargut, which is spoken mainly in China, are characterised phonetically by the con-

[1] See R. Bonaparte, *Documents de l'épigraphie mongole des XIIIe et XIVe siècles* (Paris, 1895).
[2] See A. Rudnev, 'A Buriat Epic' (*MSFOu*, LII, Helsinki, 1924).

version of Common Mongolian *ts*, *tš*, *dz*, *dž*, into *s*, *š*, *z*, *ž* (i.e. loss of affrication through loss of the initial dental plosive) and by the change of *s* into *h*(*x*). There are two main dialects—the Northern (Cisbaikalian) and the Southern (Transbaikalian)— and these are so discrepant that communication is not always possible between them. The vowel phonemes of Literary Buryat,[1] which uses a modified Cyrillic script, are varied and include diphthongs and a rounded member of the front series (ẏ = [ʏ]). They are marshalled according to the requirements of vowel harmony into contrasted front and back types, *i*, both long and short, being treated as neutral. The consonantal system is simpler owing to the absence of certain labials (*p*, *f*, *v*) and velars (*k*, *n*). Expiratory stress falls on the first syllable and is independent of vowel length, but the final syllable carries a tone, which gives the impression that it is stressed. Noun and pronoun are declined here, as in the other forms of Mongolian, and the adjective is invariable for case. The Buryat system of declension is straightforward and has a limited range of case-forms. Possessive suffixes exist side by side with absolute possessive pronouns (e.g. *tanai ger* 'your house', *gerheetnai* 'out of your house'). The verb distinguishes tense-aspect and mood and isolates participle and gerund. The syntactic pattern of the language shows the major members of the sentence (subject and finite verb) normally enclosing the minor, the verb coming last (e.g. *xašan morimnai xaišaa arljaab* 'where did our lazy horse stray to?', which shows the attributive adjective preceding its noun).

Kalmyk also has two main dialectal forms—Derbet and Torgout—but these differ little from each other. The phonetic peculiarities are a qualitative distinction between stressed and unstressed vowels (the latter covered by the ə-phoneme), rigid vowel harmony, and the occasional variability of the base as in flexion (e.g. nom. sing. *modn* 'tree', instr. *modār*, dat.-loc. *modndə*). The first syllable is strongly stressed, which leaves the others weakened, though the inflections can be made prominent

[1] See Г. Д. Санжеев, *Грамматика бурят-монгольского языка* (Москва-Ленинград, 1941).

by emphasis. Nouns and pronouns are declined in paradigms of eight oblique cases, including a sociative and a directive, whose functions are multiplied by postpositional government. The declension of the personal pronouns is not dissimilar to that of inflected languages (e.g. nom. *bi* 'I', gen. *minə*, dat.-loc. *nandə*). Kalmyk verbs exhibit a modal variety, which discriminates between a *dubitativus optans* of probability and a *dubitativus abhorrens*, but they are less rich in tenses, of which there are fundamentally two—the past and the present. The language also uses four participles and many hypotactic *converba* (e.g. *bā̈w-ās bā̈G* 'as it is, let it be so')[1]. Syntax insists on a strict

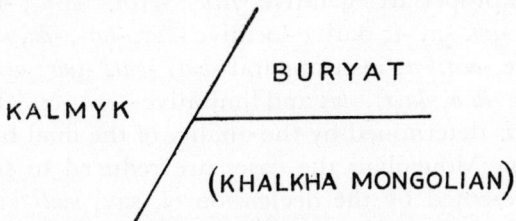

Fig. 8. Diagram of the Mongolian languages.

word-order, and the less important categories (qualifier, object, complement) precede the more important, viz. the qualified and the verb. The Kalmyk vocabulary shows Russian and, to a less extent, Turkic and Tibetan influence. The modern literature and press are based on the Torgout dialect and at first used the Cyrillic script, to which they have returned after experimenting with a modified Latin one.

The phonetic structure of Mongolian, like that of other types of Altaic, is grounded in the laws of vowel harmony, i.e. the adaptation of suffix vowels to those of the base on the principle of the antithetic 'hard-soft' classification of vowels. In Mongolian the 'hard', or back series *a, o, u* is paralleled by the 'soft', or front series *e* (*ä*), *ö, ü*, and these, as in Manchurian, Turkic, and Korean,[2] determine the quality of adjacent velar plosives, i.e. *q* and *g* [G] are found in association with the first group,

[1] See G. J. Ramstedt, *Kalmückisches Wörterbuch* (Helsinki, 1935), pp. xvii–xx.
[2] G. J. Ramstedt, *A Korean Grammar* (Helsinki, 1939), p. 25.

k and *g'* with the second. Unlike Turkic, Mongolian treats *i* as a neutral vowel, i.e. as one capable of associating indifferently with both types of the vowel dichotomy (cf. Hungarian). Contrary to Turkic practice again, the agglutinative principle is not rigidly applied: consonantal alternation, a first step towards flexion, is found in such pairs as *balgasun* 'town' (cf. Khalkha Mong. *balgas*) and *balgat* 'towns', *nöx'ür* 'companion' (cf. Khalkha Mong. *nökör*, Bur. *nüxer*) and *nöx'üt* 'companions'.[1] Suffixation is as detailed as in Turkish, but the order of the suffixes is not quite the same: Turkish gives precedence to possessive, Mongolian to case suffixes. The noun cases in Mongolian proper are: genitive *-ji(n)*, *-gi(n)*, *-u(n)*, *-i*, *-ai*, etc.; accusative *-igi*, *-ji*, *-i*; dative-locative *-dur*, *-tur-*, *-du*, *-tu*, *-da*, *-ta*, *-a*; ablative *-ača*, *-a*; instrumental *-bar*, *-gar*, *-ijar*; cooperative, or sociative *-lu'a*, *-la(r)*, *-lo*; and limitative *-čege*, *-čej*.[2] The choice of endings is determined by the quality of the final base-vowel. In Khalkha Mongolian the cases are reduced to six oblique forms represented by the declension of, say, *mal* 'cattle', viz. gen. sing. *malyn*, dat.-loc. *mald*, acc. *malyg*, abl. *malaas*, instr. *malaar*, soc. *maltai*. The Mongolian verbal base is given by the imperative. The conjugation of Mongolian proper displays a variety of temporal (including future and preterite) and especially of modal forms (including a prescriptive, a precative, and a benedictive), but person and number are rarely expressed, except in Buryat and Kalmyk (cf. Manchu). G. J. Ramstedt[3] distinguishes predicative from nominative usage in the Mongolian verb, the former qualified as definitive (finite) by Russian grammarians, the latter discriminating between *nomina verbalia* (participial forms) and *converba*, i.e. adverbial forms corresponding to the gerundive locutions in Turkish. The *converba* too contribute to the scarcity of syndetic constructions. In the sentence, adjective and attributive genitive precede the noun, object and complement precede the verb: the sentence begins

---

[1] J. Deny, 'Langues mongoles' in A. Meillet and M. Cohen, *Les langues du monde* (Paris, 1924), pp. 226–7.

[2] J. Deny, op. cit.

[3] *Kalmückisches Wörterbuch* (Helsinki, 1935).

with adverbs and ends with the verb, which closes and punctuates the predicative complex. The system of numeration[1] shows marked lexical divergences from Manchurian and Turkic, not to mention Uralian (cf. Mong. *nigen* 'one', Khalkha Mong. *nege*, with Manch. *emu*,[2] Turk. *bir*). It is curiously significant and not wholly unexpected that Šmits (op. cit.) explains the Mongolian word for 'five' *tabun* (cf. Khalkha Mong. *tava(n)*, Bur. *taban*) as being derived from a base *tav-* (cf. *tavar* 'span') meaning 'hand'.[3]

4

Turkic (Turanian) counts more members than any other branch of Altaic, and the area it covers is vast and extends, with interruptions, from the Mediterranean to the river Kolyma and the East Siberian Sea. The total number of Turkic speakers in 1897, including those living outside Russia, was over thirty millions, and there is every reason to believe that this number has both steadily and considerably increased since then. L. Tesnière gives it as thirty-nine millions at the end of 1926.[4] Over half of these now live in the U.S.S.R.—in Siberia, Central Asia, South and East Russia, and the Caucasus. This catalogue of names, incidentally, offers a geographical classification of the Turkic languages, but such a classification must necessarily be unsatisfactory, because it does not consider linguistic criteria. In 1929 A. Sauvageot,[5] following Gyula Németh, the Hungarian turcologist, suggested detaching the extreme eastern Yakut from the extreme western Chuvash as independent units (the *s*-group) from a loose and scattered grouping of the remainder (*j*-group). This classification, reproduced by C. Tagliavini in the *Enciclopedia Italiana*, is too general. But there is still

[1] See P. Schmidt, 'Altaische Zahlwörter' (*MSFOu*, LXVII, Helsinki, 1927).
[2] Cf. Mong. *emüne* 'in front', Khalkha Mong. *emne*.
[3] Turkish *bes* 'five' is an Indo-European loan-word (cf. Pers. *pandž*), but *elli* 'fifty' recalls *el* 'hand'. The synonymy of 'five' and 'hand' is illustrated *inter alia* by Austronesian *lima/rima*.
[4] 'Statistique des langues de l'Europe' in A. Meillet, *Les langues dans l'Europe nouvelle*[2] (Paris, 1928).
[5] 'Ural-Altaic (*sic*) Languages' (*Encyclopaedia Britannica*, XXII, 1929[14]).

W. Radloff's (into Eastern, Western, and Central Asiatic),[1] as improved by P. M. Melioranskij for the Russian 'Brockhaus-Efron Encyclopaedia', by F. E. Korš,[2] and more recently by A. N. Samojlovič.[3] This uses phonetic as well as morphological data, and has received the sanction of Soviet turcology. There are, in terms of this classification, five groups of Turkic languages: (1) the South-Western (i.e. the non-Soviet Osmanli, the Azerbaijani, Turkmen, Khorezmi of Khiva, Turuk of Fergana and Uzbekistan, Gagauzi of Bessarabia, and Krymchak, or South Crimean Tartar); (2) the North-Western (i.e. Oirot, or Altai,[4] Baraba, Tartar of the Volga-Kama area, Bashkir, Tepter, Mishar, Kazakh, Kirgiz,[5] Nogay, Tobol Tartar, Karakalpak, Karachay-Balkar, Kumyk, North Crimean Tartar, and the Karaim of Poland and the Crimea); (3) the South-Eastern (i.e. Uzbek, and the largely non-Soviet Neo-Uiguric dialects of Taranchi, or Ili, Kashgar, Turfan, Ami, Khotan, and Lobnor); (4) the North-Eastern (i.e. Shor, Tuva,[6] Sary-Yugur in China, Khakass, and Yakut); and (5) Chuvash, the modern descendant of Bolgar. It will be observed that this classification recognises the distinctness of Chuvash, if not of Yakut, and admits three of Radloff's divisions, viz. the Western (Kipchak), the Eastern (Altai), and the Central Asiatic (Uzbek), although the membership of Radloff's groups is not reproduced in full.[7] Radloff puts

[1] *Phonetik der nördlichen Türksprachen* (Leipzig, 1883).
[2] ‚Классификация турецких племен по языкам' (*Этногр. обозрение,* Москва, 1910).
[3] *Некоторые дополнения к классификации турецких языков* (Петроград, 1922).
[4] Altai is a Turkic language allied to the adjacent Teleut, Tuba, and Kumanda. It should not be confused with Altaic. Nor is Turkic Oirot synonymous with Mongolian Oirat (Kalmyk).
[5] K. H. Menges (see *Qaraqalpaq Grammar*, 1, New York, 1947) places Kirgiz (Qyrɣyz) in Samojlovič's South-Eastern group along with Uzbek (Özbek) and Old Uigur.
[6] Spoken in the now annexed satellite republic of Tannu Tuva (capital Kyzyl), formerly Chinese Uryankhai, north-west of the Mongolian People's Republic. It is known also as Soyot or Soyon.
[7] Radloff has also influenced V. A. Bogorodickij's classification, which recognises, e.g., a Central Asiatic group (see *Введение в татарское языкознание в связи с другими тюркскими языками,* Казань, 1934).

Tuva (Uryankhai), for instance, in the Eastern group, and Khorezmi in the Central Asiatic. The phonetic tests used in effecting the classification are—the presence or absence of voiced or voiceless plosives and affricates initially (e.g. voiceless plosives are used in Radloff's Eastern group, voiced plosives in the Southern group: *pir/bir* 'one'); the quality of vowels, which is largely determined by the strictness with which the principles of vowel harmony are applied (e.g. in Radloff's Central Asiatic and Southern groups *o* and *ö* occur only under stress); the choice of hush or hiss sibilants, i.e. *š/tš* or *s/ts*; the sonority or voicelessness of intervocalic consonants (e.g. in the Eastern group they are all voiced); the choice of one or other of the interchangeable *z*, *t*, *d*, and *j* (e.g. *azaq*, *ataq*, *adaq*, *ajaq* 'leg'); the existence of velar *l* (lacking in Central Asiatic); and the retention of archaic *v* (in the Southern group), which has become either *p* or *f* in the majority of Turkic languages. Samojlovič's classification involves the use of key-words like *tau/tağ/dağ* 'mountain' and *bol/ol* 'to be', and the apophonic (Ablaut) series *z-t-d-j* for subdivision. Thus Oirot (Altai) belongs to the North-Western group of *tau*-dialects, Koibal to the *z*-subgroup of the North-East group of *bol*-dialects.

The earliest known attempt to classify the Turkic languages was made by the lexicographer Maḥmūd-al-Kāšgharī for his Turco-Arabic glossary about 1073.[1] He distinguished between a Western group (comprising Oguz, the precursor of modern Turkish, Pecheneg, Kipchak, and Turco-Bolgar) and an Eastern group (comprising Uigur, Kashgar, etc.). The affiliation of Turkish to Oguz reveals how relatively slight linguistic changes have been in at least one form of Turkic during nine centuries. In spite of this and of other information furnished by the fourteenth-century *Codex Cumanicus* (a Latin-Persian-Turkish vocabulary) and the runiform Orkhon inscriptions interpreted by the Danish scholar V. Thomsen in 1893, Turkic historical grammar is still rudimentary, and up to now nothing comparable in mass and analysis to the work done by

---

[1] *Dīwān lughāt al-turk*. See B. Atalay, *Divanü lûgat-it-türk tercümesi*, I–III (Ankara, 1939–41) and *Divanü lûgat-it-türk tipkibasimi* (Ankara, 1941).

K. Brugmann and H. Hirt for Indo-European and of C. Brockelmann for Semitic has been written.[1]

In contrast to Uralian and even to its own immediate congeners, Turkic is very uniform in time and space. Its separation from Mongolian appears to be ancient in view of the scarcity of parallels in vocabulary: the numerals, as we have seen, are totally different. On the whole the common words are shorter in Turkic, longer in Mongolian (cf. Turk. *dağ* 'mountain', Kirg. *tau*, with Mong. *dabaga* 'mountain pass', Khalkha Mong. *davaa(n)*). But for all these and other dissimilarities, the relationship between Turkic and Mongolian remains intimate and indisputable. Pronouns, case suffixes, and sentence structure exhibit an obvious family likeness. Noun and verb forms are built up by agglutination, which is pointed by vowel harmony (e.g. Turk. *öldürmeyelim* 'let us not kill'; *dostunuz* 'your friend'). The laws of vowel harmony affect the same eight vowels—a front series represented by $e(ä)$, i, $ö$, $ü$, and a complementary back series consisting of a, $ı(y)$, o, u. The forms of adjustment involve assimilations between the front and the back series, open and close types, and rounded and neutral types. The result of the interplay of these assimilations is that the same suffix can have four different vowel-variants, viz. a, $e(ä)$, o, $ö$, if it is open, and $ı(y)$, u, i, $ü$, if it is close. In contrast to the variety of vowels, the Turkic consonantal system is fairly simple. Peculiar consonants are found chiefly in those languages which have been in close contact with representatives of other stocks, for instance North Caucasian. Karachay has strongly aspirated plosives (p', t', k', q', $č'$), Balkar has 'interdentals' ([θ], [ð]), Karaim the palatal plosive [c], Taranchi (in Eastern Turkestan) the uvular vibrant (*r-grasseye'*), and Abakan (an Oirot dialect) initial *mb*, as in Albanian, Melanesian, and Bantu. Turkic suffixation is more agglutinative than either Mongolian or Manchurian: base and suffix constitute a single, though well articulated, whole,

---

[1] K. Brugmann, *Grundriss der vergleichenden Grammatik der indogermanischen Sprachen* (Berlin-Leipzig, 1906–30); H. Hirt, *Indogermanische Grammatik* (Heidelberg, 1921–29); C. Brockelmann, *Grundriss der vergleichenden Grammatik der semitischen Sprachen* (Berlin, 1908–13).

whereas in the more easterly varieties of Altaic, as in Palaeoasiatic, the fusion of parts is less complete. The noun suffixes describe a comparatively restricted number of declensional cases—genitive (*-(n)iŋ, -(n)in, -n*: Turk. *ev-in* 'of the house'), accusative (*-ig, -eg, -(j)i, -ni*: Turk. *ev-i*; cf. Yak. *-ne, -te, -le*), dative (*-ge, -ke, -(j)e*: Turk. *ev-e*), locative (*-de, -te*: Turk. *ev-de*; cf. Yak. *-ne, -ine*) and ablative (*-den, -din*: Turk. *ev-den*).[1] The plural endings *-lar/-ler* (e.g. Turk. *baş-lar* 'heads', *göz-ler* 'eyes') have parallel secondary formations, which illustrate the characteristic Turkic alternation of dental, 'liquid', and nasal consonants. Noun and verb share the same pronominal suffixes, the noun to indicate possession, the verb to indicate person (e.g. Turk. *ev-im* 'my house', *sever-im* 'I love'). The other suffixes denote tense (e.g. Turk. *sev-dim* 'I loved'), negation (e.g. Turk. *sev-me-mek* 'not to love'), and voice (e.g. Turk. *sev-il-mek* 'to be loved'). The nominal category however dominates the verbal in Turkic, with the result that the finite verb is less common than participial constructions.[2] The position of the suffixes, nominal and verbal, tends to vary: Yakut, for instance, inserts the negative *-pa-* (cf. Turk. *-ma-*) immediately after the verbal base and before the other suffixes, whereas allied forms of Turkic, e.g. Turkish itself, prefer a position farther removed from the base. Unlike Uralian, Turkic is largely free from irregularities, apart from those imposed by the demands of vowel harmony. In this respect it is widely different from Indo-European, towards which geographical proximity and perhaps a still to be established genetic relationship have urged the less regular Uralian. While the Uralian base tolerates variation (e.g. Finn. *käsi/kät-/käd-* 'hand') and the Uralian inflections are invariable for both numbers, the Turkic base and suffixes are units compacted with transparent precision.[3] Compounds are rarer in

[1] J. Deny, 'Langues turques' in *Les langues du monde* (Paris, 1924), p. 206.
[2] K. Grönbech, *Die türkische Sprachbau* (Copenhagen, 1936).
[3] The 'agglutination' in Papuan, as described by A. Capell ('Word-Building and Agglutination in South-Eastern Papua', *BSOS*, IX, 3, London, 1937–9), is of a different sort. The examples he adduces illustrate the amalgamation of units which are for the most part semantically self-sufficient.

Turkic than in Uralian, and this is illustrated most clearly by a comparison of the cultured extra-Soviet languages—Turkish on the one hand, and Finnish and Hungarian on the other. The tendency to agglutination, of which Turkic is the supreme example in linguistic literature, increases as we proceed from north-east to south-west, from Yakutia to Anatolia. At the same time the Turkic verb acquires a greater complexity (cf. the 'extremes' of Yakut and Turkish in this particular). But besides graded characteristics we find idiosyncrasies. The Central Asiatic forms of Turkic are remarkable for phonetic abbreviation. Yakut, though isolated and aberrant, is not outstandingly conservative: thus it has lost its genitive-case suffix and replaced it with a pronominal periphrasis singularly resembling a familiar Dutch and Low German construction (cf. Yak. *örüs bas-a* 'the horse's head' with African Dutch *dag se werk* 'day's work', Low Germ. *den' Herr sin Engel* 'the angel of the Lord').[1] Chuvash, on the western march of the Turkic world, also has a distinct individuality, less because of geographical isolation than because it is, as research has proved, a Turkic language with a Uralian 'substratum'.

The interresemblance of the Turkic languages was till recently accentuated by their standardised Arabic spelling with Persian values, which imperfectly represented the phonetic diversity of colloquial speech. But long before they adopted the Arabic script, Turkic-speakers had been familiar with two other alphabets of Semitic origin, which may be qualified as 'national' in the sense in which the Mongolian and the Manchu are. These Turkic alphabets are the runiform *kök türk* ('Urban Turkic')[2] of the Orkhon and Yenisei inscriptions and the Uigur, or Neo-

[1] The Papuan language Bongu (in Northern New Guinea, east of Madang) offers a parallel in *bul andam ingi* 'pig its fodder'. See A. Hanke, *Grammatik und Vokabularium der Bongu-Sprache* (Berlin, 1909).

[2] This was also a court language, with special words for courtly use, e.g. *ašar* 'to eat' instead of the common *jir* (see C. Brockelmann, 'Hofsprache in Altturkistan', *Donum Natalicium Schrijnen*, 1, Nijmegen-Utrecht, 1929). The same differences are found in Javanese (cf. the *boso kromo* 'high language' with the *boso ngoko* 'low language'), Polynesian, Micronesian, Fijian, and Dravidian.

Sogdian, which derive from Persian Aramaic. The runiform alphabet was known in the sixth century. Its characters are written without ligatures, from right to left, and the period is indicated by a colon. There are about forty characters, and they are so devised as to reproduce the peculiar phenomena of vowel harmony. The inscriptions are funerary and cut in tall stone monuments dedicated to the memory of Turkic kagans. They are our principal source for the history of the Turkic kingdom on the Orkhon river (a Selenga affluent in Mongolia) in the eighth century. Discovered over 200 years ago by the Swede Strahlenberg, and studied by three expeditions, including W. Radloff's, between 1889 and 1891,[1] they were deciphered by V. Thomsen only in 1893.[2] Thomsen thought the characters to be ultimately of Aramaic (Nestorian Sogdian) origin. The Uigur alphabet[3] seems to have overlapped the runiform at a later stage and derives, according to F. Müller,[4] not from the Estrangelo Syriac of the Nestorian missionaries, but from the Sogdian. In its turn it served as a model for the Mongolian and the Manchu characters. It has fourteen letters and, in accordance with Semitic practice, does not indicate vowels, but suggests them through the quality of adjacent consonants (cf. the Russian indication of palatalised consonants by vowel symbols). The Uigur alphabet was used for Buddhist literature and later even for Mohammedan texts before it was finally discarded for the Persian-Arabic. Among the oldest surviving works in this alphabet is the Kashgar court-chamberlain

[1] See *Inscriptions de l'Orkhon* (Helsinki, 1890).
[2] 'Inscriptions de l'Orkhon dechiffrées' (*MSFOu*, v, Helsinki, 1894–6); 'Turcica. Etudes concernant l'interprétation des inscriptions turques de la Mongolie et de la Sibérie' (*MSFOu*, xxxvii, Helsinki, 1916). Consult also O. Donner, 'Sur l'origine de l'alphabet turc du Nord de l'Asie' (*JSFOu*, xiv, Helsinki, 1896); A. Vámbéry, 'Noten zu den alttürkischsen Inschriften der Mongolei und Sibirien' (*MSFOu*, xii, Helsinki, 1897–8); Н. Г. Малицкий, *О связи тюркских тамг (письмен) с орхонскими письменами* (Ташкент, 1897–8); W. Radloff, *Die alttürkischen Inschriften der Mongolei*, i–iii (St Petersburg, 1894–9).
[3] A. von Le Coq, *Kurze Einführung in die uigurische Schriftkunde* (Berlin, 1919).
[4] *Uigurica*, i–ii (Berlin, 1908–10).

Yusuf's didactic *Kudatku Bilik* (or *Qutadgu Bilig*, 1069).[1] At a very much later date (fifteenth–seventeenth centuries) it was occasionally used to represent Chagatai (Old Uzbek), a literary language which flourished at Samarkand, Bukhara, and Herat (Afghanistan), and was also resorted to by the Mogul emperor Babur.[2]

Modern Turkic languages, when reduced to writing, have generally had recourse to the Arabic script. This usage was the outcome of the paramount Turkish and Mohammedan influence, and the script was given its Turkish values. In some cases (e.g. in Bashkir, Kirgiz, Chuvash, Yakut, Gagauzi, and even Volga Tartar), where that influence was not exclusive, a modified Cyrillic alphabet is found, as in translations of the Scriptures. After the October Revolution the latinisation of the limited and inadequate Arabic alphabet was initiated. This however was not the first attempt at alphabetic reform. In the middle of the nineteenth century the Azerbaijani writer Mirza Fatali Achundov proposed the replacement of the Arabic alphabet by a judicious mixture of Latin and Cyrillic characters, but his proposal was ignored. In 1922 reforms were inaugurated at Baku, and by 1924 the new Latin script had been introduced into schools in Azerbaijan. During the next three years latinised alphabets were adopted by the Turkic Karachays, the Indo-European Ossetes (Ossetinians), and the North Caucasian Adyge, Chechen, Ingush, and Abkhaz peoples. Societies and study circles of 'Friends of the New Alphabet' (*yanalif*), were started among the extra-Caucasian Turkic peoples, for instance the Volga Tartars, Bashkirs, Turkmens, Uzbeks, Kazakhs, and Crimean Tartars.[3] In due course all those Soviet nationalities that had at one time used the Arabic alphabet adopted the Latin. This script was also taken up by other peoples, which already had letters of their own, notably the Kalmyks, Buryats, even the

---

[1] See W. Radloff, *Das Kudatku Bilik des Jusuf Chass-Hadschib aus Bälasagun*, I–II (St Petersburg, 1891–1910).

[2] See Á. Vámbéry, *Čagataische Sprachstudien* (Leipzig, 1867) and *Uigurische Sprachmonumente und das Kudatku Bilik* (Leipzig, 1870).

[3] See Ф. Агадзе и К. Каракашлы, *Очерк по истории развития нового алфавита и его достижения* (Казань, 1928).

Jews and the Chinese of the U.S.S.R., and it became the basis of alphabets devised for a number of lately illiterate tribes. The Turkic Latin-letter systems were unified in 1927. There are thirty-three letters in all, including c ([tʃ]) and ç ([ʤ]), whose values are reversed in Turkish, ə, q, ʜ ([ɣ]), ŋ ([ŋ]), ө ([ø]), ş ([ʃ]), ƶ ([ʒ]), and ь ([ɯ]). Errors were inevitably committed in the framing of the new alphabets, for instance the awkward, multiliteral systems compiled for the North Caucasian languages Kabardin (Kabardinian) and Circassian (Kyakh), and especially the Tajiki alphabet; and on the whole even the unified Turkic alphabet, like the Tagalog and Fijian scripts of the Spanish and English missionaries respectively, or the English and Dutch spellings of various types of Indonesian (e.g. Malay), is inadequate because of the phonetic misconnections of several of the characters (e.g. ç for [ʤ], ө for [ø], ь for [ɯ], ƶ for [ʒ], and especially Yakut q for [x], ʃ for [ɣ], з for [ʤ], x for [œ], w for [yö], and ıo for [uo].[1] After 1929, with the gradual recrudescence of Russian nationalism in the U.S.S.R., several peoples, particularly those living in close contact with Russians, gave up the Latin character, with its Western 'overtones', for the Cyrillic. Thus the Kabardins adopted Cyrillic in 1935–6, the Oirots, Shors (Russ. Šorcy), and Nogays in 1937, and after that other Soviet nationalities followed suit. The change-over was particularly common in the 1940's. It is obviously easier to write one's mother-tongue with traditional Russian letters than with an odd and unskilful medley of characters elaborated from an exotic system by some 'compromising' alphabetic commission. And so 'latinisation', which Lenin had described in 1922 as 'the great revolution in the East', and which had aided in the 'liquidation' of illiteracy, was largely abandoned for a more familiar and practical method of representing the spoken word. In Turkey however the stimulus of the alphabetic reforms in Azerbaijan in 1924 led to the ultimate abandonment of the Arabic script. Mustafa Kemal set up a committee to study the matter of alphabetic reform in 1927. The reform itself began in

[1] See E. Lewy, 'Die Türksprachen' (1926) in M. Heepe, *Lautzeichen und ihre Anwendung in verschiedenen Sprachgebieten* (Berlin, 1928).

Turkey in the following year with a decree imposing the use of the new character on press and business. The Latin alphabet was introduced into Outer Mongolia and Tannu Tuva in 1930 and subsequently correlated with those of the Buryats and Kalmyks. In the 1940's the Cyrillic replaced it in both areas.

The earliest attempt to represent a Turkic language phonetically is the *Codex Cumanicus* (fourteenth century), in which the medieval Latin characters are skilfully adapted to symbolise Turkic phonemes. In 1857 Castrén applied his tested transcription to the representation of the Turkic Koibal and Karagass. In the later nineteenth century W. Radloff, following Otto Böhtlingk, began a more intensive study of the Turkic languages of Siberia and used Cyrillic to represent them.[1] Yakut was first transcribed by Böhtlingk in 1851, and his transcription was taken over almost *in extenso* by the Russo-German scholar E. K. Pekarskij for his monumental Yakut dictionary in 1907.[2] Compared with this, the Soviet alphabet for Yakut, though accurate in principle, is weird in execution. When the Orkhon 'runes' were deciphered late in the nineteenth century, Thomsen chose a Latin transliteration to reproduce them, Radloff a Cyrillic one. This tendency of Western scholars to use Latin and of Russians to use Cyrillic continued till the 1920's, when, as we have already noticed, the Russians temporarily abandoned Cyrillic for Latin.

Of the numerous varieties of Turkic, most of which are confined within the frontiers of the U.S.S.R., Yakut (Sakha),[3] spoken in the immense Yakut Autonomous Republic (capital Yakutskay, Russ. Yakutsk), which approximately coincides with the Lena basin, is regarded as one of the more isolated types. It represents the North-Eastern group and is remarkable *inter alia* for the perfection to which it carries the Altaic and Uralian device of vowel harmony, with its balanced vowel-series. This

---

[1] *Proben der Volksliteratur der türkischen Stämme Südsibiriens*, I–X (St Petersburg, 1866–1907).

[2] *Словарь якутского языка*, I–III (СПБ, Ленинград, 1907–30).

[3] This name is also given to themselves by the turkicised Dolgans of the Taimyr (or Dolgan-Nenets) National Area.

language exhibits archaic features: for instance, the suffix -*tar* of the conditional participle is paralleled by -*sar* in the Orkhon inscriptions. Another thing the two languages, past and present, have in common is the confusion of the ablative and locative cases. Yakut has initial *s* for the *j* and *ç* (*dž*) of other Turkic types (e.g. Yak. *suoł* 'road'; cf. Turkmen *jōł*, Nog. *džoł*, Volga Tart. *žoł*) and intervocalic *t* for *j/d* (cf. Yak. *atag* 'leg' with Turkmen *ajaq*, Orkhon *adag*, Shor *aðag*). The language has preserved original long consonants, like Turkmen, and to some extent like Karachay and Mishar, and it has diphthongised *e* and *o*. The Yakut vocabulary discloses Palaeoasiatic as well as Altaic contacts, the latter represented by Mongolian and Tungus loans. Mongolian has also modified Yakut morphology, for instance some features of conjugation. Since the Revolution the Latin character has replaced both the earlier Cyrillic and the phonetic transcription invented and employed by the Yakut S. P. Novgorodov, but Pekarskij's dictionary was continued and completed in his own Cyrillic character.

In contrast to the North-Eastern group, the North-Western is well represented. Its easternmost type is Oirot. This is a general name for the related dialects of a group of tribes—Altai, Teleut, Abakan, Tuba, and Chelkan—which numbered c. 48,000 in 1939. There was no Oirot writing till the Revolution, which established an Oirot Autonomous Province (capital Oirottura) in 1922, founded schools, and introduced a press. At first Oirot was written in Cyrillic characters, which in 1929–30 gave way to Latin and were restored in 1938. The language has been described in detail by N. M. Dyrenkova.[1] Phonetically Oirot is interesting for its long and short vowels, palatal plosive (written *d'*, e.g. *d'er* 'earth'; cf. Turk. *yer*), and velar nasal (η). Its 'Kipchak' affiliations may be seen in the forms *kün* 'day' and *tau* 'mountain'. The system of noun declension is complicated by the presence of an instrumental and a comparative case (e.g. instr. *keme-le*, comp. *keme-dij* < *keme* 'boat'), and it has a parallel in the declension of the numerals. The Oirot verbal system is well articulated from its finite forms to the 'peripheral'

[1] *Грамматика ойротского языка* (Москва-Ленинград, 1940).

participles and gerunds. The negative suffix, unlike the characteristic Turkic -*ma*-, is -*pa*-/-*ba*- (e.g. *čyk-pa-gam* 'I did not go out'; cf. Yakut). Asyndetism is relieved by the use of the copulative conjunctions *da/de*, *la/le*, and *baza* 'and'.

The more southerly members of the North-Eastern group, spoken mainly in the northern part of Central Asia, are Kazakh, Karakalpak, and Kirgiz, which are associated respectively with the federal republic of Kazakhstan (capital Alma-Ata, formerly Verny), the Karakalpak Autonomous Republic (capital Nukus) and the federal republic of Kirgizia (capital Frunze, formerly Pishpek).

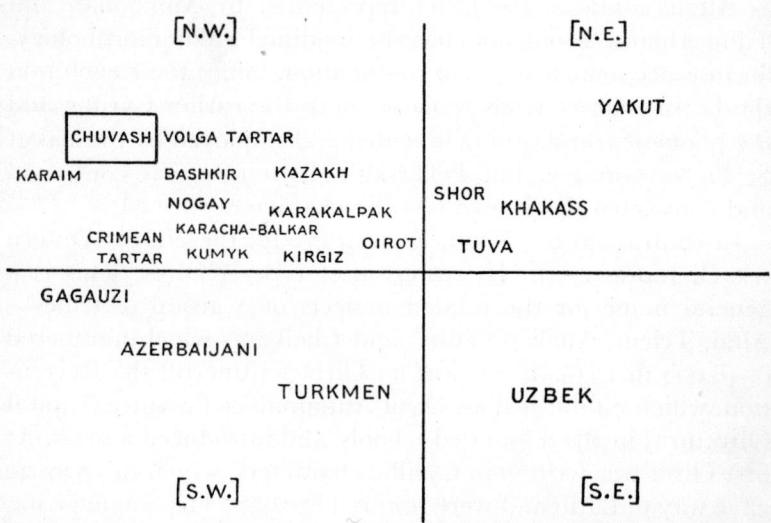

Fig. 9. Diagram of the Turkic languages.

Kazakh, the earlier Kazak-Kirgiz, was known corruptly as Kirgiz-Kaisak in the eighteenth century (cf. the opening of Deržavin's 'Ode to Felica', i.e. Catherine II). To-day it is numerically one of the strongest Turkic languages of the U.S.S.R. It has dialectal forms, for instance the Aral variety, but so far these have not been properly investigated. The Aral dialect has ǯ (*dž*) for the normal Kazakh *ž*, as well as special affixes, e.g.

aldъmъz for the more usual *aldьq* 'we took'. Kazakh proper, like most other Turkic languages, subjects its vowels to the strict laws of vowel harmony. It diphthongises or elides them to avoid hiatus (e.g. *kara at* 'black horse' > *kar'at*). Its consonantal system is characterised by the absence of initial *d* and *g* (e.g. *tau* 'mountain', *keldi* 'he came'; cf. Turk. *dağ, geldi*), *b* for Turkish *v* (e.g. *bermek* 'to give'; cf. Turk. *vermek*), and final *ŋ* for *n* (e.g. *onuŋ* 'his'; cf. Karak. *onun*). Kazakh declension includes a comparative case in *-dai/-dei* in its paradigm and extends to the pronoun, but not to the adjective, according to general Turkic usage. The system of possessive suffixes is fully developed. In the verb we observe a predominance of tense over mood: past and future exhibit two types each, and the tense system is complicated by being carried into the non-finite grammatical categories, including the gerund, where it is best interpreted however in terms of aspect (e.g. perf. gerund *baryp* 'having gone', imperf. gerund *bara* 'going'). Kazakh syntax, like that of other Turkic languages, illustrates the prevalence of participial constructions. Kazakh has had a literature from feudal Islamic times. It was particularly vigorous in the late nineteenth century, when the Kazakhs revolted against Tsarist oppression. To-day Kazakh has a full modern literature, with an eminent representative in the epic poet Džambul Džabajev.

Karakalpak is used both on its own territory, an administrative subdivision of Uzbekistan, and in Uzbekistan itself. It is most closely related to Nogay (q.v.) and Kazakh, and its vocabulary has been influenced by the latter.[1] Karakalpak has a typical Turkic set of paired vowels; diphthongises vowels initially (e.g. *e* becomes *i̯e*, *o* becomes *u̯o*: *ier* 'man', *u̯on* 'ten'; cf. Chuvash); has twenty-two consonants, again like Nogay; and differs from Kazakh in having the plural ending *-lar* (cf. Turkish), where Kazakh uses *-dar* (e.g. *qъzlar* 'girls'; cf. Kaz. *qъzdar*). Morphologically Karakalpak shows signs of Uzbek influence (e.g. the debitative suffix *-çaq*; *bolaçaq* 'must be') and has an interesting participial form in *-tuɣun* (e.g. *baratuɣun* 'going'). In 1928 Karakalpak adopted the Latin character

---

[1] K. H. Menges (op. cit.) regards Karakalpak as a Kazakh dialect.

and rapidly evolved a literary language on the basis of its Northern dialect. A recent Russian-Karakalpak dictionary[1] represents the language in Cyrillic.

Kirgiz was called Kara-Kirgiz till the Revolution, and Kazakh was known as Kirgiz. The Kirgiz are historically one of the oldest Turkic tribes, but their language has been relatively little studied till lately.[2] It closely resembles Oirot, has strict vowel harmony, tolerates *o* and *ö* in other syllables than the first, and has *s* where its cognates have *š*. The last and certain other phonetic peculiarities recall Kazakh. The Arabic alphabet in which Kirgiz had been written was latinised after the Revolution, and a press (e.g. the newspaper *Kьzьl Kьrgьzstan* 'Red Kirgizstan') and literature have sprung up in Frunze.

West of the Caspian Sea representatives of the North-Western group of Turkic are to be found in the Caucasus, on the Volga and its eastern affluents, and in the Crimea. The Caucasian types include Kumyk, Karachay, Balkar, and Nogay.

The Kumyk of Northern Daghestan, wherever it is not in competition with the North Caucasian Awar, serves as a medium of intercourse to the various peoples of North-East Caucasia, besides being the mother-tongue of over 100,000 speakers, who use one of three dialects—Khasav-Yurt, Buinak, and Khaidak. Like the other Turkic languages of the Caucasus, it made use of the Latin script ('the new Daghestan alphabet'), based on the form adopted in Azerbaijan, till the late 1930's. The phonetic system of Kumyk resembles that of Nogay in some points (e.g. *v* is bilabial). Kumyk *k* and *g* are strongly palatalised (e.g. *g'el'mek* 'to come'), and of the initial correlatives *t/d* and *k/g*, it prefers the 'peripheral' distribution *t/g* (e.g. *tau* 'mountain', *gün* 'day') to the more 'regular' Oguz-type *d/g*, illustrated by Turkmen and Azerbaijani, or the Kipchak-type *t/k*, illustrated by Uzbek, Kazakh, and Nogay (e.g. Nog. *tau*

---

[1] Н. А. Баскаков, У. А. Кожуров и С. Б. Бекназаров, *Русско-каракалпакский словарь* (Москва, 1947).

[2] See А. Шайданов и И. А. Батманов, *Элементарные основы киргизского языка* (Фрунзе-Ташкент, 1938²); И. А. Батманов, *Грамматика киргизского языка*, I–II (Фрунзе, 1939–40); К. К. Юдахин, *Киргизско-русский словарь* (Москва, 1940).

'mountain', *kün* 'day'). The morphology and syntax are typically Turkic down to the use of gerundial constructions to secure the effect of a durative aspect (e.g. *jazyp tura* 'he keeps on writing') and of the numeral *bir* 'one' to express indefiniteness (cf. *bir kitap oxumaq* 'to read a book' with *kitapny oxumaq* 'to read the book', where *-ny* is the gen.-acc. ending of the direct object).

Karachay is the language of the now dissolved Karachay Autonomous Province in the Stavropol' (formerly Orjonikidze) Region and is also spoken outside its own narrow bounds. It is related to Balkar, and Samojlovič (op. cit.) puts it in the North-Western (Kipchak) group of *tau*-languages. The phonetic and morphological systems of Karachay and Balkar seem to have been influenced by Ossetic and North Caucasian (Caucasian). It is surmised that both languages descend from Cumanic (Polovecian): the alternation of *ts/tš* and *dz/dž*, for instance, is found also in the fourteenth century *Codex Cumanicus*. Both Karachay and Balkar have the Caucasian vigesimal system of numeration, a future participle, and a conditional-future form with a dative-allative affix. The Latin alphabet was introduced here in 1924, and a press and literature have come into existence since then. The literary language is called Karachay-Balkar, and has been described by U. D. Alijev.[1]

Nogay is used in the Daghestan Autonomous Republic (capital Makhachkala) and in Circassia. The Crimean Nogays now speak Krymchak (South Crimean Tartar), a South-West Turkic type, the Astrakhan Nogays speak Volga Tartar. There are three dialects of the surviving Nogay, viz. White (*Ak*) Nogay, in the autonomous Circassia (q.v.), Black (*Kara*) Nogay, in Daghestan, and Central Nogay, also in Daghestan. The first of these differs markedly from the other two. All three dialects have the following phonetic features: *e* and *o* are diphthongised to *i̯e* and *u̯o*, but not regularly as in Kazakh and Karakalpak; there is interdialectal alternation of *j/ž/dž* (e.g. White Nogay has *ž*: *žol* 'road') and some syllabic metathesis as between

[1] У. Д. Алиев, *Карачаево-балкарская грамматика* (Кисловодск, 1930).

White and Black Nogay (cf. W.Nog. *tezere* 'lake' with B.Nog. *tereze*); *i* and *u* have each a lowered articulation, as in Kazakh; *v* is bilabial; and pronunciation hesitates between *s* and *š*, where Kazakh always has *s* and Volga Tartar *š* (e.g. *bas* or *baš* 'head'). Morphologically, Nogay has the customary Turkic system of declension, eked out with postpositions and complicated by suffixed possessive pronouns (e.g. loc. sing. *tas-ta* 'in stone'; nom. sing. *at-ymyz* 'our horse'), shows dialectal variation in the plural suffixes (e.g. W. and B.Nog. *-lar*, C.Nog. *-lar/-nar*: *tonlar* 'sheepskin coats', *tonnar*), and is well provided with conjugational forms distinguishing mood and tense. Literary Nogay was established in 1928, at first in two dialects. Now the tendency has set in to have a unified literary language. The Latin character prevailed in Nogay till 1937, when a modified Cyrillic was adopted, with the Russian 'hard' and 'soft' signs as the indices of velarised consonants and front vowels respectively (e.g. къара–*qara* 'black', уьйуьм–*üjüm* 'my house').

Of the East Russian types of Turkic, Bashkir is confined more or less to the Bashkir Autonomous Republic (capital Ufa). According to Samojlovič, it belongs, with the three types of Caucasian Turkic which have just been considered, to the well-articulated North-Western division. Its closest congener is the more northerly Volga Tartar (q.v.), and some scholars even reduce Bashkir to the status of a Volga Tartar dialect (cf. the 'ratio' between Russian and Ukrainian). Besides the six common Turkic vowels *a, e* (*ä*), *u, ü, y, i*, Bashkir has an open *o*, a centralised *i*, and two intermediate sounds between *o* and *u*, all of them products of the metaphonic transformation (*Umlaut*) of Common Turkic *a, o, ö*. All four vowel-phonemes occur also in Volgar Tartar, and the details of vowel harmony are identical in both languages. The chief differences between Bashkir and Volga Tartar are in their phonetic systems: in Bashkir *č* becomes *s* (cf. Bash. *säsän* 'orator' with V.Tart. *čäčän*), $s > h$ initially (cf. Bash. *hin* with V.Tart. *sin* 'thou'), $s > \theta$ medially (cf. Bash. *uθal* 'bad' with V.Tart. *usal*), $z > ð$ (cf. Bash. *hað* 'a musical instrument' with V.Tart. *saz*), and initial $dž > j$ (cf. Bash. *jir* 'earth' with V.Tart. *džir*). Combinative changes in Bashkir include that of *l* into *t/d* (e.g. *jigit-tar* 'horsemen') and of *n* into *d* (e.g. the accusative ending *-ny* becomes *-dy*: *kul-dy* 'hand'). Bashkir has twenty-four consonants, including *w*, *θ*, *ð*, *q*, *x*, *ɣ*, *n*, and a palatal and a velar *l*. Its morphology and syntax resemble those of Volga Tartar; the vocabulary is slightly different. Till recently the Bashkirs wrote Tartar. They have a rich folk-lore, including balladry, for instance songs about Salavat Juslajev, a companion of the redoubtable Jemel'ka Pugačov (see Puškin's novelette 'The Captain's Daughter'). At the present time Bashkir has a political and technical as well as an imaginative literature, the last strongly influenced by Russian, but also drawing on vernacular folk-lore. The Bashkir Learned Society, founded in 1925, is partly interested in the study of the language and publishes, besides its 'Proceedings', the periodical *Bašqort Ajmağy* ('The Bashkir Race'). The Arabic letters were at first modified in Literary Bashkir as in Tartar, to indicate vowels, but the vowelless Semitic script is an essentially inadequate medium for representing the vocalic diversity of Turkic languages.

Like Bashkir, the Tartar dialects belong to the North-Western division of Turkic. They include some languages spoken in Western Siberia, for instance Tyumen', Tobol, and Ishim Tartar, but are confined mainly to the Volga tracts and to the Crimea, except the southern coastal strip, which speaks a South-Western type.[1] The Volga Tartar *par excellence* is the language of Kazan', spoken by the descendants of the Golden Horde. The phonetics of this language is illustrated by G. Weil's voice-recordings of Tartar speakers.[2] The *č* and *dž* sounds are palatalised, *u̯* ([w]) occurs, and there is a glottal plosive. Most vowels may be long or short, and they include the characteristic short *ä* as well as several types of diphthongs, in which the second element may be *i*, *u*, or *y* (which Weil spells *î*). The phonetic texts show that the language raises and lengthens

[1] See А. Н. Самойлович, *Опыт краткой крымско-татарской грамматики* (Петроград, 1916). Some of the outstanding peculiarities of this language are: (1) the change of *ö*, *ü* into *o*, *u* (e.g. *koj* 'village', *kun* 'day'); (2) loss of initial *h* (e.g. *ava* 'air'); (3) the coincidence of predicative and possessive forms in the 1st sing. (e.g. *oqam* 'I am a teacher; my teacher').

[2] *Tatarische Texte* (Berlin-Leipzig, 1930).

e and *o* to *ī* and *ū* in certain positions (e.g. *ūn* 'ten' for Turkish *on* and *īlli* 'fifty' for Turk. *elli*). Morphologically and syntactically Volga Tartar might serve as a typical representative of literary Turkic.[1]

The type of Turkic found near Astrakhan' is mixed with Nogay and inherits elements from the language of the historically important Khazars. The same influence may be discerned in the Northern and Central types of Crimean Tartar: these are nearer to Tartar proper, whereas the Southern is more like the Gagauzi of Bessarabia and Turkish.

Volga Tartar culture, the most notable of all Tartar cultures, was suppressed after Ivan IV had conquered Kazan' in 1552, and its eclipse lasted till the eighteenth century, when the Tartars fell under the sway of the feudal culture of Bukhara and produced a galaxy of Mohammedan poets and thinkers. The rampant nationalism of the nineteenth century led to an all-round literary development and the multiplication of periodicals. At the present time the Tartars have a large realistic literature, which reflects post-revolutionary fashions in Russian. In the Crimea too the late nineteenth century saw the beginnings of journalism, when Izmail Gasprinskij, the prophet of a united Turania, founded 'Tardžiman' in 1883. This newspaper continued to appear till 1918, though a decline in Crimean Tartar literature had set in after the 1905 revolution. From 1920 till 1941 however there was a revival of writing and printing. A contributor to the 'Minor Soviet Encyclopaedia'[2] mentions the existence of a conflict between Tartar 'nationalism', identified with 'bourgeois' opinion, and Russian 'communism'. This appears to have been a familiar phenomenon in the post-revolutionary literatures of so many national communities in the U.S.S.R.

Isolated from the North-Western group of Turkic and distinctly *sui generis* is Chuvash, spoken by considerably over a million and a quarter speakers in the autonomous republic

[1] М. Курбангалиев и Р. Газизов, *Систематическая грамматика татарского языка* (Казань, 1932).

[2] *Малая советская энциклопедия*, VIII (Москва, 1930), p. 695.

of that name (capital Cheboksary) and in the adjacent Tartary (capital Kazan') and elsewhere. This language, according to a consensus of scholarly opinion, is descended from Bolgar[1] and therefore represents the type of language which the Balkan Bulgarians ultimately discarded for Slavonic.[2] The idiosyncrasies of Chuvash include traces of Finnic influence and a laxer vowel harmony (cf. Uzbek). Phonetically it resembles Volga Tartar in its 'reduced' (centralised and central) vowels, notably *ö* [ö] and *ĕ* [ë], e.g. Upper Chuv. *s'öltör* 'star' (cf. V.Tart. *jöndös*, Turk. *yıldız*) and *čĕlxe* 'tongue, language' (cf. V.Tart. *təl*). Chuvash is remarkable for the non-existence of long vowels, vowel-sequences, and the 'suprasegmental' voice-phoneme, as a result of which written *k* may be pronounced [k]/[g], written *p*—[p]/[b], and written *š*—[ʃ]/[ʒ], according to the position of the consonant (e.g. *upa* 'bear' is realised as *uba*, *jultaš* 'comrade' as *juldaš*). Consonants, unlike vowels, may be long (e.g. *atte* 'father', *sukkăr* 'blind'). As in the East Finnic Mordvin and Cheremiss,[3] consonants are palatalised in contact with *i* and *ü* (e.g. *il'* 'take', *üt'* 'body', *k'in'* 'daughter-in-law'). In Chuvash declension the accusative case may formally coincide with either the nominative ('indefinite' accusative) or the dative ('definite' accusative). The plural suffix is *-sem* (dialectal *-sam*/ *-sem*), which is usually preceded, where necessary, by the possessive suffix and followed by only the case ending (e.g. *yvăl-am-sem* 'my sons') in contrast to the Turkic practice of inserting the plural suffix between the stem and the possessive suffix (cf. Kalmyk *kük-m-näm* 'to my girl'). The negative particle *an* is prepositive, as in Mongolian. A peculiarity of the Chuvash

---

[1] See Н. И. Ашмарин, *Болгары и чуваши* (Казань, 1902); B. Munkácsi, 'A Volgar bolgárokról' (*Etnographia*, XIV, Budapest, 1903).

[2] This seems to be the only important instance of a Turkic language having been abandoned by its speakers. On the other hand, there are several instances of alien peoples, e.g. Samoyeds, Finns (Somians), Greeks, Persians, and Caucasians, being turkicised.

[3] See N. Trubetzkoy, 'Das mordwinische phonologische System verglichen mit dem russischen' (*Charisteria G. Mathesio*, Prague, 1932); В. А. Богородицкий, ,Характеристика звуковой системы марийского языка' (*ИАН, отд. лит. и яз.*, т. III, вып. 6, Москва, 1944).

verb is the decay of the conditional mood, of which only the form of the 2nd person singular survives and has been extended to the other persons (e.g. *epĕ, esĕ, văl pus'lasan* 'if I, thou, he should begin'). Unlike the other Turkic languages, Chuvash does not require predicative pronominal suffixes (e.g. *epĕ puian* 'I am rich', cf. V.Tart. *mīn bajmyn*, Turk. *ben zenginim*).

Anciently Bolgar-Chuvash influenced neighbouring Uralian languages: there are some 200 Bolgar loan-words in Hungarian,[1] and Chuvash has marked the vocabularies of Votyak, Cheremiss, and Mordvin,[2] which for several centuries were in the cultural orbit of Bolgar the Great. These loan-words help us to follow Chuvash phonetic changes. The language itself has Arabic and Persian borrowings, which appear to have entered it through Tartar, as well as Uralian (mainly East Finnic) and Russian ones. It is spoken in two dialects—the Upper or *o*-dialect (*Viryal*) and the Lower or *u*-dialect (*Anatri*), between which the phonetic difference is small (cf. Upper Chuv. *olma* 'apple' with Lower Chuv. *ulma*, and U.Chuv. *porne* 'finger' with L.Chuv. *purne*). Chuvash literature began in the eighteenth century, and a modification of the Cyrillic alphabet was used to represent the language. This alphabet was further modified in the 1870's by the Chuvash, I. J. Jakovlev, who made use of diacritic marks. Pre-revolutionary Chuvash literature is for the most part a translated one, but since the Revolution it has put on originality and comprises fiction, journalism, and scholarly writing. The study of the language is pursued by the Chuvash Research Institute.

At the opposite extremity of the Turkic-speaking area is the relatively isolated and numerically very significant language of

---

[1] See Z. Gombocz, 'Die bulgarisch-türkischen Lehnwörter in der ungarischen Sprache' (*MSFOu*, xxx, Helsinki, 1912); G. Fehér, 'Bulgarisch-ungarische Beziehungen in dem V–XI Jahrhundert' (*Keleti Szemle*, xix, Budapest, 1921).

[2] See Y. Wichmann, 'Die tschuwassischen Lehnwörter in den permischen Sprachen' (*MSFOu*, xxi, Helsinki, 1920); M. Räsänen, 'Die tschuwassischen Lehnwörter im Tscheremissischen' (*MSFOu*, xlviii, Helsinki, 1913); H. Paasonen, 'Die türkischen Lehnwörter im Mordwinischen' (*JSFOu*, xv, Helsinki, 1897).

the Uzbeks, which is used by about five million speakers, not only in Soviet Uzbekistan (capital Tashkent), but also in Chinese Turkestan, and even in Afghanistan.[1] It is far the most important form of South-Eastern Turkic. Two dialects are distinguished: the *o*-dialect of Tashkent, Samarkand, Bukhara, and Kokand substitutes an open [ɔ] for the common Turkic *a*, which is retained by the marginal *a*-dialect (cf. *bor* 'there is' with *bar*). The *o*-dialect may be roughly described as central, the *a*-dialect, in its *jok* ('no') and *džok* subgroups, as north-western and southern respectively. Both forms of Uzbek (Uzbeki) have been influenced, at least in vocabulary, by the Iranic Tajiki (q.v.) and have forfeited the characteristically Turkic vowel harmony. The literary language is based on a development of Chagatai as used by the Uzbeks of Tashkent and goes back to the fifteenth century, but the rapid growth of a modern literature has created a literary medium closer to the everyday speech of the urban masses. This was made possible in part by the abandonment of the Arabic alphabet for the Latin in 1928 and for the Cyrillic in 1940.

South and west of Uzbekistan lies the immediately contiguous territory of the federal republic of Turkmenistan (capital Ashkhabad), the home of Turkmen (Turkmeni, Turcoman), which, with Azerbaijani (q.v.), Gagauzi, and Turkish, constitutes the South-Western division of Turkic. It is spoken not only in Turkmenistan, but in Anatolia, in Persia (Iran) and, like Uzbek, in Afghanistan. Even in its native habitat it offers considerable dialectal diversity. Consonantal assimilations and contracted forms differentiate the literary form of the language, which took shape in the seventeenth century, from the spoken. The standard pronunciation carefully distinguishes long vowels from short and exhibits the usual Turkic vowel harmony. The system of consonants substitutes 'interdental' for dental and bilabial for labio-dental sounds. From the morphological standpoint an interesting peculiarity is the elision of the dative-directive case-ending after an open syllable (e.g. *geči*+*e* 'night'

---

[1] See G. Jarring, *Uzbek Texts from Afghan Turkestan* (*Lunds Universitets årsskrift*, N.f., avd. 1, XXXIV, 2, Lund, 1937).

gečä). Syntactically Turkmen is remarkable for its extensive use of the quasi-ergative construction (e.g. *meniŋ jazan kitabym* 'the book I wrote'), in which the participle (here *jazan*) is devoid of a morpheme to express the passive voice and links up with the object by juxtaposition. The vocabulary of Literary Turkmen comprises three principal ingredients—Turkic, Persian-Arabic, and Russian. The Turkic includes loans from Chagatai (Old Uzbek). As in the case of other cultivated Turkic languages, three alphabets have been successively used to write Turkmen, viz. the Arabic, the Latin (from 1927), and the Cyrillic (since 1940).

Opposite the Caspian coast of Turkmenistan lies the coastline of the Soviet federal republic of Azerbaijan (capital Baku), where a population of over 2,250,000 makes use of the most important Turkic language of the Caucasus. Like Turkmen and Turkish, it represents the South-Western division of Turkic, but is not without its own distinguishing marks. Azerbaijani has nine vowels, preserves the archaic final *b* and *ŋ*, aspirates voiceless plosives under foreign, perhaps Armenian and Georgian influence, has nasal vowels in some dialects, occasionally transgresses against the strict rules of vowel harmony, and offers a number of morphological archaisms (e.g. the difference between the present and the future tense stems: *alyr* 'takes', *alar* 'will take'; *olur* 'is', *olar* 'will be'). The classificatory key-words 'day' and 'mountain' appear in this language as *kün* and *daγ* respectively. There are several distinct Azerbaijani dialects, three of them spoken in Russian Azerbaijan, the remainder in the north-western Persian province of the same name, where the majority of Azerbaijani-speakers are settled. Very naturally a strong Persian influence colours the vocabulary and syntax of the language. Azerbaijani literature goes back to the sixteenth century and is abundant, expecially in the drama. There are also many newspapers. In 1922 the pioneer Latin script, which served as a model for the latinisation of Turkish, was introduced, and the reforms of Achundov were finally realised, though not exactly as he had conceived them. A Cyrillic alphabet of thirty-six letters has been substituted for the Latin since then.[1]

[1] See Г. Гусейнов, *Азербайджанско-русский словарь* (Баку, 1941).

Map 4. North and South Caucasian languages.

CHAPTER V

NORTH CAUCASIAN LANGUAGES

I

Of the various Turkic languages, the North-Western types, Karachay, Balkar, and Kumyk, and the South-Western type, Azerbaijani, are near neighbours of the languages of North and South Caucasian stock, all of which are spoken within the congested area of the Caucasus. Summarising the researches of Baron P. K. Uslar, R. von Erckert, N. J. Marr, A. Dirr, and others, Prince N. Troubetzkoy (Trubeckoj)[1] distinguishes three major types of languages in use there, exclusive of Turkic and Indo-European, viz. North-East, North-West, and South Caucasian. The North-East Caucasian, or Checheno-Lezginian type comprises the Chechen, Ingush, and Tsova-Tush (Bats) of the former Chechen-Ingush Autonomous Republic (now the Grozny province) and the Lezginian complex, consisting of Awaro-Andian (twelve languages spoken in North-West Daghestan),[2] Dargwa,[3] Kubachi, Lak (also called Kazikumukh),[4] and Archi in Central Daghestan, and the Samur group, i.e. Lezgin proper, in its two principal dialects Kyuri and Akhti, Agul, Tabassaran, Budukh (Budug), Jek,[5] Rutul (Mykhad), Tsakhur, Khinalugh, which is spoken in a single village, and Udi, which is the language of two villages, in South-East Daghestan. Some

---

[1] 'Langues caucasiques septentrionales' in the symposium *Les langues du monde* (Paris, 1924), pp. 327–42.
[2] Viz. Awar, Andi, Botlikh, Godoberi, Karata, Akhwakh (Alwal), Kwandi (Bagulal), Chamalal, Tindal (Tindi), Dido (Tsets), Khwarshi, Kapuchi (Beshitl).
[3] Or Dargin, of which Khyurkili is the best-studied variety.
[4] A corruption of Haji Qumuq, i.e. Pilgrim Kumyk, a misnomer due to the error of regarding its speakers as Turkic. The title 'Kazi' (Haji) is applied to them, because they were the first people in the Caucasus to embrace Islam.
[5] Including Khaputli and Kryz.

investigators, among them Marr[1] and G. Dumézil,[2] prefer to separate the Chechenian from the Lezginian types by treating the latter as more properly East Caucasian, and the former as Central Caucasian. All these languages are structurally and lexically related among themselves and more distantly to North-West Caucasian, or Abkhazo-Circassian. To the last group belong the more southerly Abkhaz, with its dialects,[3] in the Abkhaz Autonomous Republic (capital Sukhumi), which is federated with Georgia, and the more northerly Adyge, spoken in two forms—Kabardin, in the Kabarda Autonomous Republic (capital Nal'chik), and Circassian (Cherkess, Kyakh), in the Circassian and the Adyge Autonomous Republics (capitals Cherkessk and Maikop respectively). A third type of North-West Caucasian is usually listed, viz. Ubykh, which is now almost extinct along the north-east coast of the Black Sea and survives chiefly in Asia Minor.[4]

South Caucasian (Iverian), the only well-articulated language-stock in the Caucasus, consists of Georgian and its congeners Mingrelian (Megrel) and Laz (Chan), now sometimes covered by the inclusive name Zan,[5] and the rather more divergent Svanetian (Svan). These languages are spoken as varieties of a single structural type in the Georgian Federal Republic (capital Tbilisi, formerly Tiflis).

The North-East and North-West Caucasian languages are fundamentally cognate and may be regarded as two distinct ramifications of North Caucasian (more properly Caucasian), but investigation has not yet demonstrated the affinities of this and the so-called South Caucasian, which accordingly must be treated as an independent stock. To the latter the historical and

---

[1] ‚Яфетические языки' (*Большая Советская Энциклопедия*, т. LXV, Москва, 1931).

[2] *Introduction à la grammaire comparée des langues caucasiennes du Nord* (Paris, 1933).

[3] Samurzakan, Abzhu, and Bzyb.

[4] See G. Dumézil, *La langue des Oubykhs* (Paris, 1931).

[5] See А. Чикобава, ‚О лингвистических чертах картвельских языков' (*ИАН, отд. лит. и яз.*, т. VII, вып. 1, Москва-Ленинград, 1948).

less confusing name Iverian (Čikobava[1] has 'Ibero-Caucasian'), as well as Kartvelian, which derives from the self-designation of the Georgians, are sometimes given.

North Caucasian is remarkable phonetically for a minimum of vowel phonemes and a profusion of consonants: Circassian, for instance, has fifty-seven consonants, which include ejective and 'pulmonic' variants of the characteristic lateral affricate [tɬ], as well as numerous labialised, palatalised, velarised, and glottalised types of plosives and fricatives. Morphologically all North Caucasian languages oppose a *casus agens* (agentive), the subject of a transitive verb, to a *casus patiens*, the subject of an intransitive verb or the object of a transitive one, and their purely verbal bases (radicals) are 'uniliteral', i.e. they consist of a single consonant. Besides these shared elements of structure and function, the North Caucasian languages have a considerable common vocabulary.

2

The North-East Caucasian languages, to take the more easterly first, exhibit the consonantal excess and complementary vocalic simplicity already referred to, the Awar system, for instance, containing fifty phonemes, which however are not readily combinable, except at rudimentary levels (e.g. a 'liquid' and another consonant). The most striking trait of these languages is the division of nouns into from two to eight classes[2] (cf. Bantu and some forms of Papuan, e.g. in Southern Bougainville), each distinguished by a special consonant or consonants (one for the singular, the other for the plural), which are affixed to members of all the grammatical categories associated with a given noun, and thus establish a formal nexus in gender and number among the members of the syntactic complex. This may be illustrated from Awar (q.v.) in which w is the masculine, j the feminine index: *dow tši wugo ruq'ow* 'this man is in the house'

---

[1] Op. cit.
[2] A. Dirr, 'Über die Klassen (Geschlechter) in den kaukasischen Sprachen' (*Archives internationales d'Ethnographie*, xviii, Leiden, 1908).

and *doj ttš'užu jigo ruq'oj* 'this woman is in the house'.[1] Nominal and verbal flexion operates by means of suffixes added to appropriate bases, of which the noun may have four (e.g. the Lak patiens sing. *barts'* 'wolf'; *burts'i-l*; pat. plur. *barts'ru*; gen. plur. *burts'irdi-l*), and the verb may have two (durative and perfective). The personal pronouns have an even more irregular system (cf. the Awar patiens *mun* 'thee' with the corresponding agens *dutsa* 'thou'), and only the adjectives, demonstrative pronouns, and numerals present a more uniform (agglutinative) type of flexion. The nominal declension is well articulated (e.g. Agul has twenty-five, Awar thirty, and Tabassaran thirty-five cases, including a plethora of local, or spatial ones), and the entire system pivots, in Caucasian style, on the syntactic and morphematic antithesis of *casus agens* and *casus patiens*. The verbal radicals are preceded by prefixes indicating aspect and class and are followed by suffixes of tense and mood. The North-East Caucasian languages, except Lak and Dargwa, do not make a distinction between personal and impersonal forms of the verb and have no personal flexion. Two languages, Tabassaran and Udi, introduce pronominal enclitics as substitutes for the latter, presumably under alien influence.

As representatives of North-East Caucasian we may take the already cited Awar, Lezgin, and Agul. Awar has, we have learnt, fifty phonemes, only five of which are vowels. The consonantal system is abundant in both occlusive and constrictive types (including affricates), and the latter may be either long or short. Among peculiar phonemes are the pharyngals, almost as in Arabic, the ejectives, made with simultaneous glottal closure (*t'*, *k'*, *ts'*, *tš'*), and the specifically Awar laterals, including [tɬ] (indicated by *ł*), and the glottalised lateral plosive *q'*, which N. F. Jakovlev has qualified as a 'creak' (*skripjaščij zvuk*). The language distinguishes noun classes based on the intersection of the human/non-human, animate/inanimate, and masculine/feminine dichotomies. Each class has its own consonantal index (*w* represents the masculine, *j* the

[1] The apostrophe (') stands for glottal closure, the 'hard breathing' (') for aspiration.

feminine, *b* the neuter, and *r* and *l* the plural of all genders, e.g. *k'udijaw tši* 'big man'; *k'udijaj ttš'užu* 'big woman'; *k'udijab ruq'* 'big house'; *k'udijal tšujal* 'big horses'). Awar declension recognises four grammatical cases, including an ergative (e.g. *čijas tts'alula t'ex'* 'the man reads the book, lit. the book is read by the man'), and five sets of local cases, each with three correlates (e.g. the first set contains the locative, allative, and elative). The personal pronouns are also declined in full. The Awar verbal category comprises finite and non-finite (participial) forms, associated with one or other of three tenses and capable of expressing a restricted number of moods, viz. indicative, imperative, optative, and necessitative. The participles are declined like adjectives, and the class indices are attached to them for attributive concord (e.g. *bosarab t'ex'* 'a bought book', where we have the neuter index -(*a*)*b*; *araw tši* 'the man who went away'; *araj ttš'užu* 'the woman who went away').

Lezgin belongs, as we have seen, to the Samur river language-group in the Daghestan Autonomous Republic (capital Makhachkala) and is represented by two principal dialects Kyuri (Küri) and Akhti. The name 'Lezgin' is of Turkic origin. The specific features of this language, shared with Budukh, Jek, Rutul, and Tsakhur, are a phonetic discrimination between labialised and non-labialised consonants (e.g. Kyuri q^war 'mare' and *qar* 'hail'), the alternation of consonants in flexion (e.g. *qib* 'frog', *qipèr* 'frogs'), and a general tendency towards phonetic and grammatical simplification. In the west this tendency is not strong: Tsakhur and Rutul have an archaic morphology, with four classifiers and numerous paradigms. Among other features of these conservative types is the expression of the future tense by the infinitive preceded by a personal pronoun, as in the Hamitic Somali.[1] But the north-eastern languages, including Lezgin itself, have strictly speaking no noun classes (Tabassaran discriminates only between human and non-human), though their system of declension is complex enough, consisting of four abstract cases (absolute, ergative, dative, and

[1] See W. Czermak, 'Zum Gebrauche des Infinitivs als Futurum im Somali' (*Donum Natalicium Schrijnen*, I, Nijmegen-Utrecht, 1929).

genitive) and as many as twelve spatial ones, with numerous, mainly locative postpositions besides. The Lezgin adjective is indeclinable when connected with a noun, but declined when absolute. Comparison is functional for the most part, but one of the items compared does stand in the ablative case. As in other Caucasian languages, numeration is vigesimal. The verb has neither person nor number, and hypotaxis is replaced by participial constructions. Sentence syntax is determined by the force of the verb: the subject of an intransitive verb is in the absolute case (e.g. Lezg. *quš-ar t'awā suda* 'birds are flying across the sky'), that of a transitive verb in the ergative (e.g. Lezg. *za adaz p'ul gana* 'by me to him money is given'), and that of a *verbum sentiendi* in the dative (cf. Georgian case-syntax infra).

Another type of North-East Caucasian closely related to Lezgin is Agul, spoken to the north of the Lezgin, to the south of the Dargwa, and to the west of the Tabassaran area. The number of Agul speakers in 1920 was computed at rather under 8000, and these spoke the language in one or other of four varieties. The literary form described by R. Šaumjan,[1] viz. Agul proper, may be taken as typical not only of the Agul dialects, but of the Lezginian type of North-East Caucasian. Its phonetic system opposes six vowels, including *ä*, *ü*, *y*, to a massive complex of seventy-eight consonants and their audible variants, which include glottalised plosives and affricates, uvular, pharyngal, and glottal sounds, several of them with parallels in the Georgian and Armenian phonetic systems, and imperfectly voiced consonants, described by Russian investigators as 'neutral' (e.g. *ṫ*, *τ*, *κ*). The system of declension is more involved than that of Lezgin, even of Tabassaran, having twenty-five oblique cases, each with a distinctive morpheme. The cases are mostly spatial, and among them we find such unusual names as 'adhesive' (e.g. *babaw* 'to the mother' from nom. *bab* 'mother'), 'obessive', 'exablative', 'superallative', and 'collative' (e.g. *dada-faj* 'with father' from nom. *dad* 'father'). The adjective, when attributive, is indeclinable, but

[1] Р. Шаумян, *Грамматический очерк агульского языка* (Москва-Ленинград, 1941).

it illustrates all the case-forms, singular and plural, when absolute. Declension also governs the Agul pronoun. The verb, in contrast to the noun, exhibits a relatively simple system with a small number of moods, but considerable variety of tense (e.g. it has two present tenses, four preterites, and a future). Compound verbs, combining noun and auxiliary verb, are found alongside of simple ones. Person is not distinguished in the verb morphematically, but number has its characteristic exponent (e.g. imperat. sing. *dyw* 'pull'; imperat. plur. *dywaj*). The negative particle is attached to the verb as a prefix (e.g. infin. *akas* 'to do', *dakas* 'not to do').

The Samur group of languages, to which Lezgin and Agul belong, is now in process of decline and giving ground to the Turkic Azerbaijani, the *lingua franca* of Transcaucasia. The archaic Archi, which is important for the comparative study of North-East Caucasian, the Christian Udi, which is permeated with Armenian loan-words and inflects the verb for person, and the little-studied Khinalugh are all tiny fragments of North Caucasian speech apparently doomed to early extinction.

The Chechenian, or North-Central Caucasian group of languages, though it forms a unit with the Lezginian, is also the link between North-East and North-West Caucasian. This is particularly noticeable in its systems of declension and conjugation, which are relatively simpler than those of Lezginian type. There is a sort of geographical continuity between all three groups of North Caucasian languages, and the facts of Kabardin, the easternmost type of the North-West Caucasian group, tally best with those of the North-Central.

Chechen (*naxtš'uin muott'*) and its congeners Ingush and Tsova-Tush (Bats) are closely related phonetically and in their forms. Chechen however has long vowels where Tsova-Tush does not distinguish length, and these vowels appear not only singly, but in diphthongs.[1] Chechen consonants are fewer than those of Tsova-Tush. Both languages are partial to 'consonant-clusters'. All three types of North-Central Caucasian use six classifiers, of which only two (masculine and feminine) have

[1] A. Schiefner, *Tschetschenzische Studien* (St Petersburg, 1864).

semantic value, and seventeen cases, including an equative, a conversive, an elative, and a motive. The verb confronts semelfactive (punctual) with iterative, singular with collective categories; the participles play a predominant role in syntax; and the vocabulary shows admixture with adjacent languages. In Chechen there is a great variety of thematic forms, unified only by the presence of the common radical consonant. These irregularities, which are the rule and not the exception (e.g. Chech. nom. sing. *sai* 'deer', gen. *sēŋ*, instr. *sē*; nom. plur. *sieš*), make Chechen, according to Troubetzkoy, one of the most difficult of Caucasian languages to learn, and this may account for its relative lack of expansive force, although numerically it is the principal language of the Northern Caucasus with c. 320,000 speakers (1926). Chechen has two main dialects—Lowland and Highland—the first phonetically similar to Ingush. Literary Chechen is based on the Lowland speech of Great Chechenia (Russ. Чечня). In 1926 the Latin alphabet was substituted for the Arabic, which had been current till then. Newspapers and a mostly translated educational and political literature exist.

3

North-West Caucasian (Abkhazo-Circassian), unlike North-East Caucasian, is distinguished by its consonantal groupings, particularly its labialised hush-sibilants (Fr. *chuintantes*), which, among the North-East Caucasian languages, are found only in Tabassaran, and its voiced and voiceless labial vibrants, e.g. Abkhaz ρ, as in the North and East European equivalent of 'whoa', and Ubykh τ, its voiceless counterpart.

The southern variety of North-West Caucasian, Abkhaz, with its seventy-five predominantly consonantal phonemes, is phonetically one of the most difficult and least harmonious languages of the Caucasus. It was first described in its Bzyb dialect by Baron P. K. Uslar,[1] who used a hybrid Latin-Cyrillic-Georgian alphabet to symbolise its phonetic complexities. As

---

[1] *Этнография Кавказа. Языкознание. Абхазский язык* (Тифлис, 1887).

usual in Caucasian, both Northern and Southern, a simple vowel-system is opposed to and modified by an extremely involved system of consonants, which include labialised and glottalised phonemes, a diversity of affricates, and two bilabial vibrants (e.g. *aτá* 'hay', where the voiceless consonant is sounded by vibrating the lips). Abkhaz structure does not recognise declension, but exhibits the presence of the class dichotomies human/non-human and masculine/feminine, which

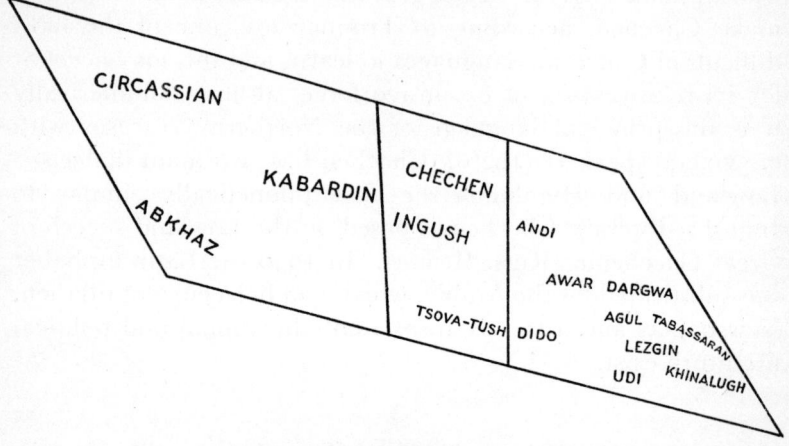

Fig. 10. Diagram of the North Caucasian languages.

complicate the pronominal paradigm, has a postpositive definite article (e.g. *rasá* 'nut', *rasák* 'the nut'; *ámca* 'fire', *mcak* 'the fire'), and enriches its verbal system by adding aspect to tense and incorporating the direct object in the predicative complex (e.g. *i-l-tš'a-s-ts'-ueit'* 'I am putting it in his mouth, lit. it(i)-him(l)-mouth($tš'y$)-I(s)-put(ts')-ing($ueit'$)'). Abkhaz had a missionary alphabet of sixty characters before this was reformed to do justice to the phonetic variety of the spoken language. In the revised alphabet a literature has sprung up, and there are already several prominent authors.

The other term of the compound synonym for 'North-West Caucasian' is 'Circassian', and this covers the two literary languages Adyge and Kabardin (*qeberdei jabze*). But in point of fact the more inclusive term is 'Adyge', which, as we have already seen, distinguishes two dialectal forms—Circassian, or Adyge proper (*kjax'ə abze*) and Kabardin. These dialects are qualified in geographical terms as 'Lowland' and 'Highland' respectively.[1] Most Adyge speakers, like the expatriate Ubykhs, now live not only in the Caucasus, their original habitat, but in Turkey, where many of their ancestors fled in 1864–6, after the Russian annexation of their homeland.

Kabardin, the Highland and more easterly variety of Adyge,[2] has three basic vowels *a*, *ə*, *y*, and a number of 'derivative' ones, i.e. variants adapted to different phonetic environments (viz. *i*, *e*, *o*, *u*). Its consonants, which are numerous and varied, show in some cases the presence of glottal closure, indicated in the new Cyrillic alphabet by I (e.g. фIэфIын, i.e. [f'əf'in] 'to wish'). The noun system is characterised by the existence of a definite ending with anaphoric value (viz. -*r* and -*m*: *šy-r* 'the horse', *psy-m* 'the river') and by declensional paradigms of relatively small dimensions (nine cases). There is no morphological difference between noun and adjective. The contrast between absolute and ergative forms, characteristic of the noun declension, recurs in the pronoun. The Kabardin verb has personal suffixes, plural indices, spatial affixes, and a negative form, and distinguishes eight moods, eight tenses (including three preterites), and the transitive-intransitive antithesis, which gives rise to a subjective, an objective, and an intermediate subjective-objective 'construction' (Russ. *stroj*).

The Circassian (Adyge proper)[3] phonetic system resembles that of Kabardin in having the same seven vowels, represented in the present-day Cyrillic spelling by nine characters (including ю and я). These vowels are variously 'realised' according to their position in a word. The system of consonants is as complex as in the cognate types, having fifty-seven distinct phonemes

[1] See Н. Ф. Яковлев, ‚Краткий обзор черкесских (адыгейских) наречий' (*Зап. сев.-кавк. краеведческого инст.* I, Ростов н/Д., 1928).

[2] See Г. Турчанинов и М. Цагов, *Грамматика кабардинского языка*, I (Москва-Ленинград, 1946).

[3] See Н. Яковлев и Д. Ашхамаф, *Грамматика адыгейского литературного языка* (Москва-Ленинград, 1941).

through the interaction of a variety of 'suprasegmentals' (e.g. voice, glottal closure, labialisation). Morphologically we observe a complex verbal system, expressing several forms of the past tense without recourse to auxiliaries, two varieties of the future, implying a contrast between fact and possibility, and four varieties of the conditional mood. The modal structure of the verb also includes special forms for the indicative, imperative, and optative, as well as for Jakovlev's (op. cit.) 'affirmative', 'confirmative', 'negative', and 'interrogative' moods. Some of these, viz. the last four, have nine tenses each. In acute contrast to the complexity of the verb, Circassian declension is quite simple. The case paradigm of nouns and adjectives presents only three types—active, passive, and instrumental—in both numbers. The active and passive cases are often formally identical (e.g. act. and pass. sing. *uan* 'saddle'; instr. *uanek'e*). But this simplification is counterbalanced by a formal discrimination between definiteness and indefiniteness (e.g. *unè* 'house', *une-r* 'the house'). Class and gender are both absent, but the pronominal system, with four persons, including a reflexive, is richly developed and its connection with the noun is established by possessive prefixes (e.g. *si-k'ale* 'my son', *i-k'al* 'his son', *ti-k'ale* 'our son'). The Circassian vocabulary is sometimes wanting in single terms for the simpler notions: thus 'beard' is *za-k'e* 'mouth-tail', 'face' is *na-p'e* 'eye-nose', and 'tear' *ne-p'e* 'eye-water'. In 1908 the Arabic character was first used to represent the language and it remained in use till 1925, when, after a conference at Kislovodsk, the Latin alphabet with diacritics was introduced, to be replaced subsequently by Cyrillic.

CHAPTER VI

SOUTH CAUCASIAN LANGUAGES

South Caucasian (Iverian) is now spoken by about two million speakers, who represent an ancient language-community known to old Greek as Ἴβηρες (Iberi). This name survives in the stunted Armenian form 'Virk'' ('Georgians'), in which the aspirated final consonant is the plural sign. N. J. Marr, partly Georgian himself, identifies 'Iber'/'Iver' with 'Imer', as in Imerian (Imeretian), a Georgian dialect, and even with 'Kimer' (Cimmerian), but this seems far-fetched, although less so than is usual with this erratic thinker.[1] The connection of Georgian with a comparatively distant medieval past however is established by a fifth-century inscription at Bolnis Sion and especially by its literature, which has been known since the tenth century in association with two distinctly formed alphabets—the ecclesiastical and angular 'khutsuri' ('priestly hand'), found in both uncial and minuscule form, and the civil and rounded 'mkhedruli' ('knightly hand'), which is said to be the invention of the Georgian king Parnavaz. The mkhedruli alphabet of thirty-nine signs is possibly older than the khutsuri, traditionally thought to have been devised by the Armenian bishop St Mesrop. Both alphabets derive, like the Armenian, from a Greek-modified Semitic pattern and are arranged mostly in Semitic order, the non-Semitic sounds coming at the end of the series. An attempt to latinise the mkhedruli in 1926 did not reach beyond typewriting and business correspondence. Till the early 1920's Georgian was the only South Caucasian language with a literary culture. Since then all the other types of South Caucasian have received an alphabet and a literary language, and the literature of both Georgian and its cognates has been considerably enriched in many directions.

Georgian (Kartvelian) appears in several dialectal forms, one

[1] ‚Новый поворот в работе по яфетической теории‘ (*ИАН*, Москва, 1931).

of which, viz. Imerian, has already been alluded to. The others are Gurian, Pshav, Thush (not interchangeable with Tsova-Tush, or Bats, a North Caucasian language), Khevzur, Ingilo (the last four bordering geographically on Lezgin), Mthiul, Rachin, Kakhetin, and Meskh. Mingrelian (Megrel) and Laz (Chan), the latter spoken in the Ajar Autonomous Republic (capital Batumi, formerly Batum) and mainly in Turkish Lazistan, are connected almost as dialects, though separated by a considerable distance. The present-day fashion is to regard them as two forms of a common Zan. The conservative and divergent Svanetian (Svan), on the other hand, exhibits less family likeness and is kept apart. It is in immediate contact with North-West Caucasian.

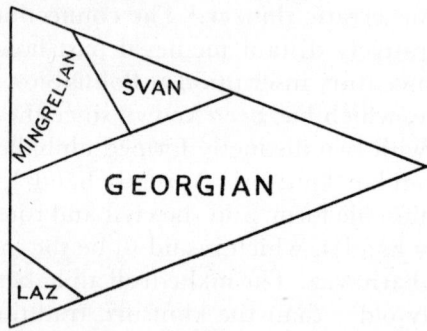

Fig. 11. Diagram of the South Caucasian languages.

In common with the Indo-European Armenian (q.v.), Georgian has three sets of plosives—voiced, voiceless aspirated, and glottalised (e.g. b, p', p')—represented in the customary three types of plosives, bilabial, dental and velar, and in two sets of affricates of sibilant type (ts' and $t\check{s}'$). Georgian also has the pair of velar fricatives x/γ, a voiceless, but unaspirated uvular plosive (q), and a v which tends to become bilabial. The vowels—a, e, i, o, u—are of the usual type, and, as in North Caucasian, it is the consonants which determine the phonetic physiognomy of the language. Compared with Old Georgian, the modern language has simplified its phonetic structure, but it still preserves a predilection for difficult consonantal conglomerates like *bavšv-s* 'to the child', *st'sdebian* 'they are wrong', and *brt'šqv-inav-da* 'shone', and what G. S. Achvlediani[1] calls 'decessive harmonic complexes' (e.g. *tsk*, *tšk*, *dzg*, *džg*, etc.).

F. N. Finck has described Georgian as *gruppenflektierend*, i.e. as illustrating 'glomerative', or 'group' flexion, which he contrasts with the 'radical' flexion of Arabic and the 'thematic' flexion of Greek.[2] In all three cases the flexional element is an essential component of a word, undetachable from the stem with the clean edges of a Turkic suffix or a Bantu prefix. Yet this does not imply that Georgian is an inflected language like Indo-European or Semitic, or rather that it is inflected to the same degree. Structurally it is intermediate between the Indo-European and the Uralian type and has autonomous features, but some recent investigators, like A. Čikobava (op. cit.), prefer to treat it as a purely agglutinative language.

Georgian has no gender, and its nominal flexion is moderately rich in case forms, of which, according to B. T. Rudenko,[3] there are seven, including an ergative, an instrumental, and a directive (final), but excluding an accusative, which is represented by the dative. Marr and M. Brière, in their monumental grammar,[4] recognise secondary cases—a locative, an inessive (Finck's 'adessive'), a superessive, a disjunctive (Finck's 'ablative'), a limitative (Finck's 'terminative'), and a comitative (Finck's 'sociative'). Finck himself (op. cit.) lists eleven cases with an additional one in the plural. The case endings were formerly postpositions: Old Georgian, it would appear, had only two cases, a nominative (absolute) and an oblique in the plural, and its noun was invariable in the singular. The modern suffixes are identical in both numbers (e.g. nom. *-i*, gen. *-is(a)*, dat.-acc. *-s(a)*, erg. *-a(n)*, instr. *-it'(a)*, dir. *-ad(a)*, voc. *-o*). The plural indices are *-ebi* and *-ni* (e.g. *saxli* 'house', *saxlebi* 'houses'; *kata* 'cat', *kateni* 'cats', cf. O.Geor. *katani*). The adjective, as

---

[1] See A. Čikobava, op. cit.
[2] *Die Haupttypen des Sprachbaus* (Leipzig, 1923²). Finck's other two terms are *wurzelflektierend* and *stammflektierend*.
[3] *Грамматика грузинского языка* (Москва-Ленинград, 1940).
[4] *La langue géorgienne* (Paris, 1931).

attribute, precedes the noun and remains indeclinable if the noun is pluralised with the ending *-ebi*. The noun is singular after numerals,[1] which embody the vigesimal system. Postpositions are used besides case-suffixes and govern particular cases (e.g. *gan* 'by' takes the genitive: *mamis(a) gan* 'by the father'). The verb uses affixes distinct from the nominal, to indicate, besides the meaning contained in the root, the ideas of time (including a future), mood (including the optative and the subjunctive), person (shown by a prefix), direct and indirect objects (by means of an infix), voice, and aspect. There are two conjugations, subjective and objective (Finck's *Tat- und Empfindungsverben*), each with its own set of personal prefixes. The subjective conjugation is the more regular and developed of the two. Georgian conjugation is more complicated than its declension and is characterised by the use of prefixes (e.g. the occasional future prefixes *da-, ga-*) as well as of suffixes.[2] The prefixes predominate. The subject of a transitive verb figures in the ergative case, and of an intransitive verb in the dative. There is also a curious variation of the cases of logical subject and object according to tense, for instance in the present tense the subject is nominative, the object dative-accusative; in the perfect the subject is dative, the object nominative; and in the aorist the subject is ergative, the object nominative (cf. Svan). The characteristic prefixes attached to the base are the directive vowels *a* (which has causative force, e.g. *vdšam* 'I eat'; *vadšev* 'I feed'), reflexive or intransitive *i* (e.g. *vban* 'I wash'; *viban pirs* 'I wash my face'), *u* (indirect object), and *e* (past reflexive). The meaning of these prefixes is clearer in the older literary language than in present-day speech. As will have been seen from the foregoing examples, *a* and *u* relate to the 3rd person, *i* and *e* to the 1st, i.e. the front vowels indicate nearness, the back vowels distance (cf. *v-a-ts'er* 'I write for another'; *v-i-ts'er* 'I write for myself'). There are two kinds of negative particles (e.g. *nu ts'er* 'do not

[1] E.g. *ot'xi katsi* 'four men, lit. four man'. Cf. Hung. *négy ember*; Pers. *č(ah)ār mard*; Arm. *tšors mart'*.
[2] Suffixes also occur in adjectival comparison and in the derivation of ordinals from cardinals, e.g. *rva* 'eight', *me-rv-e* 'eighth'.

write'; *ara* 'not'), as in Armenian and Persian, Albanian and Greek. Questions are often introduced by the interrogative particles *hom* and *gana* (cf. Est. *kas*, Latv. *vai*, Lith. *ar*, Pol. *czy*). The Georgian vocabulary contains many Armenian, Persian, Greek, and Arabic borrowings.

Mingrelian (Megrel) is spoken at Poti and north of the Rion river as far as the Abkhaz and Svanetian borders. It has been encroached on by the Georgian dialects Gurian and Imerian, and uses many Georgian loan-words. There are in Mingrelian a number of phonemes alien to Georgian, for instance the glottal plosive (Arab. *hamza*), the central vowel ə, and a strongly palatalised *l*, as well as hush-sibilants corresponding to the Georgian hiss-sibilants (cf. the *s*/*š* antithesis in Finnish and Carelian). The language has special cases of declension, viz. a directive, ablative, and destinative, the last a kind of ethic dative. In Mingrelian syntax the conjunction comes at the end of the subordinate clause. Georgian was the only literary language of the Mingrelians, as of the Laz speakers, descendants of the ancient Colchians of the Greek Golden-Fleece legend, and the Svanetians till 1930, when newspapers began to be published in these vernaculars. Mingrelian is also used in elementary schools.

CHAPTER VII

INDO-EUROPEAN LANGUAGES

I

Immediately flanking Georgian on the north is Ossetic, the language of the North Ossete Autonomous Republic (capital Dzaujikau, formerly Vladikavkaz) and of the South Ossete Autonomous Province (capital Stalinir, formerly Tskhinval) in Georgia, which bestride the central Caucasus range, and flanking it on the south is Armenian, which is now largely concentrated in the Armenian Federal Republic (capital Erevan). Both Ossetic, with over 350,000 speakers, and Armenian, with over two millions, are Indo-European languages: Ossetic is a member of the Iranic branch and cognate with Persian and its dialects Talysh and Tat, which are spoken in Soviet Azerbaijan, as well as with Tajiki and the Pamiri dialects of the federal republic of Tajikistan (capital Stalinabad, formerly Dyushambe); Armenian stands isolated, like the Albanian, Hellenic, and Tokharian branches of Indo-European.

The connection of Ossetic (Os, Ir) with the language of the ancient Alans,[1] a Sarmatian tribe mentioned in the sixth century by Jordanes, may be demonstrated circuitously by adducing the vocabulary it shares with Hungarian.[2] It is well known that the Hungarians and the Alans were medieval neighbours and allies before the former finally migrated to and settled down in Slavonic Pannonia, i.e. the major Danubian plain. And the name 'Alan' has been equated with 'Ārya' and with the Ossetic 'Ir'.

Ossetic resembles the geographically eastern types of Iranic, especially Sogdian and its modern descendant Yaghnobi, and displays a Caucasian taste for consonantal groupings, though

---

[1] Turkic-speakers still call the Ossetes (Ossetinians) Alans.

[2] See H. Sköld, 'Die ossetischen Lehnwörter im Ungarischen' (*Lunds Universitets årsskrift*, N.F., avd. 1, xx, 4, Lund, 1925).

these are not nearly so complex as in North and South Caucasian because of the presence of alleviating vowels. The chief dialectal, mainly phonetic differences are between West Ossetic (Digor) and East Ossetic (Tagaur), which is numerically the more important of the two and the basis of the literary language. The vowel system of both dialects is of a conservative Indo-European type, with front rounded vowels absent altogether. Length is a 'suprasegmental' phoneme and occurs in diphthongs as well as in pure vowels (e.g. *ūi/ui* and *ī/i*). The consonantal system contains uvulars (e.g. *q*) and has absorbed 'Caucasian' ejectives, or 'abruptives' (*p'*, *t'*, *k'*, *ts'*, *tš'*). Unlike the other Iranic languages which have mostly simplified their system of declension, Ossetic, as between its dialects, retains eight cases, including an interior and an exterior locative and a sociative (in Tagaur), and ekes these out with a large number of prepositions and postpositions. The attributive adjective is invariable (e.g. *xorz ūs* 'a good woman'; gen. *xorz ūsi*; dat. *xorz ūsän*). The verb, except from the standpoint of word-formation, is straightforward, distinguishes subjunctive from indicative, and constructs its tenses chiefly by suffixation, though typical Indo-European compound tenses, juxtaposing participial forms with finite auxiliaries, also occur. Ossetic (Tagaur) texts and Scriptural translations in Cyrillic had been in existence for two generations before the Revolution led to the creation of a modern literature and press.

Talysh belongs, with the more northerly Tat and the North Persian dialects Gilaki, Mazandarani, and Samnani, to the Caspian group of Iranic. Texts however reveal the greater affinity of Talysh and Tat in contrast to the others and at the same time the linguistic autonomy of both. The short vowels in Talysh show hesitations (e.g. *dil/del* 'heart', *zelf/zulf* 'lock of hair'); *ā* has become *ǭ* (e.g. *ǭv* 'water'); *r* often lapses (e.g. *dāi* 'tree', cf. Pers. *dār*); and *x* is replaced by *h* (e.g. *hešī* 'sun'; cf. Pers. *xoršīd*). As in Persian, there is no gender, and the system of declension is formally limited to the opposition of *casus rectus* and *casus obliquus*, singular and plural. Unlike its congeners, Talysh has *az* for 'I' (cf. Tat *mū*, *mya*; Pers. *man*). Its verbal system recalls both Tat and Persian, but naturally has peculiarities of its own (e.g. *-ōn, -an* in the 2nd person plur. of the pres. indicative for Tat *-īd, -ind*, Pers. *-id*).

The Tat of Azerbaijan, north of Baku, is, like Talysh, a divergent variety of Persian. It has been fully described by V. Miller.[1] The Tat vowel-system contains close and open sounds, front rounded vowels, and the Russian-type *y* (ы), which give it a complexity unknown to Persian. Its consonantal system illustrates widespread palatalisation, but on the whole resembles that of Persian and shares with the latter sounds borrowed from Turkic and Arabic. The paradigm of nominal declension recognises genitive, dative, and accusative cases, which are indicated by suffixes. All other case-relations are expressed with the aid of prepositions (e.g. *ve* 'with', *bä* 'in(to)'). Adjective is joined to noun by the suffix *-a* (e.g. *xub-a xuna* 'good house'). The Tat verb, like the Persian, is characteristically Indo-European and distinguishes a variety of tenses, including the future. The invariable verbal forms comprise the infinitive (in *-n*) and gerunds (in *-äni* and *-ä*). There are a great many prepositions and postpositions.

Tajiki, which is spoken in Afghanistan, south of the Hindu Kush, as well as on Soviet territory, is regarded by most students of it as a Persian dialect. It differs from Persian phonetically, showing velars absent in the latter, and also in structure and in vocabulary, having been influenced by Turkic, notably Uzbek. Tajiki is not entirely confined to the natives of Tajikistan, but is also used by Central Asiatic Jews[2] and Gypsies and by a considerable number of Arabs. The Tajiki of Afghanistan was most probably introduced there by immigrants from the north. Till 1929 Tajikistan was an autonomous enclave of Uzbekistan, but is now an independent federal republic of the Union. Persian had been its official language and the Arabic its official script till the Latin alphabet displaced the latter in 1927 and the local dialect was given a literary shape.

[1] *Татские этюды,* II (Москва, 1907).
[2] See И. И. Зарубин, „Очерк разговорного языка самаркандских евреев' (*Иран*, II, Ленинград, 1928).

The Tajiki phonemes include long and short vowels, contrasted open and close *o*, and an Iranic consonantal system, with postvelar *x/ɣ*, uvular *q*, the paired affricates *tš/dž*, and a *v* tending to become bilabial in rapid articulation. Structurally Tajiki recalls Tat and Persian, but presents at the same time one or two idiosyncrasies, for instance the pronominal plurals *māyān* 'we', *šumāyān* 'you' (cf. Pers. *mā, šomā*), the ending -*t* in the 3rd person singular of the present tense instead of Persian -*d*, the presence of Turkic elements in the syntax, and the curious non-Turkic interchange of finite verb and infinitive.

Related to Tajiki are a large number of Iranic dialects spoken in the high valleys of the Pamirs. They have been listed by H. Reichelt[1] and G. A. Grierson,[2] who single out Yaghnobi, Wanchi, Yazghulami, the Shughni group (i.e. Shughni proper, Rushani, Bartangi, and Oroshori), Sargilami, Ishkashmi (Zebaki), Wakhi, and Minjani (Munji), the last two in Afghanistan. These dialects are spoken by mainly bilingual tribes, whose second language is Tajiki, and the dialects are naturally shrinking to the encroachment of the latter. Wanchi is now probably extinct. In the Yazghulam valley even the children speak a Persian, as well as their vernacular Pamiri dialect, and among Shughni speakers Persian is the liturgical language. The Shughni group of four dialects falls into two divisions, to the northern of which the Sarikoli of Chinese Turkestan shows considerable resemblance. Shughni and several other Pamiri dialects have been provided with an odd-looking Latin alphabet and school textbooks by the Soviet authorities.[3]

Shughni (Shughnani) may be isolated here to illustrate Pamiri structural features. According to W. Geiger[4] a systematic distinction is drawn between long and short vowels; the

---

[1] 'Iranisch' in *Grundriss der indogermanischen Sprach- und Altertumskunde*, II, 4 (Berlin, 1927²). See also W. Geiger und E. Kuhn, *Grundriss der iranischen Philologie*, I–II (Strassburg, 1895–1901).

[2] *Linguistic Survey of India*, x (Calcutta, 1921).

[3] E.g. A. Djakof (D'jakov), *Xugnǝni alifbǝ kudaken çat* 'A Shughni ABC for Children' (Stalinabad, 1931).

[4] 'Die Pamir-Dialekte' in *Grundriss der iranischen Philologie*, I, 2 (Strassburg, 1898–1901).

rounded *â* ([ɔ]) appears where, for instance, Sarikoli has *ā*; and the consonantal series includes *w*, the dental fricatives *θ/ð*, a full set of sibilants, and the velars *x/γ*. Word-formation is based on a limited number of formants, which are most in evidence in verbal composition. The system of declension confronts a common (epicene) case with a dative (in *-ar*, *-er*, *-ir*), and the singular with the plural (e.g. *čīd* 'house', *čad-īn* 'houses'). These oppositions are everything that survives of the Indo-European nominal paradigm, which is as 'impoverished' as in Persian itself. Other Pamiri dialects, for instance Wakhi and Sarikoli, exhibit a *rectus-obliquus* antithesis in the plural (e.g. Wakhi nom.

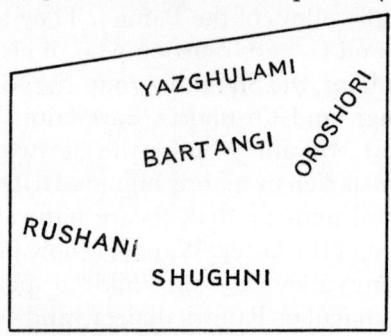

Fig. 12. Diagram of the Pamiri dialects.

plur. *xūn* 'houses', obl. plur. *xūn-aw*). This antithesis occurs also in some of the Shughni personal pronouns (e.g. nom. sing. *vuz* 'I', obl. sing. *mu*; nom. sing. *ya* 'she', obl. sing. *vam*). The verbal paradigm in the present indicative recalls the Persian pattern, and the Persian moods and tenses recur, with the preterite serving also as the future. There is less Arabic influence in the Shughni than in the Persian vocabulary, and this may be seen in the use, say, of *et* 'and' for Persian *va*.

The name 'Ghalchah' has been applied to the Pamiri group by British investigators, including Grierson, but, according to W. Lentz,[1] this name as a national appellation is unknown in Tajikistan. The Pamir tribes, R. B. Shaw wrote in 1876, 'are

[1] *Pamir-Dialekte. I. Materialien zur Kenntnis der Schugni-Gruppe* (Göttingen, 1933).

all classed by their Turki (i.e. Turkic) neighbours under the general designation Ghalchah'.[1] The name appears to be accepted by European scholarship as synonymous with 'hillman', but Lentz declares it to be a pejorative nickname with the sense of 'loafer' and even 'coward'.

2

The Armenian dialect used in the U.S.S.R. is the Eastern, in contrast to the expatriate Western dialect (derived from Cilician) in European Turkey, including Istanbul, where there are said to be over 250,000 Armenians. These dialects are a lineal bifurcation of the colloquial language (*ašcharabar*) corresponding to literary Old Armenian (*grabar*), which had a peculiar uncial alphabet of Greco-Semitic origin devised by Bishop Mesrop and a sacred literature as early as the fifth century, though the first MSS. belong to the ninth. Old, or Classical Armenian[2] is a strictly literary dialect, like Bishop Wulfila's Scriptural Gothic, and as such it is remarkable for its formal regularity. Middle Armenian (twelfth to fifteenth centuries) is similar to it grammatically, and it is from this that the two modern literary languages evolved in the course of the nineteenth century. They are nearer to the spoken idiom, which is in use not only in the Armenian Federal Republic, but in the adjacent Azerbaijan and Georgia, as well as on the Turkish and Persian sides of the frontier. Alphabetic reforms were initiated in Armenia in 1926, but could not be fully carried out, and the traditional alphabet retains its former authority. A large modern literature exists.

In the opinion of N. J. Marr,[3] Armenian arose in the sixth century B.C. as a hybrid of Indo-European and the aboriginal

---

[1] 'On the Ghalchah Languages, Wakhī and Sariḳolī' (*Journal of the Asiatic Society of Bengal*, XLV, 1876).

[2] See Н. Я. Марр, *Грамматика древнеармянского языка* (СПБ, 1903); A. Meillet, *Esquisse d'une grammaire de l'arménien classique* (Vienna, 1903) and *Altarmenisches Elementarbuch* (Heidelberg, 1913).

[3] *Яфетические элементы в языке Армении* (СПБ, 1911); , Армянская культура, ее корни и доисторические связи по данным языкознания' (*Язык и история*, 1, Ленинград, 1936).

Caucasian language ('Japhetic') of its present habitat. History however does not venture to follow 'linguistic palaeontology' so far. The Indo-European character of the language was established by Petermann and Windischmann in the 1830's, but it continued to be regarded as Iranic till, in the later nineteenth century, H. Hübschmann[1] defined it as an independent branch of Indo-European, intermediate between Slavonic and Iranic. Phonetically Eastern Armenian, like the other varieties of this language, resembles Germanic in its shifted ('permutated') plosives (cf. *tasn* with 'ten', *kev* with 'cow', *hajr* with 'father'). According to E. Sievers,[2] 'the unvoiced *b*, *d*, *g* alternate *promiscue* with the voiced forms in the spoken language, but this does not lead to confusion with the aspirated *pʻ*, *tʻ*, *kʻ*.' The dialect shares its sets of aspirated and glottalised plosives with Georgian. There are two kinds of apical *r*, as in Spanish (e.g. *nor* 'new', *tsʼarr* 'tree'; cf. Span. *pero* 'but', *perro* 'dog'). The vowel system is simple, includes the central *ə*, and shows a tendency to diphthongise *e* and *o* initially. This tendency has gone so far as to give rise to *je* and *vo*. Unlike the other Indo-European languages, except Persian, Armenian has no grammatical gender, but, like the Scandinavian (Nordic) group, some Balkan languages (viz. Albanian, Bulgarian, and Rumanian), Mordvin, Ethiopian (Ge'ez), and Basque, it uses a postpositive definite article (e.g. *majr-ə* 'the mother', *vortʻi-n* 'the son'). The attributive adjective is invariable, as in English and Georgian, and nouns following numerals remain singular (e.g. *jerekʻ jeɣbajr* 'three brothers, lit. brother'). There are seven cases of the noun, including two local cases, and animate nouns have an accusative formally identical with the dative (cf. the Russian genitive-accusative of animate nouns). There are postpositions as well as prepositions (e.g. *šunə senjaki medž e* 'the dog is in the room'). The Armenian verb recognises a progressive form in the present tense, as in English (e.g. *na kartʻum e* 'he is reading'). In conjugation the personal pronouns are omitted. There are two negative particles -*tšə* and *mi*, the latter reserved

[1] *Armenische Studien* (Leipzig, 1883).
[2] *Grundzüge der Phonetik* (Leipzig, 1901).

for the imperative (cf. Georgian and Persian). The finite verb comes at the end of its clause (e.g. *ašakert'ə t'uxt' jev gəritš tšuni* 'the pupil has neither paper nor pen', where *tšuni* means 'hasn't'). Participial constructions, due most probably to Caucasian influence, are common. The vocabulary is chequered with many Persian as well as non-Indo-European elements.

Fig. 13. Diagram of the Indo-European languages.

3

On the north-western confines of European Russia, as it were counterbalancing the Indo-European languages of the Caucasus, which we have just reviewed, are the two surviving representatives of the diminutive Baltic branch—Latvian and Lithuanian. The Baltic languages, like the neighbouring Estonian, are spoken in newly annexed territories and underwent a rapid independent development between 1918 and 1940. Latvian is the official language of the Latvian S.S. Republic (capital Riga), and a variety of it called Curian (Latv. *kursenieku valoda*)[1] is spoken by a bilingual fishing population on the Kurische Nehrung in East Prussia. Lithuanian is used in the Lithuanian S.S. Republic

[1] See J. Plāķis, *Kursenieku valoda* (Riga, 1927).

(capital Vilnius, formerly Vil'na) and in the Memel (Lith. Klaipėda) area, or Kaliningrad (Königsberg) province, north of the Neman (Lith. Nemunas). Of the two languages, Lithuanian is the more conservative and on that account has been very thoroughly investigated by European, chiefly German scholarship.

It is customary among Indo-European specialists to hyphenate Baltic and Slavonic, and there appears to be some justification for this, because the resemblances between the two distinct language-groups are greater than those between either of them and any third congener.[1] But the relationship is certainly not quite so close as the one existing between Indic and Iranic. The affinities between Baltic and Slavonic are not only phonetic and morphological, but lexical, and these are perhaps the most striking as they are the most numerous (cf. Latv. *galva* 'head' with Russ. *golova*, Lith. *ieškóti* 'to seek' with Russ. *iskat'*). Both Baltic languages have a great many loans from Slavonic and a few from Old Germanic; Latvian, like Estonian, still uses many from Low German,[2] including the conjunction *un* 'and', and it has also absorbed a substantial body of Livonian words (e.g. *maksāt* 'to pay', *kāzas* 'wedding', *puisis* 'lad', *vajaga* 'it is necessary'); Lithuanian is richer in borrowings from Polish and Russian.

Several Baltic tribes and languages have become extinct in historical times. Among such tribes were the Prussians, whose scantily and imperfectly recorded language survived into the seventeenth century, the Curonians (Latv. Kurši, Lith. Kuršiai) of Western Curonia (Latv. Kurzeme), the Γαλίνδαι of Ptolemy,[3] whose name is found even in Central Russia (cf. O.Russ. Goljad'), and the Yatvingians, who are referred to as 'Jatvjazi' in Russian annals up to the thirteenth century.

[1] The pros and cons of the thesis of Balto-Slavonic unity may be read in A. Senn, 'On the Degree of Kinship between Slavic and Baltic' (*The Slavonic Year-Book*, Menasha, 1941). See also O. Szemerényi, 'Sur l'unité linguistique balto-slave' (*Etudes slaves et roumaines*, I, 2-3, Budapest, 1948).

[2] See J. Sehwers, *Die deutschen Lehnwörter im Lettischen* (Zürich, 1918).

[3] *Claudii Ptolemaei Geographia*, ed. C. F. A. Nobbe, tomus I, Lipsiae, 1843. See my article 'Medieval Baltic Tribes' (*American Slavic and East European Review*, VIII, 2, 1949).

Latvian, like its northern neighbour, has been known in writing since the sixteenth century, but its modern literature is little more than a century old. Unlike Estonian, which has changed only one letter (substituting *v* for *w*), it has modified its alphabet of German origin by replacing the Gothic with Latin characters, rejecting the monophonic consonant-groups and the transliteral strokes, and introducing diacritic signs, mainly from Czech. Latvian is spoken in several dialects—the Eastern, or Upper (*augšzemnieku*, 'Latgalian'), the Central (*vidus*), and the Western (*tāmnieku*). The Central dialect of Jelgava (Mitau) is the literary language, but its spoken form, as used in the capital, Riga, has undergone certain changes under the influence of other dialects. The Eastern dialect has many phonetic peculiarities, including a very different grouping of vowels and the presence of the diphthong *yu*, which resembles Standard Estonian *õu* (cf. *myusu* 'our' with the Central and literary *mūsu*). The Western dialect, with its Livonian 'substratum', has lost the twofold (masculine-feminine) gender and simplified the verbal system by the wholesale abandonment of characteristic endings. Literary Latvian, phonetically, shows a well-articulated system of consonants, including the relatively unfamiliar palatal plosives (*ķ*, *ģ*), found in Hungarian (*ty*, *gy*), also the affricates *c*, *dz*, *č*, and a less notable vowel system, which diphthongises originally long *ē* and *ō* into *ie* and *uo* (written *o*), like the North-Eastern, or Viru dialect of Estonian, opposes [æ] (written *e*) to the closer *e* in a sort of vowel harmony, and has three diphthongs of the *i*-series (*ai*, *ei*, *ui*) as against one of the *u*-series (*au*). The stress, as in West Finnic, is protosyllabic, but the characteristic Baltic tones (Latv. *intonācijas*) survive, though their incidence is not always the same as in Lithuanian. One of the three Latvian tones is merely the glottal plosive, or 'broken tone' (*lauztā intonācija*), severing the continuity of a long vowel (e.g. *kâts* 'handle'), and is the outcome of an accentual-tonal shift (cf. Latv. *galva* 'head' with Lith. *galvà*); the other two, viz. the level (*stieptā*) and the falling (*krītošā*),[1] correspond

[1] The difference between the glottalised 'tone' and the falling tone has been lost in the Western (Latv. *tāmnieku*) dialect. See G. (i.e. J.) Plāķis,

respectively to the falling (ˊ) and the rising tone (˜) of Lithuanian.

Morphologically Latvian is less complex than Lithuanian: it has rather fewer noun cases (six as against seven, the instrumental being formally identical with the accusative) and no dual number, but the same twofold adjectival paradigm, i.e. the indefinite and the definite (e.g. masc. nom. sing. indef. *liels,* def. *lielais;* fem. nom. sing. indef. *liela,* def. *lielā* 'big, the big'), the same two genders, masculine and feminine (Old Prussian also had a neuter), similar personalised demonstratives serving as the 3rd person forms of the personal pronoun (Latv. *viņš* 'he', *viņa* 'she'; Lith. *jìs* 'he', *jì* 'she'), and a common form for the 3rd singular and plural of the verb (e.g. Latv. *viņš ir* 'he is', *viņi ir* 'they are'; cf. Lith. *jìs, jiẽ yrà*). In contrast to Lithuanian, Latvian has no special superlative form, but uses a modified comparative, like spoken Estonian (e.g. masc. nom. sing. *liels, lielāks, vislielākais* 'big, bigger, biggest'; cf. Est. *suur, suurem, kõige suurem*). The verb, as in Lithuanian, has a reflexive form for the old middle voice, a conditional, and a relative, or 'oblique' mood for *oratio obliqua* (cf. Estonian), a single preterite tense and a 'sigmatic' future; it uses an entire series of inseparable prefixes, like Slavonic (contrast German and Hungarian), declines its participles like adjectives, and has a typically Indo-European set of numerals based on decimal numeration.

Lithuanian has two considerable dialect-groups: Low Lithuanian (*žemaičių tarmė*) and High Lithuanian (*augštaičių tarmė*), the first spoken in the valley of the lower Nemunas (Russ. Neman, Germ. Memel) in East Prussia, the second in the province of Kaunas (Kovno) and in parts of the Suvalkai (Pol. Suwałki) and Vilnius (Vil'na) provinces. Most Lithuanians, other than the numerous emigrants overseas, were concentrated in the Lithuanian Republic before the Soviet annexation, and others were drawn in with the acquisition of part of the Vilnius province in 1939. The present Lithuanian S.S. Republic contains most of the European Lithuanians.

'Les dialectes lettons: le dialecte de Tām' (*Revue des études slaves,* IV, Paris, 1924).

Literary Lithuanian is based on the High Lithuanian spoken round Kaunas, which has been the approximate geographical centre of the Lithuanian-speaking lands since the beginnings of historical record, and during the twenty-odd years of political independence had reached a high degree of literary and academic culture, vying in pliancy with Latvian and Estonian. But Lithuanian written documents in various dialects ascend to the sixteenth century (e.g. M. Mažvydas)[1] and include the work of the poet K. Donelaitis in the eighteenth.

Lithuanian has practically the same compact system of vowels as Latvian, including *o* (absent in Latvian except orthographically), [æ] (written *e*), and *ė* (long, close *ẹ̄*, also not in Latvian), practically the same consonants, but with a palatalised series, like Russian, and the affricate *dž*, unknown to Latvian. There is a predominance of hush over hiss sibilants (cf. Lith. *àš* 'I' with Latv. *es*), and the older forms of Lithuanian appear to have had nasal vowels, whose symbols still survive, but with oral values. The Lithuanian accent is 'free', and its tones comprise one rising (e.g. *gintãras* 'amber') and a pair of falling ones, the two latter being distinguished by the length or shortness of the syllable to which they belong (e.g. *rýtas* 'morning' and *grìkai* 'buckwheat'). Unlike the Latvian and Serbian tones, the Lithuanian ones do not exactly correspond to those of Old Greek: where the last had a circumflex accent, i.e. a compound rising-falling tone, Latvian and Serbian have a falling one, whereas Literary, or High Lithuanian has a rising one,[2] and where Old Greek had an acute accent, or rising tone, Lithuanian has a falling tone in contrast to the conservative rising tone of Serbian and the level or the 'broken' tone of Latvian.

Morphologically Lithuanian is richer and more varied than Latvian, though, as in the latter, the system of declension is not complicated by a neuter gender. There are seven cases, each with singular and plural forms, and the dual number often has three distinct case-forms. Besides these, there are still two not

---

[1] G. Gerullis, *Mosvid. Die ältesten litauischen Sprachdenkmäler bis zum Jahre 1570* (Heidelberg, 1923) and *Senieji lietuvių skaitymai*, I (Kaunas, 1927).

[2] Low Lithuanian (Samogitian) appears to have a rising-falling tone here.

quite obsolete local cases associated with the postpositional particles -*na* and -*p*, illative and allative (e.g. *namúosna* 'homewards', *kunigōp* 'to the priest'). The adjective has an indefinite (e.g. *báltas-baltà* 'white') and a longer definite variety (e.g. *baltàsis-baltóji* 'the white'), which is formed by attaching the 3rd person form of the personal pronoun (*jìs, jì*) to the indefinite as base (cf. Slavonic), with certain phonetic and tonal adjustments. Adjectival comparison in Lithuanian clearly distinguishes comparative and superlative (e.g. masc. nom. sing. *didèsnis* 'bigger', *didžiáusias* 'biggest'). The numerals exhibit curious types in the second decade (e.g. *vienúolika* 'eleven', *dvýlika* 'twelve'), which present an exact parallel to two Gothic forms, viz. *áinlif* and *twalif*. In both cases the second part of the word means 'left over'. Gothic replaces -*lif* with *taíhun* 'ten' in the remaining numbers of the decade, but Lithuanian carries -*lika* right through to *devyniólika* 'nineteen'. The Lithuanian verb, like the noun, has a dual number, and the forms of the 3rd person in all three numbers are identical. The conjugation is mainly thematic, but there are also remnants of ancient athematic forms in the singular of the verb 'to be' (*esmì, esù* 'am', *esì* 'art', *ẽsti* 'is'). As in Latvian, the middle voice is expressed by reflexive forms associated with a reflexive pronoun affix -*s(i)*, which however shows more mobility than in Latvian and can be an infix as well as a suffix. The tenses comprise present, preterite, imperfect, and future forms, the last 'sigmatic' as in Latvian (e.g. pres. tense *dìrbu* 'I work', fut. *dìrbsiu* 'I shall work'). There are numerous participles, including a preterite passive (e.g. *dìrbtas* 'worked, done'; cf. the active form *dìrbęs* 'worked') and a gerundive, or debitative (e.g. *dìrbtinas* 'to be worked, done'). The participles, like the adjectives, have a definite and an indefinite form in all tenses and in both voices (e.g. masc. nom. sing. *dìrbąs* 'working', *dìrbęs* 'worked', *dìrbdavęs* 'was working,' *dìrbsiąs* 'about to work'), and all these are declinable in full. There are also parallel indeclinable forms in all tenses (e.g. *dìrbant, dìrbus, dìrbdavus, dìrbsiant*). The Lithuanian moods include a conditional (e.g. *dìrbčiau* 'I should work') and an optative (e.g. *tedìrba* 'let him work'), which is paraphrased in Latvian by the particle *lai* 'let'; there are two kinds of infinitive (e.g. *dìrbti, dìrbte*) and a supine (e.g. *dìrbtų*). Compound tenses, perfect and pluperfect, with participial constructions have been modelled, as in Latvian, on West European prototypes, and these complicate still further the already complex verbal system.

Lexically Lithuanian is considerably indebted to Slavonic influence,[1] owes a body of loans to German,[2] and, unlike Latvian, has few contacts with Livonian.

4

The remaining Indo-European language-type spoken in the U.S.S.R. is the East Slavonic, to which the *lingua franca*, Russian, the mother-tongue of about half the total inhabitants, belongs. East Slavonic consists of three varieties, whose effective separation goes back to approximately the fourteenth century, viz. Russian, White Russian, and Ukrainian. It was customary under the monarchy to treat these three as allotropic forms of the same language, but each of them has a literary dialect of its own, and this is predominant in its own territory for administrative and educational purposes.

Roughly reproducing the political dichotomy of Novgorod and Muscovy, Russian, the descendant of the Old Russian dialects of the Kriviči, Slověne, and Vjatiči, has, since the Middle Ages, distinguished a Northern from a Southern subsidiary dialect, the dividing line between the two describing a curve from near Pskov in the west to the middle Sura, and from there on to Stalingrad and the lower Volga. The Northern dialect, which is also the 'basic' Russian of Siberia, is the more conservative and adheres in pronunciation to the accepted spelling: unaccented *o* and the plosive consonant *g* (г) remain (e.g. [mo'ros] 'frost', [go'ra] 'hill'); unaccented *e* (< *ě*) tends to become *i* (e.g. ['mjisto] for *mesto* 'place') and unaccented *e* (< *e*),

[1] See A. Brückner, *Litu-Slavische Studien. I. Die slavischen Fremdwörter im Litauischen* (Weimar, 1877); P. Skardžius, *Die slavischen Lehnwörter im Altlitauischen* (Kaunas, 1931).
[2] See K. Alminauskas, *Die Germanismen des Litauischen*, 1 (Kaunas, 1935).

followed by a non-palatalised consonant, to become *jo/'o* (*ë*) (e.g. [ṣo'lo] for *seló* 'village'); orthographic *ae* and *oe* often forfeit the second as a distinct term; palatalised consonants are preserved before suffixes (e.g. *car'stvo* 'kingdom'), and it is only in a restricted southerly tract of the Northern dialect area, viz. the 'steppe island' of the provinces (*oblasti*) of Yaroslavl', Vladimir, and Kostroma, that the peculiarly northern *cokan'je* (*c*-articulation), i.e. the substitution of hiss-sibilants for hush-sibilants—*ts* (ц) for *tš* (ч) and *vice versa*—or the use of an intermediate 'blurred' affricate, is not found. In Southern Russian *o* and *e* (< *e* and *ě*) are pronounced *a* and *ja/'a* (я) respectively when unaccented (e.g. [a'na] for *on'a* 'she'; [ṗa'ro] for *peró* 'pen'), *g* (г) becomes a fricative as in Greek, *v* (в) and *u* (у) are interchangeable (e.g. *uzjal* for *vzjal* 'took'; *vkral* for *ukral* 'stole'), the final *t* (т) of the 3rd person singular and plural of the present tense is either palatalised or omitted (e.g. *idet'* or *ide* 'comes'), the genitive ending of pronouns and adjectives -*go* (-го) does not change into -*vo*, as in the Northern dialect, but is pronounced with the velar sound, and phonetic levelling has led to the lapse of the neuter gender. The Moscow dialect, on which Literary Russian has been based since the fifteenth century, represents a transitional, compromise dialect blending the 'reduced' Southern vowelling (Russ. *akan'je*) with the Northern values of the consonants (e.g. *g* is pronounced as a plosive).

Literary Russian has its dated beginnings in the eleventh century and has been subjected till recently to the subtle, varied, and continuous influence of the liturgical language, known to the faithful as Church Slavonic and representing a development from a medieval form of Macedonian Bulgarian. In a great many cases this has resulted in the creation of lexical doublets, the abstract, metaphoric member of each word-pair being generally of Church Slavonic, the simple member of Russian, origin. Church Slavonic influence on Russian is paralleled by Latin influence on the Romance languages and English and by Arabic-Persian influence on the Urdu form of Hindustani. During the seventeenth century, after having spread to Siberia, as English had spread to North America, Russian began to experience the impact of West European culture. The earliest European words were adopted in Polish forms, but ever since the eighteenth century the borrowings have been made from the original sources or through the medium of French, and have been especially numerous since the 'latinising' Revolution. Though much simplified since the eleventh century, when it resembled the coeval Old Church Slavonic (Old Bulgarian) in grammatical involution, Literary Russian is still a conservatively inflected language as compared with present-day English, French, and even German. Its nominal flexion is more complex than its verbal, but the verb, as if in compensation, has been subtilised by the perfected mechanism of aspect, and the syntax has been considerably altered since the end of the eighteenth century by the deliberate pursuit of French models.

White Russian, the modern representative of the medieval dialect of the Dregoviči, is spoken in the expanded White Russian Federal Republic (capital Minsk), i.e. roughly in the basins of the upper Western Dvina and the upper Dnieper. It came into currency as a literary language in the Grand Duchy of Lithuania in the fourteenth century and was used, along with medieval Latin as the official language, because the majority of the inhabitants of that country were White Russians.[1] After the dynastic union of Lithuania and Poland in 1386, and till the nineteenth century, literary White Russian very gradually declined in importance under the pressure of Polish and ultimately fell into disuse with the break-up of Poland. Recreated independently in the middle of the nineteenth century on the basis of a south-western dialect, it has tended, at least in the practice of some writers, to diverge deliberately from the pattern of both Russian and Ukrainian, its immediate congeners (cf. literary Portuguese in relation to Spanish). On the whole White Russian has more in common with Russian than with Ukrainian: it is an *a*-language and

[1] C. S. Stang, *Die westrussische Kanzleisprache des Grossfürstentums Litauen* (Oslo, 1935).

distinguishes *i* (і) from *y* (ы), like South Russian, and it recalls this dialect also in making its *g* fricative ([ɣ]), interchanging *v* (в) and *u* (у) before consonants, and preserving the velar consonant in the adjectival case-ending *-go*. The last three features, together with the change of final velar *l* into *w*, the lapse of *-t* in the ending of the 3rd person singular of the present indicative, and the preservation of the vocative case, connect White Russian with Ukrainian. A peculiarity which White Russian shares only with the latter is the reproduction of stressed historical *y* (ы) where Russian has *o* (e.g. masc. nom. sing. *pusty* 'empty' for Russian *pustoj*). The language also has affinities with Polish (e.g. *t/d* before front vowels are palatalised into affricates *c'*(*ts'*)/*dz'*: *pacjani* 'pull', Russ. *potjani*; *ljudzi* 'people', Russ. *ljudi*) and has substantially increased its literary vocabulary by borrowing from that source. White Russian orthography is more phonetic than Russian and recognises *a*-vowelling (e.g. *vada* 'water'), *ja* (я) for unaccented *e*, affrication (i.e. *ts/dz* for Russian *t/d*), and *y̌*, or *w* (ў), for Russian *v* (в).

Ukrainian derives from the eleventh-century East Slavonic dialect of the Velynjane and Dulěby of Volynia and Galicia and is to-day the domestic and official language of the thirty to forty million subjects of the Ukrainian Federal Republic (capital Kiev). It is also spoken in the recently annexed territories of Galicia and Subcarpathian Ruthenia. The present literary form of the language does not go back beyond the eighteenth century and has no lineal connection with Ukrainian literature before that time. During the later nineteenth century it was proscribed as subversive by the Tsarist *régime*, and this led to the concentration of exiled Ukrainian writers in Lemberg (Pol. Lwów, Ukr. L′viv), the cultural focus of Austrian Galicia, and the Imperial Austrian Government, for political reasons, welcomed and furthered the literary cultivation of Ukrainian, better known then as Ruthenian. The language, as written in Lemberg, absorbed many words and terms peculiar to Polish, some of which were discarded when Ukrainian was revived at home after the repeal of the government ban in 1906.

In common with Russian and White Russian, Ukrainian exhibits the irregular and mobile accentuation characteristic of East Slavonic as well as other East Slavonic features, like initial *o* for *je/e* (cf. *ozero* 'lake' with O.C.S. *jezero*), pleophony or 'full vowelling' (e.g. *horod* 'town' for O.C.S. *grad*), and the absence of vowel length. Phonetically Ukrainian illustrates the coincidence of *i* and *y* in a close central vowel of Polish type (e.g. *lycho* 'misfortune'), also the change of closed original *e* and *o* (i.e. underived from the 'surds' ь and ъ respectively) into *i* (cf. *vil* 'ox' with Russian *vol*, *pič′* 'stove' with Russian *peč′*) and the transformation of velar *l* into [w] before a consonant (cf. вовк 'wolf' with Russ. волк). The palatalisation of consonants, so characteristic of Russian, has been notably reduced. It accounts for the coincidence of *i* and *y*, and the use of 'hard' *e* for Russian 'soft' *e* (i.e. one preceded by *j* or a palatalised consonant). Like Northern Russian, Ukrainian pronounces written unstressed *o* as *o* (Russ. *okan′je* '*o*-vowelling') and changes *e* (derived from *ě*) into *i* (cf. *obid* 'dinner', *did* 'grandfather', *rika* 'river' with Russian *obed*, *ded*, *reka*); like White Russian, it sibilates velars before *i* in the oblique cases of nouns, does not palatalise *r*, has *xv* for *f*, and has developed long consonants from the original juxtaposition of consonant and *j* (cf. Ukr. *suddja* 'judge' with W.Russ. *sudz′dzja*).

The Soviet policy of consistently encouraging the literary use of regional idioms gave an impetus to White Russian and Ukrainian studies after the Revolution. Universities and academies, at which these languages, like Georgian at Tbilisi and Armenian at Erevan, became the media of scientific exposition, were founded, and White Russian and Ukrainian schools and periodicals multiplied. Writing in 1918 under the vivid impression of revolutionary events, A. Meillet[1] regretted the linguistic decentralisation in the U.S.S.R., but consoled himself with the conviction that Russian would survive this apparent reverse. His regret was gratuitous even at that time. The expansion of Russian, attested over so many centuries, seems, whether desirable or not, to be an inevitable process,

[1] *Les langues dans l'Europe nouvelle* (Paris, 1918).

if only because the language remains the exclusive common medium of communication between one Soviet people and another. Its forcible tuition, once part of the centralising policy of the Tsars, quite naturally bred distaste for it among the many non-Russians on whom it was imposed, and linguistic nationalism went to intensify its political counterpart. The present-day government, on the contrary, aims generally at appeasing ethnic and linguistic minorities by taking an interest in the development of their languages. Nevertheless this policy is subtly expansionist in result, if not in purpose. The sense of inferiority which speakers of the minor languages feel towards the all-embracing *lingua franca*, its practical value to them, and the psychologically 'emancipating' effect of its possession inspire the more gifted and ambitious among them to make the effort to acquire it, and this process, started in school (Russian being everywhere an obligatory subject) and fostered by the radio, is accelerated by army life, which was unknown before the Revolution to some nationalities (e.g. to those of Central Asia), and by the frequent and chequered migration of labour to regions that are being industrially exploited in various parts of the Union. In view of all these things there can hardly be any doubt, to quote Meillet, 'that the future of Russian is assured', and that decidedly without any 'conflicts and difficulties', even the purely imaginary ones, which he seems to believe this always numerically powerful language 'has never been spared'.

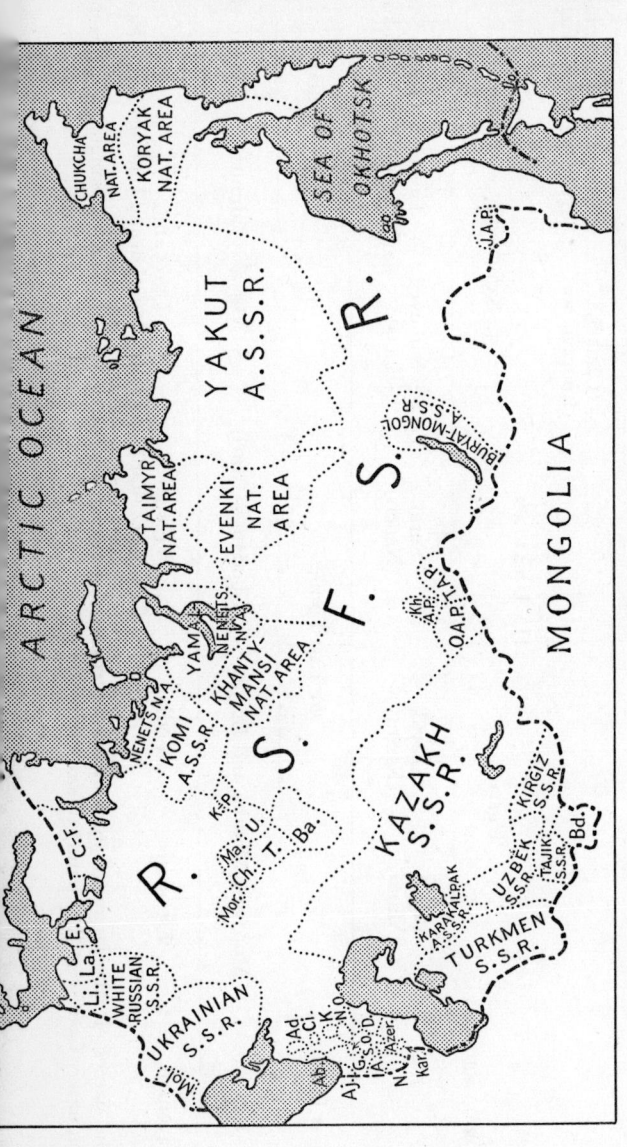

A.	Armenian S.S.R.	D.	Daghestan A.S.S.R.	Ma.	Mari A.S.S.R.
Ab.	Abkhaz A.S.S.R.	E.	Estonian S.S.R.	Mol.	Moldavian S.S.R.
Ad.	Adyge Auton. Province	G.	Georgian S.S.R.	Mor.	Mordva A.S.S.R.
Aj.	Ajar A.S.S.R.	J.A.P.	Jewish Aut. Province.	N.	Nakhichevan A.S.S.R.
Azer.	Azerbaijan S.S.R.	K.	Kabarda A.S.S.R.	N.O.	North Ossete A.S.S.R.
Ba.	Bashkir A.S.S.R.	Kar.	High Karabakh Aut. Prov.	O.A.P.	Oirot Aut. Prov.
Bd.	High Badakhshan Aut. Prov.	K.-P.	Komi-Permyak Nat. Area.	S.O.	South Ossete Aut. Prov.
C.-F.	Carelo-Finnish S.S.R.	Kh.A.P.	Khakass Aut. Prov.	T.	Tartar A.S.S.R.
Ch.	Chuvash A.S.S.R.	La.	Latvian S.S.R.	T.A.P.	Tuva Auton. Prov.
Ci.	Circassian Aut. Prov.	Li.	Lithuanian S.S.R.	U.	Udmurt A.S.S.R.

Map 5. Administrative divisions of the U.S.S.R.

APPENDIX I
TABULAR SUMMARY[1]

I. PALAEOASIATIC

1. Yenisei Ostyak (Ket)
2. Yukagir (Odul)
3. Gilyak (Nivkh)
4. Ainu
5. Chukotian
   - Chukcha (Luoravetlan)
   - Koryak (Nymylan)
   - Kamchadal (Itel'men)

II. URALIAN

2. Ugrian
   - Vogul (Mansi)
   - Ostyak (Khanty)

3. Samoyedic
   - Yurak (Nenets)
   - Yenisei Samoyed (Enets)
   - Tavgi (Nganasan)
   - Ostyak Samoyed (Sel'kup)

1. Finnic (Somian)
   - (a) West Finnic
     - Livonian
     - Estonian
     - Vodian
     - Vepsian (with Ludian)
     - Carelian (with Olonecian and Ingrian)
     - Kola Lappish (Saam)
   - (b) East Finnic
     - Mordvin (Moksha and Erzya)
     - Cheremiss (Mari)
   - (c) Permian
     - Votyak (Udmurt)
     - Zyryan (Komi)

[1] The names of each language stock are arranged, as in the text, from east to west, and the languages in each stock approximately from west (left hand) to east (right hand).

III. Altaic

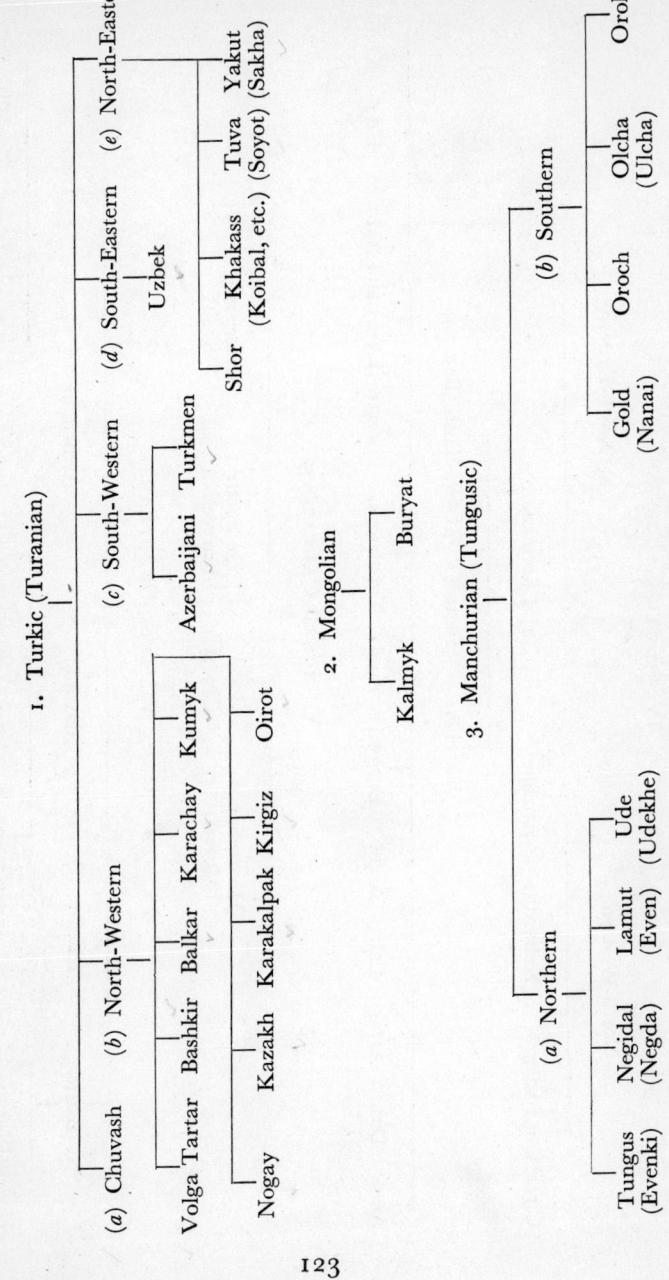

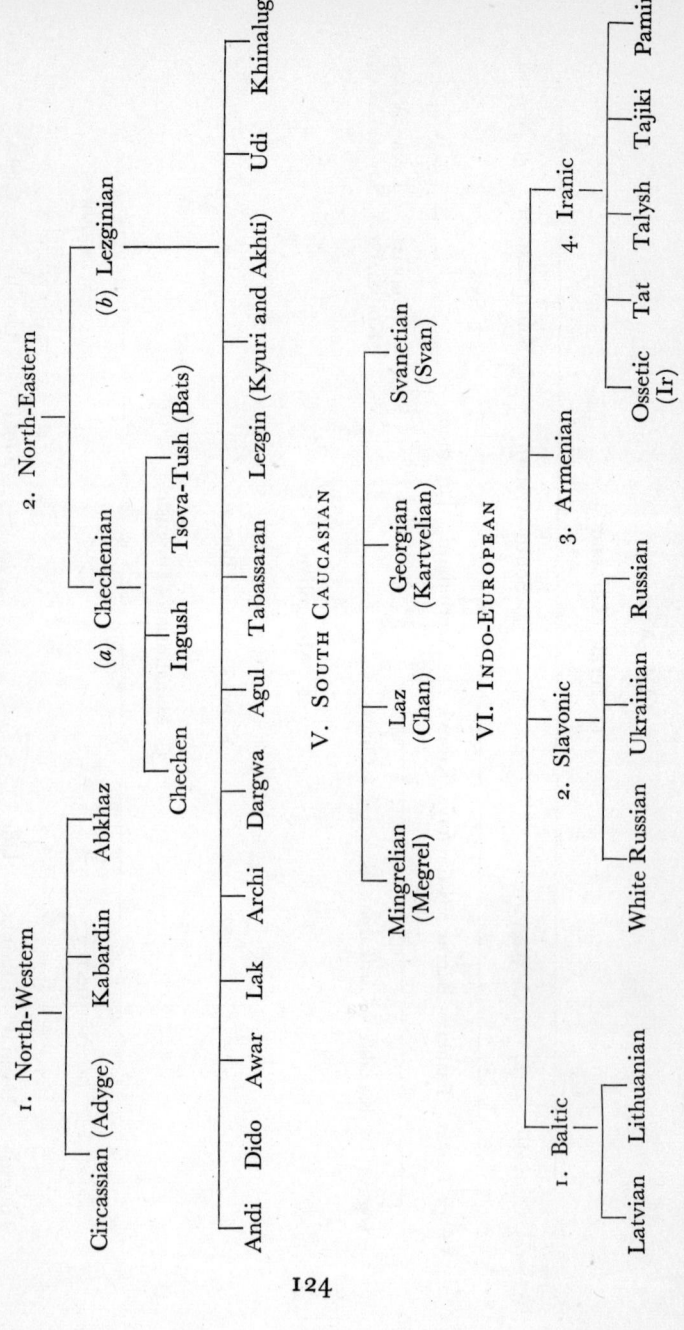

APPENDIX II

LANGUAGE STATISTICS

The figures in this table are no more than approximate and do not all belong to the same year. In most cases the latest figure has been preferred and, where estimates compete, generally the higher. Statistics contained in the following works have been collated, viz.: (1) J. Szinnyei, *Finnisch-ugrische Sprachwissenschaft*, Berlin, 1922²; (2) F. N. Finck, *Die Sprachstämme des Erdkreises*, Leipzig, 1923³; (3) A. Meillet & M. Cohen, *Les langues du monde*, Paris, 1924; (4) A. Kannisto, U. T. Sirelius, E. N. Setälä & Y. Wichmann, *Suomen suku*, I, Helsinki, 1926; (5) *Большая Советская Энциклопедия*, Москва, 1926–47; (6) И. И. Зарубин, *Список народностей СССР*, Ленинград, 1927; (7) L. Tesnière, 'Statistique des langues de l'Europe' (in A. Meillet, *Les langues dans l'Europe nouvelle*, Paris, 1928²), (8) Д. Коркмасов, *Письменность и революция*, I, Москва-Ленинград, 1933; (9) Г. Н. Прокофьев, *Языки и письменность народов Севера*, I, Ленинград, 1937; (10) *Iso Tietosanakirja*, XII, Helsinki, 1937.

Language Group	Language	Number of Speakers	Year
I. Palaeoasiatic			
Chukotian	Chukcha (Luoravetlan)	12,300	1926
	Koryak (Nymylan)	7,500	1926
	Kamchadal	800	1926
—			
	Yukagir (Odul)	500	1926
	Gilyak (Nivkh)	4,000	1926
	Ainu	1,500	1935
	Yenisei Ostyak (Ket)	1,500	1926
II. Uralian			
Samoyedic	Yurak (Nenets)	18,000	1926
	Yenisei Samoyed (Enets)	250	1926
	Tavgi (Nganasan)	1,000	1926
	Ostyak Samoyed (Sel'kup)	1,600 (E. Prokof'jeva has 4,500)	1926
—			
Ugrian	Vogul (Mansi)	6,000	1926
	Ostyak (Khanty)	23,300	1926
—			
Permian	Votyak (Udmurt)	606,000	1939
	Zyryan (Komi)	409,000	1939
—			

LANGUAGES OF THE U.S.S.R.

Language Group	Language	Number of Speakers	Year
East Finnic	Mordvin	1,451,000	1939
	Cheremiss (Mari)	481,000	1939
West Finnic	Livonian	2,000	1939
	Estonian	1,200,000	1935
	Vodian	1,000	1926
	Vepsian (with Ludian)	31,000	1926
	Carelian (with Olonecian and Ingrian)	370,000	1926
	Kola Lappish (Saam)	1,800	1926

III. Altaic

Language Group	Language	Number of Speakers	Year
Manchurian (Tungusic)	Tungus (Evenki) } Negidal (Negda) }	40,000	1926
	Lamut (Even)	2,000 (V.I. Cincius has 8,000)	1926
	Ude (Udekhe)	2,000	1926
	Gold (Nanai)	9,000	1926
	Oroch	650	1926
	Olcha (Ulcha)	720	1926
	Orok	160	1926
Mongolian	Kalmyk	129,000	1926
	Buryat	236,000	1926
Turkic	Chuvash	1,368,000	1939
	Volga Tartar	4,300,000	1939
	Bashkir	843,000	1939
	Balkar	33,000	1926
	Karachay	55,000	1926
	Nogay	60,000	1910
	Kumyk	95,000	1926
	Kazakh	39,570,000	1926
	Karakalpak	186,000	1939
	Kirgiz	884,000	1939
	Oirot	48,000	1939
	Azerbaijani	2,275,000	1939
	Turkmen	812,000	1939
	Uzbek	4,844,000	1939
	Shor	13,000	1926
	Khakass	53,000	1939
	Tuva (Soyot)		
	Yakut (Sakha)	220,000	1926

LANGUAGE STATISTICS

Language Group	Language	Number of Speakers	Year
	IV. NORTH CAUCASIAN		
North-Western	Adyge (Circassian and Kabardin)	252,000	1939
	Abkhaz	59,000	1939
North-Eastern	Chechen	319,000	1926
	Ingush	74,000	1926
	Tsova-Tush (Bats)	2,000	1910
	Andi group	32,400	1920
	Dido group	11,000	1920
	Awar	159,000	1926
	Lak	40,000	1926
	Archi	800	1920
	Dargwa	108,000	1926
	Agul	8,000	1920
	Tabassaran	30,000	1926
	Lezgin (Kyuri)	165,000	1926
	Budukh	3,500	1920
	Jek	7,200	1920
	Rutul	12,000	1920
	Tsakhur	5,000	1920
	Udi	10,000	1920
	Khinalugh	2,200	1920
	V. SOUTH CAUCASIAN (IVERIAN)		
	Mingrelian (Megrel)	242,000	1926
	Laz (Chan)	2,400	1926
	Georgian	1,460,000	1926
	Svanetian (Svan)	13,000	1926
	VI. INDO-EUROPEAN (ARYAN)		
Baltic	Latvian	1,400,000	1930
	Lithuanian	1,900,000	1931
East Slavonic	White Russian	6,600,000	1926
	Ukrainian	33,900,000	1926
	Russian	80,000,000	1926
	Armenian	2,152,000	1939
Iranic	Ossetic (Ir)	354,500	1939
	Tat	125,000	1922
	Talysh	80,000	1926
	Tajiki	1,229,000	1939
	Pamiri group (Shughni, Wakhi, Yaghnobi, etc.)	19,600	1925

APPENDIX III

BIBLIOGRAPHY[1]

I. GENERAL WORKS

Aïtov, D., 'Peuples et langues de la Russie' (*Annales de géographie*, xv, Paris, 1909).
Bloomfield, L., *Language* (New York, 1933).
Большая Советская Энциклопедия, I–LXV (Москва, 1926–47).
Черняков, З. Е., *Карта распространения языков народов севера СССР* (Москва-Ленинград, 1934).
Dauzat, A., *L'Europe linguistique* (Paris, 1940).
Diringer, D., *The Alphabet* (London, 1948).
Enciclopedia Italiana, I–XXXVI (Milan-Rome, 1929–39).
Finck, F. N., *Die Haupttypen des Sprachbaus* (Leipzig, 1923²).
Finck, F. N., *Die Sprachstämme des Erdkreises* (Leipzig, 1923³).
Graaff, W., *Language and Languages* (New York, 1932).
Gray, L. H., *Foundations of Language* (New York, 1939).
Hovelacque, A., *La linguistique* (Paris, 1887⁴).
Iso Tietosanakirja, I–XV (Helsinki, 1931–9).
Jensen, H., *Die Schrift in Vergangenheit und Gegenwart* (Glückstadt-Hamburg, 1935).
Kieckers, E., *Die Sprachstämme der Erde* (Heidelberg, 1931).
Lewy, E., 'Der Bau der europäischen Sprachen' (*Proceedings of the Royal Irish Academy*, XLVIII, C. 2, Dublin, 1942).
Литературная Энциклопедия, I–IX (Москва, 1930–5).
Loukotka, Č., *Vývoj písma* (Prague, 1946).
Meillet, A., *Les langues dans l'Europe nouvelle* (Paris, 1928²).
Meillet, A. et M. Cohen, *Les langues du monde* (Paris, 1924).
Мещанинов, И. И., *Общее языкознание* (Ленинград, 1940).
Milewski, T., *Zarys językoznawstwa ogólnego*, I–II (Lublin-Cracow, 1947–8).
Müller, F., *Grundriss der Sprachwissenschaft*, I–IV (Vienna, 1876–88).
Pedersen, H., *Sprogvidenskaben i det nittende Aarhundrede* (Copenhagen, 1924).
Sayce, A. H., *Introduction to the Science of Language*, I–II (London, 1879–80).
Schmidt, J., *A nyelv és a nyelvek. Bevezetés a nyelvtudományba* (Budapest 1923).
Schmidt, W., *Die Sprachstämme und Sprachenkreise der Erde* (Heidelberg, 1926).
Steinthal, H. und F. Misteli, *Charakteristik der hauptsächlichsten Typen des Sprachbaues* (Berlin, 1893²).
Šmits, P., *Ievads valodniecībā* (Riga, 1934).
Шор, Р. О. и Н. С. Чемоданов, *Введение в языковедение* (Москва, 1945).

[1] This is tentative rather than exhaustive and does not include publications earlier than 1840. The titles are arranged in the order of the Latin alphabet.

Trombetti, A., *Elementi di glottologia*, I–II (Bologna, 1922–3).
Tucker, T. G., *Introduction to the Natural History of Language* (London, 1908).
Ушаков, Д. Н., *Краткое введение в науку о языке* (Москва, 1928⁸).

II. PALAEOASIATIC LANGUAGES

Крейнович, Е. А., *Языки и письменность народов Севера*, III (Москва-Ленинград, 1934).
Мещанинов, И. И., ‚Палеоазиатские языки' (*Изв. Акад. Наук, отд. лит. и яз.*, т. VII, вып. 6, Москва-Ленинград, 1948).

1. CHUKCHA (Luoravetlan)

Bogoras, W., 'Chukchee' (in F. Boas, *Handbook of American Indian Languages*, Pt II, Washington, 1922).
Богораз, В. Г., *Материалы по изучению чукотского языка и фольклора*, I (СПБ, 1900).
Богораз, В. Г., *Луораветланско-русский словарь* (Москва-Ленинград, 1937).
Radloff, L., 'Über die Sprache der Tschuktschen und ihr Verhältnis zum Korjakischen' (*Mémoires de l'Académie des Sciences*, VIIᵉ série, tome III, St Petersburg, 1859).
Скорик, П. Я., ‚Инкорпорация в чукотском языке как способ выражения синтаксических отношений' (*ИАН, отд. лит. и яз.*, т. VI, вып. 6, Москва-Ленинград, 1947).
Скорик, П. Я., ‚О причастиях в чукотском языке' (*ИАН, отд. лит. и яз.*, т. VII, вып. 4, Москва-Ленинград, 1948).
Скорик, П. Я., ‚О выражении субъектно-объектных отношений в чукотском языке' (*ИАН, отд. лит. и яз.*, т. VII, вып. 6, Москва-Ленинград, 1948).

2. KORYAK (Nymylan)

Bogoras, W., *Koryak Texts* (Leyden, 1917).
Корсаков, Г. М., *Нымыланско(корякско)-русский словарь* (Москва, 1939).
Корсаков, Г. М., *Самоучитель нымыланского языка* (Москва-Ленинград, 1940).
Стебницкий, С. Н., ‚Основные фонетические различия диалектов нымыланского (корякского) языка' (*Памяти В. Г. Богораза*. Сборник статей., Москва-Ленинград, 1937).

3. KAMCHADAL (Itel'men)

Стебницкий, С. Н., ‚Ительменский (камчадальский) язык' (*Инст. Народов Севера, Труды по Лингвистике*, ч. 3, Москва-Ленинград, 1934).

LANGUAGES OF THE U.S.S.R.

4. YUKAGIR (Odul)

Collinder, B., 'Jukagirisch und Uralisch' (*Uppsala Universitets årsskrift*, VIII, Uppsala, 1940).
Иохельсон, В. И., *Материалы по изучению юкагирского языка и фольклора*, I (СПБ, 1900).
Jochelson, W., 'Über die Sprache und Schrift der Jukagiren' (*Sitzungsberichte der Geographischen Gesellschaft*, Berlin, 1899).
Jochelson, W., 'Essay on the Grammar of the Yukagir Language' (*Annals of the New York Academy of Sciences*, XVI, 2, New York, 1905).
Schiefner, A., *Über die Sprache der Jukagiren* (St Petersburg, 1859).
Schiefner, A., *Beiträge zur Kenntnis der jukagirischen Sprache* (St Petersburg, 1871).

5. GILYAK (Nivkh)

Grube, W., *Giljakisches Wörterverzeichnis nebst grammatischen Bemerkungen* (St Petersburg, 1892).
Крейнович, Е. А., *Фонетика нивхского (гиляцкого) языка* (Ленинград, 1937).
Матусевич, М. И. и Л. Р. Зиндер, *Экспериментально-фонетическое исследование фонем нивхского языка* (Москва, 1935).
Штернберг, Л. Я., *Материалы по изучению гиляцкого языка и фольклора* (СПБ, 1908).

6. AINU

Batchelor, J., *An Ainu-English-Japanese Dictionary* (Tokyo, 1905).
Laufer, B., 'The Vigesimal and Decimal Systems in the Ainu Numerals' (*Journal of the Am. Orient. Soc.*, XXXVII, 1917).
Pilsudski, B., *Materials for the Study of the Ainu Language and Folklore* (Cracow, 1912).

7. YENISEI OSTYAK (Ket)

Castrén, M. A. (ed. A. Schiefner), *Versuch einer jenissei-ostjakischen und kottischen Sprachlehre nebst Wörterverzeichnis* (St Petersburg, 1858).
Lewy, E., 'Zum Jenissei-Ostjakischen' (*Ungarische Jahrbücher*, XIII, Berlin-Leipzig, 1933).
Ramstedt, G. J., 'Über den Ursprung der sogenannten Jenisej-Ostjaken' (*Journal de la Société Finno-ougrienne*, XXIV, Helsinki, 1907).

K. Donner (ed. A. J. Joki), Ketica (Mém. Soc. F-Ou. 108), Helsinki 1955

III. URALIAN LANGUAGES

Бубрих, Д. Б., ,К вопросу об отношениях между самоедскими и финноугорскими языками' (*ИАН, отд. лит. и яз.*, т. VII, вып. 6, Москва-Ленинград, 1948).
Budenz, J., 'Alaktani egyezés az ugor és szamoyéd nyelvekben' (*Hunfalvy-Album*, Budapest, 1891).
Collinder, B., *Indo-uralisches Sprachgut* (Uppsala, 1934).

BIBLIOGRAPHY

Halász, I., 'Az ugor-szamojéd nyelvrokonság kérdése' (*NyK*, XXIII–XXIV, Budapest, 1894–5).
Lehtisalo, T., 'Uralische Etymologien' (*Mémoires de la Société Finnoougrienne*, LVIII, Helsinki, 1928).
Lehtisalo, T., 'Über die primären ururalischen Ableitungssuffixe' (*MSFOu*, LXXII, Helsinki, 1936).
Mark, J., 'Die Possessivsuffixe in den uralischen Sprachen' (*JSFOu*, LII, Helsinki, 1924).
Munkácsi, B., 'Adalékok az ugor-szamojéd nyelvhasonlításhoz' (*NyK*, XXIII, Budapest, 1894).
Pedersen, H., 'Zur Frage nach der Urverwandschaft der uralischen und indogermanischen Sprachen' (*MSFOu*, LXVII, Helsinki, 1933).
Прокофьев, Г. Н., *Языки и письменность народов Севера*, 1 (Москва-Ленинград, 1937).
Ross, A. S. C., 'An Indoeuropean-Finnougrian Loanword Problem' (*Transactions of the Philological Society*, 1944, London, 1945).
Rostek, E., *Die ältesten Beziehungen des uralischen Sprachstammes zum indogermanischen* (Heidelberg, 1937).
Setälä, E. N., 'Über Art, Umfang und Alter des Stufenwechsels im Finnisch-Ugrischen und Samojedischen' (*Finnisch-Ugrische Forschungen*, XII, Helsinki, 1912).
Setälä, E. N., 'Zur Frage nach der Verwandtschaft der finnisch-ugrischen und samojedischen Sprachen' (*JSFOu*, XXX, Helsinki, 1913–18).
Winkler, H., 'Samojedisch und Finnisch' (*FUF*, XII–XIII, Helsinki, 1912–13).

A. SAMOYEDIC

Budenz, J., 'Übereinstimmungen in der finnisch-ugrischen und samojedischen Formenlehre' (*Hunfalvy-Album*, Budapest, 1891).
Castrén, M. A., *Grammatik der samojedischen Sprachen* (St Petersburg, 1854).
Castrén, M. A., *Wörterverzeichnisse aus den samojedischen Sprachen* (St Petersburg, 1855).
Donner, K., 'Zu den ältesten Berührungen zwischen Samojeden und Türken' (*JSFOu*, XL, Helsinki, 1924).
Donner, K., 'Samojedische Wörterverzeichnisse' (*MSFOu*, LXIV, Helsinki, 1932).
Donner, K., *Siperia* (Helsinki, 1933).
Donner, O., 'Die samojedischen Sprachen' (*Atti del IV congresso intern. degli orientalisti*, Rome, 1878).
Joki, A. J., *Kai Donners Kamassisches Wörterbuch* (Helsinki, 1944).
Lehtisalo, T., 'Über den Vokalismus der ersten Silbe im Juraksamojedischen' (*MSFOu*, LVI, Helsinki, 1927).
Lehtisalo, T., 'Jurak-samojedische Volksdichtung' (*MSFOu*, Helsinki, XC, 1947).
Prokofjew, G., 'Materialien zur Erforschung der ostjak-samojedischen Sprache. Die tasovsche Mundart' (*Ung. Jahrb.*, XI, Berlin-Leipzig, 1931).

Прокофьев, Г. М., *Краткая грамматика самоедского (ненецкого) языка* (Ленинград, 1934).
Прокофьев, Г. М., *Селькупская (остяко-самоедская) грамматика* (Ленинград, 1935).
Прокофьев, Г. М., *Самоучитель ненецкого языка* (Ленинград, 1936).
Прокофьев, Г. М., ,К вопросу о переходном залоге в самоедских языках' (*Памяти В. Г. Богораза*, Москва-Ленинград, 1937).
Терещенко, Н. М., *Очерк грамматики ненецкого (юрако-самоедского) языка* (Ленинград, 1947).
Winkler, H., 'Samojedisch und Finnisch' (*FUF*, xii, Helsinki, 1912).

B. Finno-Ugrian

Ahlquist, A., *Die Kulturwörter der westfinnischen Sprachen* (Helsinki, 1875).
Ahlquist, A., 'Über die Kulturwörter der obisch-ugrischen Sprachen' (*JSFOu*, viii, Helsinki, 1891).
Anderson, N., 'Studien zur Vergleichung der ugrofinnischen und indogermanischen Sprachen' (*Verhandlungen der Gelehrten Estnischen Gesellschaft*, Tartu, 1879).
Beke, Ö., 'Über den Dativ-Genetiv in den finnisch-ugrischen Sprachen' (*JSFOu*, xxx, Helsinki, 1913–18).
Бубрих, Д. В., ,Сравнительная грамматика финноугорских языков в СССР' (*Учёные записки ЛГУн.*, Ленинград, 1948).
Budenz, J., *Magyar-ugor összehasonlító szótár* (Budapest, 1873–81).
Budenz, J., *Über die Verzweigung der ugrischen Sprachen* (Göttingen, 1879).
Budenz, J., *Az ugor nyelvek összehasonlító alaktana* (Budapest, 1884–94).
Donner, O., *Vergleichendes Wörterbuch der finnisch-ugrischen Sprachen* (Helsinki, 1874–88).
Donner, O., *Die gegenseitige Verwandschaft der finnisch-ugrischen Sprachen* (Helsinki, 1879).
Donner, O., 'Die finnisch-ugrischen Völker' (*JSFOu*, i, Helsinki, 1886).
Eisen, M. J., *Eestlaste sugu* (Tartu, 1909–11).
Genetz, A., *Lautphysiologische Einführung in das Studium der westfinnischen Sprachen mit besonderer Berücksichtigung des Karelischen* (Helsinki, 1877).
Hunfalvy, P., 'On the Study of the Turanian (i.e. Finno-Ugrian) Languages' (*Trans. of the Int. Congress of Orientalists*, London, 1876).
Itkonen, T. I., *Suomensukuiset kansat* (Helsinki, 1921).
Jacobsohn, H., *Arier und Ugrofinnen* (Göttingen, 1922).
Kalima, J., *Itämerensuomalaisten kielten balttilaiset lainasanat* (Helsinki, 1936).
Kannisto, A., U. T. Sirelius, E. N. Setälä ja Y. Wichmann, *Suomen suku*, i–iii (Helsinki, 1926–34).
Karstén, J. E., *Germanisch-finnische Lehnwortstudien* (Helsinki, 1915).
Kettunen, L., *Suomen heimon kirja* (Porvoo, 1931).
Korsch, T. (i.e. F. E. Korš), 'Zur Frage von den finnisch-ugrischen Zahlwörtern für 7–10' (*JSFOu*, xxx, Helsinki, 1913–18).
Lewy, E., 'Zur finnisch-ugrischen Konjugation' (*JSFOu*, xxx, Helsinki, 1913–18).

BIBLIOGRAPHY

Manninen, I., *Suomensukuiset kansat* (Porvoo, 1929).
Manninen, I., *Soome-sugu rahvad* (Tartu, 1929).
Manninen, I., *Die finnisch-ugrischen Völker* (Leipzig, 1933).
Mikkola, J. J., 'Berührungen zwischen den westfinnischen und slavischen Sprachen' (*MSFOu*, VIII, Helsinki, 1894).
Munkácsi, B., *Árja es kaukázusi elemek a finn-magyar nyelvekben* (Budapest, 1901).
Munkácsi, B., *Verschiedenheit in den arischen Lehnwörtern der finnisch-magyarischen Sprache* (Budapest, 1903).
Ojansuu, H., *Itämerensuomalaisten kielten pronominioppi* (Turku, 1922).
Ольденбург, С. Ф. и А. И. Андреев, *Финноугорский сборник* (Ленинград, 1928).
Orbán, G., *A finnugor nyelvek számnevei* (Budapest, 1932).
Pápay, J., *A finnugor népek es nyelvek ismertetése* (Budapest, 1922).
Pápay, J., *A magyar nyelvhasonlítás története* (Budapest, 1922).
Поппе, Н. Н. и Г. А. Старцев, *Финноугорские народы* (Ленинград, 1927).
Räikkönen, E., *Heimokirja* (Helsinki, 1924).
Ross, A. S. C., 'Some Remarks on the Numerals of Finno-Ugrian' (*Transactions of the Philological Society*, 1941, London, 1943).
Setälä, E. N., *Om de finsk-ugriska språken* (Helsinki, 1888).
Setälä, E. N., *Yhteissuomalainen äännehistoria*, I–II (Helsinki, 1890–1).
Setälä, E. N., *Lisiä suomalais-ugrilaisen kielitutkimuksen historiaan* (Helsinki, 1892).
Setälä, E. N., 'Über Quantitätswechsel im Finnisch-ugrischen' (*JSFOu*, XIV, Helsinki, 1896).
Setälä, E. N., 'Zur Herkunft und Chronologie der älteren germanischen Lehnwörter in den finnisch-ugrischen Sprachen' (*JSFOu*, XXIII, Helsinki, 1905–6).
Sirelius, U. T., *Die Herkunft der Finnen. Die finnisch-ugrischen Völker* (Helsinki, 1924).
Штакельберг, Р. Р., ‚Ирано-финские лексические отношения' (*Восточные Древности*, I, 3, Москва, 1893).
Steinitz, W., *Geschichte des finnisch-ugrischen Vokalismus* (Stockholm, 1944).
Szinnyei, J., *Finnisch-ugrische Sprachwissenschaft* (Berlin, 1922[2]).
Szinnyei, J., *Magyar nyelvhasonlítás* (Budapest, 1927[7]).
Thomsen, V., *Den gotiske Sprogklasses Inflydelse på den finske* (Copenhagen, 1869).
Thomsen, V., *Berøringer mellem de finske og de baltiske (litauisk-lettiske) Sprog* (Copenhagen, 1890).
Wiklund, K. B., 'Zur Kenntnis der ältesten germanischen Lehnwörter im Finnischen und Lappischen' (*Le Monde Oriental*, V, 1910).
Wiklund, K. B., 'Finno-ugrier' (*Reallexikon der Vorgeschichte*, III, Berlin, 1925).
Winkler, H., *Die Zugehörigkeit der finnischen Sprachen zum ural-altaischen Sprachstamm* (Breslau, 1911).
Zsirai, M., *A finnugor rokonságunk* (Budapest, 1937).

LANGUAGES OF THE U.S.S.R.

1. OSTYAK (Khanty)

Ahlquist, A., *Über die Sprache der Nordostjaken* (Helsinki, 1880).
Castrén, M. A. (ed. A. Schiefner), *Versuch einer ostjakischen Sprachlehre* (St Petersburg, 1858).
Hunfalvy, P., 'Az éjszaki osztják nyelv' (*NyK*, XI, Budapest, 1875).
Paasonen, H., 'Die türkischen Lehnwörter im Ostjakischen' (*FUF*, II, Helsinki, 1902).
Paasonen, H. und K. Donner, *Ostjakisches Wörterbuch* (Helsinki, 1926).
Pápay, J., *Sammlung ostjakischer Volksdichtungen* (Budapest-Leipzig, 1905).
Pápay, J., *Északi-osztják nyeltudományok* (Budapest, 1910).
Patkanov, S. und D. R. Fuchs, *Laut- und Formenlehre der südostjakischen Dialekte* (Budapest, 1911).
Schütz, J., 'Az északi-osztják szóképzés' (*NyK*, XL, Budapest, 1910).
Steinitz, W., 'Ostjakische Volksdichtung und Erzählungen,' I (*Õpetatud Eesti Seltsi toimetused*, XXXI, Tartu, 1939).
Steinitz, W., *Ostjakische Chrestomathie* (Stockholm, 1943).
Toivonen, Y. H., 'Türkische Lehnwörter im Ostjakischen' (*JSFOu*, LII, Helsinki, 1943-4).

2. VOGUL (Mansi)

Ahlquist, A., 'Wogulishes Wörterverzeichnis' (*MSFOu*, II, Helsinki, 1891).
Ahlquist, A., (ed. Y. Wichmann), 'Wogulische Sprachtexte nebst Entwurf einer wogulischen Grammatik' (*MSFOu*, VII, Helsinki, 1894).
Чернецов, В. Н. и И. Я. Чернецова, *Краткий мансийско-русский словарь* (Москва-Ленинград, 1936).
Finczicky, I., *A vogul névmások* (Budapest, 1930).
Gombocz, Z., 'A vogul nyelv idegen elemei' (*NyK*, XXVIII, Budapest, 1898).
Gombocz, Z., 'Adalékok a vogul nyelv török elemeihez' (*NyK*, XXI, Budapest, 1902).
Gombocz, Z., 'Adalékok az obi-ugor nyelvek szókészletének eredetéhez' (*NyK*, XXXII, Budapest, 1902).
Kannisto, A., 'Ein Wörterverzeichnis eines ausgestorbenen wogulischen Dialekts in den Papieren M. A. Castréns' (*JSFOu*, XXX, Helsinki, 1913-18).
Kannisto, A., 'Die Vokalharmonie im Wogulischen' (*FUF*, XIV, Helsinki, 1914).
Kannisto, A., 'Die tatarischen Lehnwörter im Wogulischen' (*FUF*, XVII, Helsinki, 1917).
Munkácsi, B., *Vogul népköltési gyüjtemény*, I-IV (Budapest, 1892-1921).
Szabó, D., *A Vogul szóképzés* (Budapest, 1904).
Szilasi, M., *Vogul szójegyzék* (Budapest, 1896).
Trócsányi, Z., *Vogul szójegyzék* (Budapest, 1909).

3. ZYRYAN (Komi)

Castrén, M. A., *Elementa grammatices syrjaenae* (Helsinki, 1844).
Fuchs, D. R. (D. Fokos), 'Beiträge zur Grammatik der permischen Sprachen' (*JSFOu*, xxx, Helsinki, 1913–18).
Genetz, A., 'Ostpermische Sprachstudien' (*JSFOu*, xv, Helsinki, 1897).
Kalima, J., 'Die russischen Lehnwörter im Syrjänischen' (*MSFOu*, xxix, Helsinki, 1911).
Lytkin, G. S., 'Syrjänische Sprachproben' (*JSFOu*, x, Helsinki, 1892).
Lytkin, G. S., 'Zur Datierung der syrjänisch-russischen Lehnbeziehungen' (*JSFOu*, xlii, Helsinki, 1928).
Лыткин, В. И., *Материалы по коми грамматике* (Москва, 1929).
Майшев, И. И., *Грамматика коми-пермяцкого языка* (Москва-Ленинград, 1940).
Medveczky, K., 'A votják nyelv szóképzése' (*NyK*, xli, Budapest, 1912).
Молодцов, В. А., *Фонетика зырянского диалекта коми языка* (Москва, 1929).
Молодцова, М. Л., *Самоучитель языка коми (зырянского)* (Москва, 1933).
Рогов, Н., *Опыт грамматики пермяцкого языка* (Москва, 1860).
Савайтов, П., *Грамматика зырянского языка* (СПБ, 1850).
Шахов, Н. А., *Краткий коми-русский словарь* (Устьсысольск, 1924).
Wichmann, Y., 'Samojedisches Lehngut im Syrjänischen' (*FUF*, ii, Helsinki, 1902).
Wichmann, Y., 'Die tschuwassischen Lehnwörter in den permischen Sprachen' (*MSFOu*, xxi, Helsinki, 1903).
Wichmann, Y. und T. E. Uotila, *Syrjänischer Wortschatz* (Helsinki, 1942).
Wiedemann, F. J., *Syrjänisch-deutsches Wörterbuch* (St Petersburg, 1880–6).
Wiedemann, F. J., *Grammatik der syrjänischen Sprache mit Berücksichtigung ihrer Dialekte und des Wotjakischen* (St Petersburg, 1884).

4. VOTYAK (Udmurt)

Aminoff, T. G., 'Votjakilaisia kielinäytteitä' (*JSFOu*, i, Helsinki, 1886).
Aminoff, T. G. (ed. Y. Wichmann), 'Votjakin äänne- ja muotoopin luonnos' (*JSFOu*, xiv, Helsinki, 1896).
Глезденев, П. П., *Руководство по изучению удмуртского языка* (Вятка, 1921).
Горохов, П. Д., *Учебник удмуртского языка* (Ижевск, 1929).
Яковлев, И. В., *Элементарная грамматика вотяцкого языка* (Казань, 1927).
Емельяков, А. И., *Грамматика вотяцкого языка* (Ленинград, 1927).
Крылов, И., *Сравнительный словарь вотских наречий* (Вятка, 1919).
Крылов, И., *Вотско-русский словарь глазовского наречия вотяков* (Вятка, 1919).
Munkácsi, B., *Votják népköltészeti hagyományok* (Budapest, 1887).
Munkácsi, B., *A votják nyelv szótára* (Budapest, 1890–6).

Вахрушев, В. М., К. А. Корепанова, Е. Н. Ложкина, А. И. Малых и др., *Удмуртско-русский словарь* (Москва, 1948).
Wichmann, Y., 'Wotjakische Sprachproben', I–II (*JSFOu*, XI, Helsinki, 1893; XIX, Helsinki, 1901).
Wichmann, Y., *Wotjakische Chrestomathie mit Glossar* (Helsinki, 1901).
Wiedemann, F. J., *Grammatik der wotjakischen Sprache* (Tallinn, 1851).
Wiedemann, F. J., *Zur Dialektkunde der wotjakischen Sprache* (St Petersburg, 1858).

5. CHEREMISS (Mari)

Beke, Ö., *Cseremisz nyelvtan* (Budapest, 1911).
Богородицкий, В. А., ‚Характеристика звуковой системы марийского (черемисского) языка' (*ИАН, отд. лит. и яз.*, т. III, вып. 6, Москва, 1944).
Budenz, J., *Cseremisz tanulmányok* (*Nyelvtudományi Közlemények*, III–IV, Budapest, 1864–5).
Budenz, J., *Erdés és hegyi cseremisz szótár* (Budapest, 1866).
Castrén, M. A., *Elementa grammatices tscheremissae* (Kuopio, 1845).
Genetz, A., 'Ost-tscheremissische Sprachstudien', I (*JSFOu*, Helsinki, 1889).
Карамзин, Г. Г., *Материалы к изучению марийского языка* (Краснококшайск, 1925).
Карамзин, Г. Г., *Учебник марийского языка лугово-восточного наречия* (Йошкар-Ола, 1929).
Lewy, E., *Tscheremissische Grammatik* (Leipzig, 1922).
Lewy, E., *Tscheremissische Texte*, I–II (Hannover, 1925–6).
Porkka, V. (ed. A. Genetz), 'Tscheremissische Texte' (*JSFOu*, XIII, Helsinki, 1895).
Ramstedt, G. J., 'Bergtscheremissische Sprachstudien' (*MSFOu*, XVII, Helsinki, 1902).
Räsänen, M., 'Die tschuwassischen Lehnwörter im Tscheremissischen' (*MSFOu*, XLVIII, Helsinki, 1920).
Räsänen, M., 'Die tatarischen Lehnwörter im Tscheremissischen' (*MSFOu*, L, Helsinki, 1920).
Szilasi, M., *Cseremisz szótár* (Budapest, 1901).
Шорин, В. С., *Маро-русский словарь горного наречия* (Казань, 1920).
Тройцкий, В. П., *Черемисско-русский словарь* (Казань, 1894).
Васильев, Ф., *Пособие к изучению черемисского языка на луговом наречии*, I–II (Казань, 1887).
Васильев, В. М., *Черемисско-русский словарь* (Казань, 1911).
Васильев, В. М., *Записки по грамматике народа мари* (Казань, 1918).
Васильев, В. М., *Элементарная грамматика марийского языка* (Москва, 1927).
Васильев, В. М., *Марийский словарь* (Москва, 1929).
Веске, М. П., ‚Исследование о наречиях черемисского языка' (*Изв. общ. арх., ист. и этнографии*, VII, Казань, 1889).
Wichmann, Y., 'Beiträge zur tscheremissischen Nominalbildungslehre' (*JSFOu*, XXX, Helsinki, 1913–18).

BIBLIOGRAPHY

Wichmann, Y., *Tscheremissische Texte mit Wörterverzeichnis und grammatikalischem Abriss* (Helsinki, 1923).
Wichmann, Y., 'Volksdichtung und Volksbräuche der Tscheremissen' (*MSFOu*, LIX, Helsinki, 1931).
Wiedemann, F. J., *Versuch einer Grammatik der tscheremissischen Sprache* (St Petersburg, 1847).

6. MORDVIN

Ahlquist, A., *Versuch einer mokscha-mordwinischen Grammatik* (St Petersburg, 1861).
Бубрих, Д. В., *Звуки и формы эрзянской речи* (Москва, 1930).
Budenz, J., *Moksa- és erza-mordvin nyelvtan* (Budapest, 1876).
Евсевьев, М. Е., *Основы мордовской грамматики* (Москва, 1931[2]).
Евсевьев, М. Е., *Мордовско-русский словарь* (Москва, 1931).
Коляденков, М. Н. и Н. Ф. Цыганов, *Эрзянско-русский словарь* (Москва, 1949).
Paasonen, H., 'Proben der mordwinischen Volksliteratur', I–II: Erzjanischer Teil (*JSFOu*, IX, Helsinki, 1891; XII, Helsinki, 1894).
Paasonen, H., 'Die türkischen Lehnwörter im Mordwinischen' (*JSFOu*, XV, Helsinki, 1897).
Paasonen, H., 'Mordwinische Lautlehre' (*JSFOu*, XXII, Helsinki, 1903).
Paasonen, H., *Mordwinische Chrestomathie mit Glossar und grammatikalischem Abriss* (Helsinki, 1909).
Paasonen, H., P. I. Ravila und P. Siro, 'Mordwinische Volksdichtung' (*MSFOu*, LXXV, LXXXI, Helsinki, 1938–9).
Pelissier, R., *Mokšamordwinische Texte* (Berlin, 1926).
Рябов, А. П., *Эрзянско-русский словарь* (Москва, 1931).
Шахматов, А. А., *Мордовский этнографический сборник* (СПБ, 1910).
Trubetzkoy, M., 'Das mordwinische phonologische System verglichen mit dem russischen' (*Charisteria Guil. Mathesio quinquagenario...oblata*, Prague, 1932).
Wiedemann, F. J., *Grammatik der erzämordwinischen Sprache* (St Petersburg, 1865).

7. ESTONIAN

Aavik, J., *Vironkielen opas* (Porvoo, 1911).
Aavik, J., *Uute sõnade sõnastik* (Tallinn, 1921[2]).
Aavik, J., *Eesti õigekeelsuse õpik ja grammatika* (Tartu, 1936).
Fazekas, J., *Észt nyelvművelő és nyelvújító törekvések* (Debrecen, 1935).
Jõgever, J., *Eesti keele grammatika*, I–III (Tartu, 1919–20).
Hermann, K. A., *Eesti keele grammatika* (Tartu, 1884).
Kettunen, L., *Lauseliikmed eesti keeles* (Tartu, 1924).
Kettunen, L., *Oppikirja eestin ja suomen eroavaisuuksista* (Helsinki, 1926[2]).
Kettunen, L., *Eestin kielen oppikirja* (Porvoo, 1928).
Loorits, O., *Eesti keele grammatika* (Tartu, 1923).
Muuk, E., *Eesti keeleõpetus*, I (Tartu, 1927).
Muuk, E., *Lühike eesti keeleõpetus*, I (Tartu, 1927).

LANGUAGES OF THE U.S.S.R.

Muuk, E., *Väike õigekeelsus-sõnaraamat* (Stockholm, 1947[9]).
Muuk, E. ja M. Tedre, *Lühike eesti keeleõpetus*, II (Tartu, 1930).
Mägiste, J., *Soome keele osa eesti kirjakeele arenemisel* (Tartu, 1931).
Põld, H., *Eesti keeleõpetus*, I–II (Tallinn, 1915–22).
Saaberk (Saareste), A., *Tegeliku eesti foneetika alged* (Tallinn, 1920).
Saareste, A., *Leksikaalseist vahekordadest eesti murretes* (Tartu, 1924).
Saareste, A., *Eesti keeleala murdelisest liigendusest* (Tartu, 1932).
Saareste, A., *Die estnische Sprache* (Tartu, 1932).
Sell, E. und P. Seeberg-Elverfeldt, *Estnisch-deutsches Wörterbuch* (Tallinn, 1937).
Veski, J. V. (ed.), *Eesti õigekeelsuse-sõnaraamat*, I–III (Tartu, 1925–37).
Wiedemann, F. J., *Versuch über den Werro-estnischen Dialekt* (St Petersburg, 1864).
Wiedemann, F. J., *Grammatik der estnischen Sprache* (St Petersburg, 1875).
Wiedemann, F. J., *Estnisch-deutsches Wörterbuch* (Tartu-Leipzig, 1923[3]).

8. LIVONIAN

Kettunen, L., *Untersuchung über die livische Sprache*, I (Tartu, 1925).
Kettunen, L., *Livisches Wörterbuch* (Helsinki, 1938).
Posti, L., 'Liivin kielen intonatioista' (*Virittäjä*, Helsinki, 1936).
Setälä, E. N., 'A lív nép és nyelve' (*Nyelvtudományi Közlemények*, XXI, Budapest, 1890).
Wiedemann, F. J., *J. A. Sjögrens Livische Grammatik nebst Sprachproben* (St Petersburg, 1861).
Wiedemann, F. J., *J. A. Sjögrens Livisch-deutsches und deutsch-livisches Wörterbuch* (St Petersburg, 1861).

9. CARELIAN (with Olonecian and Ingrian)

Genetz, A., *Versuch einer karelischen Lautlehre* (Helsinki, 1877).
Genetz, A., *Tutkimus Venäjän Karjalan kielestä* (Helsinki, 1880).
Genetz, A., 'Tutkimus Aunuksen kielestä' (*Suomi*, II, Helsinki, 1884).
Junus, V. I., *Ižoran keelen grammatikka* (Moscow-Leningrad, 1936).
Kujola, J., *Karjalan kielen opas* (Helsinki, 1922[2]).
Kujola, J., *Tverin ja Novgorodin karjalan satuja* (Helsinki).
Leskinen, E., *Karjalan kielen näytteitä*, I–II (Helsinki, 1932–3).
Leskinen, E., *Tverin karjalaa* (Helsinki).
Leskinen, E., *Aunuksen ja Raja-Karjalan murteet* (Helsinki, 1934).
Niemi, A., *Vienan läänin runot*, I, 1–4 (Helsinki, 1908–21).
Niemi, A., *Aunuksen, Tverin ja Novgorodin karjalan runot* (Helsinki, 1927).
Ojansuu, H., *Karjalan äänneoppi* (Helsinki, 1905).
Porkka, V., *Über den ingrischen Dialekt mit Berücksichtigung der übrigen ingermannländischen Dialekte* (Helsinki, 1885).
Salminen, V., *Länsi-Inkerin häärunot* (Helsinki, 1916).
Salminen, V., *Itä- ja pohjois-Inkerin runot* (Helsinki, 1929).
Salminen, V., *Etelä-Karjalan runot*, I–III (Helsinki, 1936–9).

BIBLIOGRAPHY

10. VEPSIAN (with Ludian)

Ahlquist, A., 'Anteckningar i Nordtschudiskan' (*Acta Societatis Scient. Fenn.* VI, Helsinki, 1859).
Andrejev, F. A., *Vepskijan grammatikan openduzkirj ežmäižele i toižele klassale* (Leningrad, 1934).
Hämäläinen, M. M. i F. A. Andrejev, *Vepsan kelen grammatik kuumandele i nelländele klassale* (Leningrad, 1935).
Hämäläinen, M. M. i F. A. Andrejev, *Vepsa-venähine vajehnik* (Leningrad, 1936).
Kannisto, A., *Lyydiläisiä kielennäytteitä* (Helsinki, 1934).
Kettunen, L., 'Näytteitä etelävepsästä, I–II (Suomi, IV–V, Helsinki, 1920–5).
Kettunen, L. ja P. Siro, *Näytteitä vepsän murteista* (Helsinki, 1935).
Lönnrot, E., *Om det Nordtschudiska språket* (Helsinki, 1853).
Posti, L., 'Vepsän vokaalisoinuusta' (*Virittäjä*, Helsinki, 1935).

11. VODIAN

Ahlquist, A., *Votisk grammatik* (Helsinki, 1856).
Airila, M., 'Vatjan kielen taivutusoppi. I. Nominien taivutus' (*Suomi*, V, 17, Helsinki, 1934).
Ariste, P., 'Wotische Sprachproben' (*Õpetatud Eesti Seltsi Aastaraamat*, Tartu, 1933).
Ariste, P., 'Two Old Vocabularies of the Votic Language' (*Õpetatud Eesti Seltsi Aastaraamat*, Tartu, 1935).
Kettunen, L. ja L. Posti, *Näytteitä vatjan kielestä* (Helsinki, 1932).
Ленсу, Я. Я., ,Материалы по говорам води' (*Западнофинский сборник*, Ленинград, 1930).
Mustonen, O. A. T. (Lönnbohm), 'Muistoonpanoja vatjan kielestä' (*Virittäjä*, I, Helsinki, 1883).
Posti, L., 'Vatjan kielen k>tš äänteenmuutoksen iästä' (*Kalevalaseuran Vuosikirja*, Helsinki, 1934).
Salminen, V., *Vatjalaiset runot* (Helsinki, 1928).
Salminen, V., *Runonäytteitä vatjan kielestä* (Helsinki, 1928).

12. KOLA LAPPISH (Saam)

Abercromby, J., 'The Earliest List of Russian Lappish Words' (*JSFOu*, XIII, Helsinki, 1895).
Genetz, A., *Kuollan lapin murteiden sanakirja* (Helsinki, 1891).
Halász, I., 'Orosz-lapp nyelvtani vázlat' (*Nyelvtudományi Közlemények*, XVII, Budapest, 1883).
Itkonen, T., 'Venäjänlapin konsonanttien astevaihtelu' (*MSFOu*, XXXIX, Helsinki, 1916).
Itkonen, T., 'Kolttalaisia ja kildininlaisia satuja' (*MSFOu*, LX, Helsinki, 1931).

Lagercrantz, E., 'Strukturtypen und Gestaltwechsel im Lappischen' (*MSFOu*, LVII, Helsinki, 1927).
Nielsen, K., 'Lappalaisten murteiden tutkimisestä' (*JSFOu*, XXI, Helsinki, 1903).
Wiklund, K. B., 'Die nordischen Lehnwörter in den russisch-lappischen Dialekten' (*JSFOu*, X, Helsinki, 1892).

IV. ALTAIC LANGUAGES

Bang, W., *Uralaltaische Forschungen* (Leipzig, 1890).
Donner, O., 'Die uralaltaischen Sprachen' (*FUF*, I, Helsinki, 1901).
Grunzel, J., *Entwurf einer vergleichenden Grammatik der altaischen Sprachen* (Leipzig, 1895).
Kotwicz, W., *Les pronoms dans les langues altaïques* (Cracow, 1936).
Müller, F., *Das Personalpronomen der altaischen Sprachen* (Vienna, 1895).
Németh, J., 'Die türkisch-mongolische Hypothese' (*Zeitschrift der Deutschen Morgenländischen Gesellschaft*, LXVI, Leipzig, 1912).
Ramstedt, G. J., 'Über die Zahlwörter der altaischen Sprachen' (*JSFOu*, XXIV, Helsinki, 1907).
Ramstedt, G. J., 'Zur Verbalstammbildungslehre der mongolisch-türkischen Sprachen' (*JSFOu*, XXVIII, Helsinki, 1912).
Ramstedt, G. J., 'Die Verneinung in den altaischen Sprachen' (*MSFOu*, LI, Helsinki, 1912).
Ramstedt, G. J., 'Altailasten kielten suhde muihin kielikuntiin' (*JSFOu*, LIII, Helsinki, 1946-7).
Sauvageot, A., *Recherches sur le vocabulaire des langues ouralo-altaïques* (Paris, 1930).
Schmidt (Šmits), P., 'Altaische Zahlwörter' (*MSFOu*, LXVII, Helsinki, 1927).
Winkler, H., *Uralaltaische Völker und Sprachen* (Berlin, 1884).
Winkler, H., *Das Uralaltaische und seine Gruppen* (Berlin, 1885).
Winkler, H., 'Uralaltaische Sprachen' (*Keleti Szemle*, I, Budapest, 1900).
Winkler, H., *Der uralaltaische Sprachstamm, das Finnische und das Japanische* (Berlin, 1909).
Winkler, H., 'Tungusisch und Finnisch-Ugrisch' (*JSFOu*, XXX, Helsinki, 1913-18).

A. MANCHURIAN

Цинциус, В. И., ‚Множественное число в тунгусо-маньчжурских языках' (*Уч. зап. Лен. Гос. Ун., сер. филол. наук*, 10, Ленинград, 1946).
Цинциус, В. И., ‚Проблемы сравнительной грамматики тунгусо-маньчжурских языков' (*ИАН, отд. лит. и яз.*, т. VII, вып. 6, Москва-Ленинград, 1948).
Цинциус, В. И., *Сравнительная фонетика тунгусо-маньчжурских языков* (Ленинград, 1949).
Суник, О. П., *Очерки по синтаксису тунгусо-маньчжурских языков* (Москва, 1947).

BIBLIOGRAPHY

1. Tungus (Evenki)

Adam, L., *Grammaire de la langue toungouze* (Paris, 1874).
Бойцова, А. Ф., *Категория лица в эвенкийском языке* (Москва-Ленинград, 1940).
Castrén, M. A. (ed. A. Schiefner), *Grundzüge einer tungusischen Sprachlehre* (St Petersburg, 1856).
Поппе, Н. Н., *Материалы для исследования тунгусского языка* (Ленинград, 1927).
Титов, Е. И., *Тунгусско-русский словарь* (Иркутск, 1926).
Василевич, Г. М., *Учебник эвенкийского (тунгусского) языка* (Ленинград, 1934).
Василевич, Г. М., *Эвенкийско-русский диалектологический словарь* (Ленинград, 1934).
Василевич, Г. М., *Очерк грамматики эвенкийского (тунгусского) языка* (Москва, 1940).

2. Lamut (Even)

Цинциус, В. И., ‚Эвенский (ламутский) язык' (*Уч. зап. Лен. Гос. Ун., сер. филол. наук*, 10, Ленинград, 1946).
Левин, В. И., *Самоучитель эвенского языка* (Москва-Ленинград, 1935).

3. Gold (Nanai)

Аврорин, В. А., ‚Категория времени и вида в нанайском языке' (*Язык и Мышление*, XI, Ленинград, 1948).
Петрова, Т. И., *Очерк грамматики нанайского языка* (Москва, 1941).
Суник, О. П., ‚О языке нанайцев на р. Куре' (*ИАН, отд. лит. и яз.*, т. VII, вып. 6, Москва-Ленинград, 1948).

4. Oroch

Šmits (Schmidt), P., 'The Language of the Oroches' (*Acta Universitatis Latviensis*, XVII, Riga, 1927).

B. Mongolian

1. Buryat

Амачаев, Н. и Аламчжи Мегрен, *Новый монголо-бурятский алфавит* (СПБ, 1910).
Castrén, M. A. (ed. A. Schiefner), *Versuch einer burjätischen Sprachlehre* (St Petersburg, 1857).
Орлов, А., *Грамматика монголо-бурятского разговорного языка* (Казань, 1878).
Подгорбунский, И. А., *Материалы для грамматики разговорного бурятского языка* (Иркутск, 1910).
Подгорбунский, И. А., *Русско-монголо-бурятский словарь* (СПБ, 1911).

Поппе, Н. Н., *Бурят-монгольское языкознание* (Ленинград, 1933).
Поппе, Н. Н., *Грамматика бурят-монгольского языка* (Ленинград, 1938).
Руднев, А., *Хори-бурятский говор* (СПБ, 1913–14).
Санжеев, Г. Д., *Грамматика бурят-монгольского языка* (Москва-Ленинград, 1941).

2. Kalmyk

Бобровников, А., *Грамматика монгольско-калмыцкого языка* (Казань, 1849).
Котвич, В., *Опыт грамматики калмыцкого разговорного языка* (Петроград, 1915).
Попов, А., *Грамматика калмыцкого языка* (Казань, 1847).
Позднеев, А., *Калмыцкая хрестоматия* (СПБ, 1907).
Позднеев, А., *Краткий калмыцко-русский словарь* (СПБ, 1911).
Ramstedt, G. J., 'Kalmückische Sprachproben' (*MSFOu*, XXVII, i–ii, Helsinki, 1909–19).
Ramstedt, G. J., *Kalmückisches Wörterbuch* (Helsinki, 1935).
Санжеев, Г. Д., *Грамматика калмыцкого языка* (Москва-Ленинград, 1941).

C. Turkic

Богородицкий, В. А., *Введение в татарское языкознание в связи с другими тюркскими языками* (Казань, 1934).
Будагов, Л., *Сравнительный словарь турецко-татарских наречий*, I–II (СПБ, 1869–71).
Jarring, G., *Studien zu einer osttürkischen Lautlehre* (Leipzig-Lund, 1933).
Rachmati, G. R., 'Zur Klassifikation der Türksprachen' (*Ung. Jahrbücher*, IX, Berlin-Leipzig, 1929).
Radloff, W., *Phonetik der nördlichen Türksprachen* (Leipzig, 1882).
Radloff, W., *Einleitende Gedanken zur Darstellung der Morphologie der Türksprachen* (St Petersburg, 1906).
Радлов, В. В., *Наречия тюркских племен живущих в южной Сибири и дзунгарской степи*, I–X (СПБ, 1866–1907).
Радлов, В. В., *Опыт словаря тюркских наречий*, I–IV (СПБ, 1893–1911).

1. Yakut (Sakha)

Пекарский, Э. К., *Словарь якутского языка*, I–III (СПБ, Ленинград, 1907–30).
Radloff, W., 'Die jakutische Sprache in ihrem Verhältnisse zu den Türksprachen' (*MAS*, VIIIe série, tome vii, 7, St Petersburg, 1895).

2. Shor

Дыренкова, Н. М., *Шорский фольклор* (Москва-Ленинград, 1940).
Дыренкова, Н. М., *Грамматика шорского языка* (Москва-Ленинград, 1941).

3. Oirot

Баскаков, П. А. и Тощакова, Г. М., *Ойротско-русский словарь* (Москва, 1947).
Castrén, M. A. (ed. A. Schiefner), *Versuch einer koibalischen und karagassischen Sprachlehre* (St Petersburg, 1857).
Дыренкова, Н. М., *Грамматика ойротского языка* (Москва-Ленинград, 1940).
Шабуров, А. Г., *Учебник грамматики и правописания ойротского языка*, I–II (Новосибирск, 1938).

4. Kazakh

Архангельский, Г. В., *Грамматика казакского языка* (Ташкент, 1927).
Бегалиев, Г. Б., *Казахско-русский словарь* (Алма-Ата, 1945).
Каменгеров, *Казакско-русский словарь* (Москва-Ташкент, 1926).
Каменгеров, *Учебник казакского языка* (Ташкент, 1928).
Лаптев, И. П., *Материалы по казак-киргизскому языку* (Москва, 1900).
Мелиоранский, П. М., *Краткая грамматика казак-киргизского языка*, I–II (СПБ, 1894–7).
Шонанов, Т. Ш., *Самоучитель казакского языка для русских* (Кзыл-Орда, 1929[4]).

5. Kirgiz

Батманов, И. А., *Грамматика киргизского языка*, I–II (Фрунзе, 1939–40).
Батманов, И. А., *Фонетическая система современного киргизского языка* (Фрунзе, 1946).
Юдахин, К. К., *Киргизско-русский словарь* (Москва, 1940).
Шайданов, А. и И. А. Батманов, *Элементарные основы грамматики киргизского языка* (Фрунзе-Ташкент, 1938).
Заболонков, *Латинизированные киргизские тексты* (Ташкент, 1927).

6. Karakalpak

Баскаков, Н., *Краткая грамматика каракалпакского языка* (Туртуль, 1932).
Малов, С. Е., ,Каракалпакский язык и его изучение' (*Каракалпакия*, II, Ленинград, 1934).
Menges, K. H., *Qaraqalpaq Grammar. I. Phonology* (New York, 1947).

7. Kumyk

Чобан Заде, Б,. *Заметки о языке и словесности кумыков* (Баку, 1926).
Дмитриев, Н. К., *Грамматика кумыкского языка* (Москва-Ленинград, 1940).

8. KARACHAY AND BALKAR

Алиев, У. Д., *Карачаево-балкарская грамматика* (Кисловодск, 1930).
Байрамкулов, У., *Грамматика карачаевского языка* (Кисловодск, 1930).
Филоненко, В. И., *Грамматика балкарского языка* (Нальчик, 1940).
Карпулов, Н. А., *Краткий очерк грамматики языка балкар* (Тифлис, 1912).
Pröhle, W., 'Karatschajische Studien' (*Keleti Szemle*, IX, 1909).

9. NOGAY

Баскаков, Н. А., *Ногайский язык и его диалекты* (Москва-Ленинград, 1940).
Османов, М., *Ногайские и кумыкские тексты* (СПБ, 1883).

10. BASHKIR

Dmitriev, N. K., 'Etude sur la phonétique bachkire' (*Journal Asiatique*, CCX, Paris, 1927).
Дмитриев, Н. К., „Краткий очерк башкирской грамматики" (Н. К. Дмитриев, К. З. Ахмеров и Т. Г. Байшев, *Русско-башкирский словарь*, Москва, 1948).
Катаринский, В. В., *Краткий башкирско-русский словарь* (Оренбург, 1899–1900).
Pröhle, V., 'Baskir nyelvtanulmányok' (*Keleti Szemle*, IV–VI, Budapest, 1903–4).

11. VOLGA TARTAR

Курбангалиев, М. и Р. Газизов, *Систематическая грамматика татарского языка* (Казань, 1932).
Weil, G., *Tatarische Texte* (Berlin-Leipzig, 1936).

12. CHUVASH

Ашмарин, Н. И., *Опыт исследования чувашского синтаксиса*, I–II (Казань-Симбирск, 1903–23).
Ашмарин, Н. И., *Словарь чувашского языка*, I–IX (Казань-Чебоксары, 1928–35).
Егоров, В., *Введение в изучение чувашского языка* (Москва, 1930).
Матвеев, Т. М., „Краткий обзор чувашских диалектов" (*Яфетический Сборник*, VI, Ленинград, 1930).
Paasonen, H., *Csuvas szójegyzék* (Budapest, 1908).
Поппе, Н. Н., „Чувашский язык и его отношение к монгольскому" (*ИАН*, 18–19, Ленинград, 1924–5).
Ramstedt, G. J., 'Zur Frage nach der Stellung des Tschuwassischen' (*JSFOu*, XXXVIII, Helsinki, 1922).
Золотницкий, Н. И., *Корневой чувашско-русский словарь* (Казань, 1875).

13. Uzbek

Громатович, К. Д., *Основной учебник узбекского языка* (Ташкент, 1930²).
Jarring, G., 'The Uzbek Dialect of Qilich, Russian Turkestan' (*Lunds Universitets årsskrift*, N.S., avd. 1, xxx, 3, Lund, 1937).
Юдахин, К., *Узбекско-русский словарь* (Ташкент, 1941²).
Menges, K. H., 'Drei özbekische Texte' (*Der Islam*, xxi, Berlin-Hamburg, 1933).
Поливанов, Е. Д., *Введение в изучение узбекского языка*, I–II (Ташкент, 1925)
Поливанов, Е. Д., *Краткая грамматика узбекского языка*, I–II (Ташкент, 1926).
Решетников, В., *Современный узбекский язык* (Ташкент, 1946).

14. Turkmen

Байлиев, Х. и Б. Каррыев, *Туркмено-русский словарь* (Ашхабад, 1946).
Батырев, Ш. и М. Сакали, *Туркменско-русский словарь* (Ашхабад, 1940).
Menges, K. H., 'Einige Bemerkungen zur vergleichenden Grammatik des Türkmenischen' (*Archiv Orientální*, xi, Prague, 1939).
Поцелуевский, А., *Руководство для изучения туркменского языка* (Ашхабад, 1929).
Поцелуевский, А., *Фонетика туркменского языка* (Ашхабад, 1936).
Поцелуевский, А., *Диалекты туркменского языка* (Ашхабад, 1936).
Поцелуевский, А., *Основы синтаксиса туркменского литературного языка* (Ашхабад, 1943).

15. Azerbaijani

Гусейнов, Г., *Азербайджанско-русский словарь* (Баку, 1941).

V. NORTH CAUCASIAN LANGUAGES

Dirr, A., 'Über die Klassen (Geschlechter) in den kaukasischen Sprachen' (*Archives Internationales d'Ethnographie*, xviii, Leiden, 1908).
Dirr, A., *Einführung in das Studium der kaukasischen Sprachen* (Leipzig, 1928).
Dumézil, G., *Etudes comparatives sur les langues caucasiennes du Nord-Ouest. Morphologie* (Paris, 1932).
Dumézil, G., *Introduction à la grammaire comparée des langues caucasiennes du Nord* (Paris, 1933).
Dumézil, G., *Recherches comparatives sur le verbe caucasien* (Paris, 1933).
Erckert, R. von, *Die Sprachen des kaukasischen Stammes* (Vienna, 1895).
Trubetzkoy, N., 'Studien auf dem Gebiete der vergleichenden Lautlehre der nordkaukasischen Sprachen' (*Caucasica*, iii, Leipzig, 1926).

LANGUAGES OF THE U.S.S.R.

A. CHECHENO-LEZGINIAN (NORTH-EASTERN)

1. CHECHEN

Чуликов, *Правописание чеченского языка* (Грозный, 1927).
Яковлев, Н. Ф., *Синтаксис чеченского литературного языка* (Москва-Ленинград, 1940).
Мациев, А., *Чеченско-русский словарь* (Грозный, 1927).
Мациев, А., *Самоучитель чеченского языка* (Грозный, 1932²).
Услар, П. К., ‚Чеченский язык' (*Этнография Кавказа*, т. II, Тифлис, 1888).

2. TSOVA-TUSH (BATS)

Schiefner, A., *Versuch über die Thusch-Sprache* (St Petersburg, 1856).

3. AWAR

Бокарёв, А. А., *Синтаксис аварского языка* (Москва-Ленинград, 1949).
Schiefner, A., *Awarische Texte* (St Petersburg, 1873).
Услар, П. К., ‚Аварский язык' (*Этнография Кавказа*, т. III, Тифлис, 1889).
Жирков, Л. И., *Грамматика аварского языка* (Москва, 1924).
Жирков, Л. И., *Аварско-русский словарь* (Москва, 1936).

4. ANDI AND DIDO

Бокарёв, А. А., *Очерк грамматики чамалинского языка* (Москва-Ленинград, 1949).
Дирр (Dirr), А., ‚Краткий грамматический очерк андийского языка' (*Сборник материалов для описания местностей и племен Кавказа*, XXXV, Тифлис, 1904).
Дирр (Dirr), А., ‚Материалы для изучения языков и наречий андо-дидойской группы' (*Сборник материалов*, XL, Тифлис, 1909).

5. DARGWA (WITH KHYURKILI)

Услар, П. К., ‚Хюркилинский язык' (*Этнография Кавказа*, т. V, Тифлис, 1892).
Жирков, Л. И., *Грамматика даргинского языка* (Москва, 1926).

6. LAK

Услар, П. К., ‚Лакский язык' (*Этнография Кавказа*, т. IV, Тифлис, 1890).

7. ARCHI

Дирр, А., ‚Арчинский язык' (*Сборник материалов*, XXXIX, Тифлис, 1908).

8. LEZGIN (Kyuri)

Генко, А. Н., *Материалы по лезгинской диалектологии. Кубинское наречие* (Ленинград, 1929).
Услар, П. К., ‚Кюринский язык' (*Этнография Кавказа*, т. VI, 1896).
Жирков, Л. И., *Грамматика лезгинского языка* (Махач-кала, 1941).

9. AGUL

Дирр, А., ‚Агульский язык' (*Сборник материалов*, XXXVII, Тифлис, 1907).
Шаумян, Р., *Грамматический очерк агульского языка* (Москва-Ленинград, 1941).

10. TABASSARAN

Дирр, А., ‚Грамматический очерк табасаранского языка' (*Сборник материалов*, XXXV, Тифлис, 1905).

11. RUTUL

Дирр, А., ‚Рутульский язык' (*Сборник материалов*, XLII, Тифлис, 1912).

12. TSAKHUR

Дирр, А., ‚Цахурский язык' (*Сборник материалов*, XLIII, Тифлис, 1913).

13. UDI

Дирр, А., ‚Удинская грамматика' (*Сборник материалов*, XXXIII, Тифлис, 1904).
Schiefner, A., *Versuch über die Sprache der Uden* (St Petersburg, 1863).

B. ABKHAZO-CIRCASSIAN (NORTH-WESTERN)

1. ABKHAZ

Марр, Н. Я., *Абхазско-русский словарь* (Ленинград, 1925).
Услар, П. К., ‚Абхазский язык' (*Этнография Кавказа*, т. I, Тифлис, 1887).

2. ADYGE (KABARDIN AND CIRCASSIAN)

Jakovlev, N., 'Kurze Übersicht über die tscherkessischen (adygheischen) Dialekte und Sprachen' (*Caucasica*, VI, Leipzig, 1930).
Яковлев, Н. Ф., *Таблицы фонетики кабардинского языка* (Москва, 1923).
Яковлев, Н. Ф., *Краткая грамматика адыгейского (кяхского) языка* (Краснодар, 1930).
Яковлев, Н. и Д. Ашхамаф, *Грамматика адыгейского литературного языка* (Москва-Ленинград, 1941).

Лопатинский, Л. Г., „Краткая кабардинская грамматика' (*Сборник материалов*, XII, Тифлис, 1891).
Турчанинов, Ф. и М. Цагов, *Грамматика кабардинского языка*, I (Москва-Ленинград, 1940).

3. Ubykh

Dirr, A., 'Die Sprache der Ubychen' (*Caucasica*, IV–V, Leipzig, 1927).
Dumézil, G., *La langue des Oubykhs* (Paris, 1931).

VI. SOUTH CAUCASIAN LANGUAGES

Чикобава, А., „О лингвистических чертах картвельских языков' (*ИАН, отд. лит. и яз.*, т. VII, вып. 1, Москва-Ленинград, 1948).

1. Georgian

Багаев, К., *Опыт грузино-русского словаря* (Тифлис, 1899).
Чубинов, Д., *Грузино-русский словарь* (СПБ, 1887).
Deeters, G., *Das kharthwelische Verbum* (Leipzig, 1930).
Dirr, A., *Grammatik der modernen georgischen (grusinischen) Sprache* (Vienna, 1904).
Kluge, *Georgisch-deutsches Wörterbuch* (Leipzig, 1920).
Марр, Н. Я., *К изучению современного грузинского языка* (Ленинград, 1922).
Марр, Н. Я., *Пособие для изучения живого грузинского языка* (Ленинград, 1926).
Marr, N. et M. Brière, *La langue géorgienne* (Paris, 1931).
Meckelein, R., *Georgisch-deutsches Wörterbuch* (Berlin-Leipzig, 1928).
Руденко, Б. Т., *Грамматика грузинского языка* (Москва-Ленинград, 1940).

2. Mingrelian (Megrel)

Кипшидзе, И., *Грамматика мингрельского (иверского) языка* (СПБ, 1914).

3. Laz (Chan)

Марр, Н. Я., *Грамматика чанского (лазского) языка* (СПБ, 1914).

VII. INDO-EUROPEAN LANGUAGES

Baudiš, J., *Struktura jazyků indoevropských* (Bratislava, 1932).
Brugmann, K., *Kurze vergleichende Grammatik der indogermanischen Sprachen* (Berlin-Leipzig, 1904).
Brugmann, K. und B. Delbrück, *Grundriss der vergleichenden Grammatik der indogermanischen Sprachen*, I–V (Berlin-Leipzig, 1897–1930^2).

BIBLIOGRAPHY

Delbrück, B., *Einleitung in das Studium der indogermanischen Sprachen* (Leipzig, 1919⁶).
Hirt, H., *Indogermanische Grammatik*, I–VII (Heidelberg, 1921–37).
Kieckers, E., *Einführung in die indogermanische Sprachwissenschaft*, I (Munich, 1933).
Krahe, H., *Indogermanische Sprachwissenschaft* (Leipzig, 1943).
Kretschmer, P., *Die indogermanische Sprachwissenschaft* (Göttingen, 1925).
Meillet, A., *Les dialectes indo-européens* (Paris, 1908).
Meillet, A., *Introduction à l'étude comparative des langues indo-européennes* (Paris, 1949⁸).
Pagliaro, A., *Sommario di linguistica arioeuropea* (Rome, 1930).
Pedersen, H., 'Le groupement des dialectes indo-européens' (*Det Kgl. Danske Videnskabernes Selskab, Hist.-fil. Meddelelser*, XI, 3, Copenhagen, 1925).
Schmidt, J., *Die Verwandtschaftsverhältnisse der indogermanischen Sprachen* (Weimar, 1872).
Schrijnen, J., *Inleiding tot de studie der vergelijkende indogermaansch taalwetenschap* (Leiden, 1905).

A. Iranic

Geiger, W. und E. Kuhn, *Grundriss der iranischen Philologie*, I–II (Strassburg, 1895–1901).

1. Ossetic (Ir)

Абаев, В., „К характеристике современного осетинского языка" (*Яфетический Сборник*, VII, Ленинград, 1932).
Абаев, В., „О языке южных осетин" (*Языка Сев. Кавказа и Дагестана*, I, Москва-Ленинград, 1935).
Абаев, В. И., *Осетинский язык и фольклор*, I (Москва-Ленинград, 1949).
Christensen, A., 'Textes ossètes' (*Det Kgl. Danske Videnskabernes Selskab, Hist.-fil. Meddelelser*, VI, 1, Copenhagen, 1921).
Hübschmann, H., *Etymologie und Lautlehre der ossetischen Sprache* (Strassburg, 1887).
Миллер, В. Ф., *Осетинские этюды*, I–III (Москва, 1881–7).
Миллер, В. Ф., *Дигорские сказания* (Москва, 1902).
Миллер, В. Ф. и А. А. Фрейман, *Осетинско-русско-немецкий словарь*, I–III (Ленинград, 1927–34).
Шёгрен (Sjögren), А., *Осетинская грамматика*, I–II (СПБ, 1844).
Шифнер (Schiefner), А., *Осетинские тексты* (СПБ, 1868).

2. Talysh

Миллер, Б. В., *Талышские тексты* (Москва, 1930).

3. TAT

Миллер, Б. В., ‚Татские тексты‘ (*Иранские языки*, I, Москва-Ленинград, 1945).
Миллер, В. Ф., *Татские этюды*, I–II (Москва, 1905–7).

4. TAJIKI

Громатович, К. Д. и М. А. Дмитревский, *Учебник таджикского языка* (Ташкент, 1929).
Кузнецов, П. Е., *Сравнительная грамматика таджикского и сартовского наречий* (Ташкент, 1915).
Орфинская, В. К., ‚К характеристике фонетического состава таджикского языка‘ (*Иранские языки*, I, Москва-Ленинград, 1945).
Семёнов, А., *Краткий грамматический очерк таджикского языка* (Ташкент, 1927).
Соколова, В. С., *Фонетика таджикского языка* (Москва-Ленинград, 1949).

5. PAMIRI GROUP (SHUGHNI, ETC.)

Gauthiot, R., 'Notes sur le yazgoulami, dialecte iranien des confins du Pamir' (*Journal Asiatique*, XI, Paris, 1916).
Grierson, G. A., *Languages Spoken beyond the North-West Frontier of India* (London, 1900).
Grierson, G. A., *Ishkashmi, Zebaki, and Yazgulami* (London, 1920).
Grierson, G. A., *Linguistic Survey of India*, X (Calcutta, 1921).
Lentz, W., *Pamir-Dialekte. I. Materialien zur Kenntnis der Schugni-Gruppe* (Göttingen, 1933).
Morgenstierne, G., 'Notes on Shugni' (*Norsk Tidskrift for Sprogvidenskap*, I, Oslo, 1928).
Семёнов, А., *Материалы для изучения наречий горного Таджикистана*, I (Москва, 1901).
Shaw, R. B., 'On the Shighni Dialect' (*Journal of the Asiatic Society of Bengal*, XLVI, Calcutta, 1877).
Sköld, H., *Materialien zu den iranischen Pamirsprachen* (Lund, 1936).

B. ARMENIAN

Abeghian, A., *Neuarmenische Grammatik* (Berlin-Leipzig, 1936).
Adjarian, H., *Classification des dialectes arméniens* (Paris, 1909).
Deeters, G., 'Armenisch und Südkaukasisch' (*Caucasica*, III, Leipzig, 1926).
Dirr, A., *Praktisches Lehrbuch der ostarmenischen Sprache* (Vienna, 1910).
Feydit, F., *Grammaire de la langue arménienne moderne. Dialecte occidental* (Venice, 1935).
Feydit, F., *Manuel de langue arménienne. Arménien occidental moderne* (Paris, 1948).

BIBLIOGRAPHY

Finck, F. N., *Lehrbuch der neuarmenischen Literatursprache* (Vagarschapat, 1902).
Gulian, K. H., *Elementary Modern Armenian Grammar* (Heidelberg, 1902).
Hübschmann, H., *Armenische Grammatik. I. Armenische Etymologie* (Leipzig, 1895–7).
Macler, F., *Chrestomathie de l'arménien moderne* (Paris, 1932).
Мсерианц, А., *Армянская диалектология* (Москва, 1898).

C. BALTIC

Būga, K., *Aistiškai studijai* (St Petersburg, 1908).
Endzelīns, J., *Lekcijas par baltu valodu salīdzināmo gramatiku* (Riga, 1927).
Hjelmslev, L., *Etudes baltiques* (Copenhagen, 1932).
Matthews, W. K., 'Baltic Origins' (*Revue des études slaves*, XXIV, Paris, 1948).
Salys, A., 'Baltu kalbos' (*Lietuviškoji Enciklopedija*, II, Kaunas, 1934).
Šmits, P., *Ievads baltu filoloģijā* (Riga, 1936).

1. LATVIAN

Blese, E., *Latviešu pareizrakstības vārdnīca* (Riga, 1933).
Brandt (Brants), K. and W. K. Matthews, *A Latvian-English Dictionary* (Riga, 1930).
Ekblom, R., *Die lettischen Akzentarten* (Uppsala, 1933).
Endzelin, J., *Lettische Grammatik* (Riga, 1922; Heidelberg, 1923).
Endzelīns, J., *Latviešu valodas skaņas un formas* (Riga, 1938).
Endzelīns, J. un K. Mīlenbachs, *Latviešu gramatika* (Riga, 1934[5]).
Endzelīns, J. un K. Mīlenbachs, *Latviešu valodas mācība* (Riga, 1936[10]).
Лоя, Я. В., *Латышско-русский словарь* (Москва, 1942[2]).
Mīlenbachs, K. un J. Endzelīns, *Latviešu valodas vārdnīca*, I–IV (Riga, 1923–32).
Ozoliņš, E., *Latviešu pareizrakstības vārdnīca* (Riga, 1927, 1932).
Ozoliņš, E., *Latviski-vāciska vārdnīca* (Riga, 1935).
Plāķis, J., *Kursenieku valoda* (Riga).
Sehwers, J., *Die deutschen Lehnwörter im Lettischen* (Zürich, 1918).
Strods, *Pareizrakstības vordneica* (Riga, 1933).

2. LITHUANIAN

Alminauskas, K., *Die Germanismen des Litauischen*, I (Kaunas, 1935).
Arumaa, P., *Litauische mundartliche Texte aus der Wilnaer Gegend* (Tartu, 1936).
Baranowski (Baranauskas), A. und F. Specht, *Litauische Mundarten*, I–II (Leipzig, 1920–2).
Brückner, A., *Litu-Slavische Studien. I. Die slavischen Fremdwörter im Litauischen* (Weimar, 1877).
Būga, K., *Lietuvių kalbos žodynas*, I–II (Kaunas, 1924–5).
Busch, A. und T. Chomskas, *Litauisch-deutsches Wörterbuch*, I (Berlin-Leipzig, 1927).
Ekblom, R., *Manuel phonétique de la langue lituanienne* (Stockholm, 1922).
Ekblom, R., *Quantität und Intonation im Hochlitauischen* (Uppsala, 1925).

Fraenkel, E., *Syntax der litauischen Postpositionen und Präpositionen* (Heidelberg, 1929).
Явнис (Jaunius), К., *Грамматика литовского языка* (СПБ, 1908–16).
Gerullis, G., *Litauische Dialektstudien* (Leipzig, 1930).
Hermann, E., *Litauische Studien* (Göttingen, 1926).
Klimas, P., *Lietuvių kalbos sintaksė* (Kaunas, 1924[5]).
Kurschat, F., *Grammatik der litauischen Sprache* (Halle, 1876).
Kurschat, F., *Litauisch-deutsches Wörterbuch* (Halle, 1883).
Kurschat, F., *Litauisches Lesebuch*, I–III (Tilsit, 1911–13).
Lalis, A., *A Dictionary of the Lithuanian and English Languages*, I (Chicago, 1915[3]).
Leskien, A., *Die Bildung der Nomina im Litauischen* (Leipzig, 1891).
Leskien, A., *Litauisches Lesebuch mit Grammatik und Wörterbuch* (Heidelberg, 1919).
Niedermann, M., A. Senn und F. Brender, *Wörterbuch der litauischen Schriftsprache*, 1 (Heidelberg, 1932–).
Pedersen, H., *Etudes lituaniennes* (Copenhagen, 1933).
Plaķis, J., *Leišu valodas rokas grāmata* (Riga, 1926).
Rīteris, J., *Lietuwiski-latwiska vārdnīca* (Riga, 1929).
Rygiškių Jonas (J. Jablonskis), *Lietuvių kalbos sintaksė*, I (Seinai, 1911).
Rygiškių Jonas (J. Jablonskis), *Lietuvių kalbos gramatika* (Vilnius, 1922[2]).
Rygiškių Jonas (J. Jablonskis), *Lietuvių kalbos vadovėlis* (Kaunas, 1925).
Salys, A., 'Die žemaitischen Mundarten', I (*Tauta ir Žodis*, VI, Kaunas, 1930).
Saussure, F. de, 'A propos de l'accentuation lituanienne (*Mémoires de la Société de linguistique*, VIII, Paris, 1894).
Schwentner, E., *Die Wortfolge im Litauischen* (Heidelberg, 1922).
Senn, A., *Kleine litauische Sprachlehre* (Heidelberg, 1929).
Senn, A., *The Lithuanian Language. A Characterization* (Chicago, 1942).
Senn, A., 'Standard Lithuanian in the Making' (*The Slavonic and East European Review*, American Series, III, 2, Menasha, 1944).
Senn, A., *Lithuanian Dialectology* (Menasha, 1945).
Серейский, Б., *Систематическое руководство к изучению литовского языка* (Ковно, 1929).
Серейский, Б., *Литовско-русский словарь* (Ковно, 1933).
Skardžius, P., *Bendrinės lietuvių kalbos kirčiavimas* (Kaunas, 1936).
Torbiörnson, T., *Litauiska akcentfrågor* (Uppsala, 1936).

D. SLAVONIC

Vondrák, W., *Vergleichende slavische Grammatik*, I–II (Göttingen, 1924–8[2]).

1. RUSSIAN

Аванесов, Р. И. и В. Н. Сидоров, *Очерк грамматики русского литературного языка* (Москва, 1945).
Бархударов, С. Г., *Методические разработки по грамматике* (Москва, 1940).

BIBLIOGRAPHY

Berneker, E. und M. Vasmer, *Russische Grammatik* (Berlin, 1940⁴).
Богородицкий, В. А., *Общий курс русской грамматики* (Москва, 1935⁵).
Boyanus, S. C., *Manual of Russian Pronunciation* (London, 1946³).
Boyanus, S. C. and N. B. Jopson, *Spoken Russian* (London, 1945²).
Будде, Е. Ф., *Русский язык* (Казань, 1913).
Булаховский, Л. А., *Курс русского литературного языка* (Киев-Харьков, 1938³).
Черных, П. Я., *Русский язык в Сибири* (Иркутск, 1937).
Даль, В., *Толковый словарь живого великорусского языка*, I–IV (СПб-Москва, 1912–14⁴).
Дурново, Н. Н., *Диалектические разыскания в области великорусских говоров*, I (Москва, 1917).
Гвоздёв, А. Н. *О фонологических средствах русского языка* (*М-Л.*, 1949).
Isačenko, A. V. *Fonetika spisovnej ruštiny* (Bratislava, 1947).
Jakobson, R., *Vliv revoluce na ruský jazyk* (Prague, 1921).
Еремин, С. А. и И. А. Фалёв, *Русская диалектология. Хрестоматия* (Москва-Ленинград, 1928).
Карцевский, С., *Русский язык*, I (Прага, 1925).
Karcevski, S., *Système du verbe russe* (Prague, 1927).
Кошутић, Р., *Граматика руског језика*, I–II (Петроград, 1919²; Београд, 1914).
Mazon, A., *Morphologie des aspects du verbe russe* (Paris, 1908).
Mazon, A., *Emplois des aspects du verbe russe* (Paris, 1914).
Mazon, A., *Grammaire de la langue russe* (Paris, 1949³).
Михельсон, М., *Русская мысль и речь*, I–II (СПБ, 1912).
Овсянико-Куликовский, Д. Н., *Синтаксис русского языка* (СПБ, 1912²).
Овсянников, В. З., *Литературная речь. Толковый словарь общелитературуной фразеологии* (Москва, 1933).
Ожегов, С. И., *Словарь русского языка* (Москва, 1949).
Pawlowsky, J., *Russisch-deutsches Wörterbuch* (Riga, 1911³).
Пешковский, А. М., *Синтаксис русского языка в научном освещении* (Москва, 1928³).
Потебня, А. А., *Из записок по русской грамматике*, I–IV (Воронеж-Харьков-Москва-Ленинград, 1874–1941).
Селищев, А. М., *Диалектологический очерк Сибири*, I (Иркутск, 1921).
Селищев, А. М., *Язык революционной эпохи* (Москва, 1928).
Шахматов, А. А., *Синтаксис русского языка*, I–II (Ленинград, 1925–7).
Шахматов, А. А., *Очерк современного русского литературного языка* (Москва, 1935–40).
Щерба, Л. В., *Русские гласные в качественном и количественном отношении* (СПБ, 1912).
Tesnière, L., *Petite grammaire russe* (Paris, 1934).
Trofimov, M. V. and D. Jones, *The Pronunciation of Russian* (Cambridge, 1923).

Trubetzkoy, N., *Das morphonologische System der russischen Sprache* (Prague, 1934).
Ушаков, Д. Н. (ed.), *Толковый словарь русского языка*, I–IV (Москва, 1935–40).
Ушаков, Д. Н. и Е. И. Крючков, *Орфографический словарь* (Москва, 1945).
Виноградов, В. В., *Русский язык* (Москва, 1947).

2. WHITE RUSSIAN

Anon., *Правапіс беларускае мовы* (Менск, 1934).
Байкоў, М. і С. Некрашэвіч, *Беларуска-расійскі слоўнік* (Менск, 1925).
Карский, Е. Ф., *Обзор звуков и форм белорусской речи* (Москва, 1885).
Карский, Е. Ф., *Белоруссы*, I–III (СПБ-Петроград, 1903–21).
Карский, Е. Ф., *Белорусская речь* (Петроград, 1918).
Лёсік, Я., *Сынтакс беларускае мовы* (Менск, 1925).
Лёсік, Я., *Граматыка беларускае мовы*, I–II (Менск, 1926–7).
Носович, И. И., *Словарь белорусского наречия* (СПБ, 1870).
Пратасэвіч, У. і У. Самковіч, *Рабочая кніга па беларускай мове* (Менск, 1927).
Расторгуев, П. А., *Северско-белорусский говор* (Ленинград, 1927).
Соболевский, А. И., *Опыт русской диалектологии. Наречия великорусское и белорусское* (СПБ, 1897).

3. UKRAINIAN

Ганцов, В., *Діялектологічна класифікація українських говорів* (Київ, 1923).
Гринченко, Б., *Словарь української мови*, I–IV (Київ, 1908–9).
Дурново, Н. Н., *Хрестоматия по малорусской диалектологии* (Москва, 1913).
Хладкий, М., *Мова сучасного українського письменьства* (Харків, 1930).
Крымский, А., *Украинская грамматика*, I–II (Москва, 1907–8).
Кульбакин, С., *Украинский язык* (Харьков, 1919).
Курило, О., *Уваги до сучасної української літературної мови* (Київ, 1925[3]).
Kuzelja, Z. i J. Rudnyćkyj, *Ukraïnśko-nimećkyj slovnyk* (Leipzig, 1943).
Огиенко, И. И., *Курс украинского языка* (Киев, 1919[2]).
Огієнко, І., *Чистота й правильність української мови* (Львів, 1925).
Onatsky, E., *Grammatica ucraina teorico-pratica* (Naples, 1937).
Rudnyćkyj, J., *Lehrbuch der ukrainischen Sprache* (Leipzig, 1943[3]).
Сімович, В., *Практична граматика української мови* (Раштат, 1918).
Сімович, В., *Граматика української мови* (Київ, 1919).
Simowycz, W., *Praktische Grammatik der ukrainischen Sprache* (Vienna, 1915).

BIBLIOGRAPHY

Синявський, О., *Норми української літературної мови* (Харків-Київ, 1931).
Smal-Stockyj, S., *Ruthenische Grammatik* (Berlin, 1913).
Smal-Stockyj, S., *Ukrainisches Lesebuch* (Berlin, 1927).
Smal-Stockyj, S. und T. Gartner, *Grammatik der ruthenischen (ukrainischen) Sprache* (Vienna, 1913).
Смаль-Стоцький, С. і Ф. Ґартнер, *Граматика української мови* (Vienna, 1914^3).
Тимченко, Е., *Українська граматика*, 1 (Київ, 1918^2).
Волошин, А., *О письменном языке подкарпатских русинов* (Ужгород, 1921).
Zilyński J., *Opis fonetyczny języka ukraińskiego* (Cracow, 1932).

ADDENDA (Unclassified)

Аванесов, Р. И., *Очерки русской диалектологии*, 1 (Москва, 1949).
Braun, M., *Grundzüge der slawischen Sprachen* (Göttingen, 1947).
Бубрих, Д. В., *Грамматика литературного коми языка* (Ленинград, 1949).
Entwistle, W. J. and W. A. Morison, *Russian and the Slavonic Languages* (London, 1949).
Fraenkel, E., *Die baltischen Sprachen* (Heidelberg, 1950).
Luckyj, G. and J. B, Rudnyckyj, *A Modern Ukrainian Grammar* (Minneapolis–London, 1949).
Matthews, W. K., 'Russian Grammatical Design' (*The Slavonic and East European Review*, XXIX, 72, London, 1950).
Matthews, W. K., 'Modern Russian Dialects' (*Transactions of the Philological Society*, 1950, London, 1951).
Мещанинов, И. И. и Г. П. Сердюченко, *Языки Северного Кавказа и Дагестана* (Москва-Ленинград, 1949).
Pisani, V., *Glottologia indoeuropea* (Turin, 1949^2).
Потанкин, С. Г. и А. К. Имяреков, *Мокшанско-русский словарь* (Москва, 1949).
Реформатский, А., *Введение в языковедение* (Москва, 1947).
Trautmann, R., *Die slavischen Völker und Sprachen. Eine Einführung in die Slavistik* (Göttingen, 1947).
Винокур, Г. О., *Русское сценическое произношение* (Москва, 1948).

APPENDIX IV

INDEX OF LANGUAGES AND DIALECTS

NOTE. The initials in the Language Group column below should be interpreted as follows: P(alaeoasiatic), U(ralian), A(ltaic), N(orth) C(aucasian), S(outh) C(aucasian), and I(ndo)-E(uropean).

Language	Language Group	Language	Language Group
Abakan, see Oirot	A	Chechen	N C
Abkhaz	N C	Chelkan, see Oirot	A
Abzhu, see Abkhaz	N C	Cheremiss	U
Adyge	N C	Chukcha	P
Agul	N C	Chuvash	A
Ainu	P	Circassian, see Adyge	N C
Akhti, see Lezgin	N C	Crimean Tartar, North	A
Akhwakh	N C		
Altai, see Oirot	A	Crimean Tartar, South	A
Alwal, see Akhwakh	N C		
Anatri, see Chuvash	A	Curian, see Latvian	I-E
Andi	N C	Dargin, see Dargwa	N C
Archi	N C	Derbet, see Kalmyk	A
Armenian	I-E	Dido	N C
Awar	N C	Digor, see Ossetic	I-E
Azerbaijani	A	Dolgan, see Yakut	A
Bagulal, see Kwandi	N C	Elkenbeye, see Negda	A
Balkar	A	Enets, see Yenisei Samoyed	U
Baraba	A		
Bartangi, see Pamiri	I-E	Erzya, see Mordvin	U
Bashkir	A	Estonian	U
Bats, see Tsova-Tush	N C	Even, see Lamut	A
Beshitl, see Kapuchi	N C	Evenki, see Tungus	A
Birar	A	Gagauzi	A
Bital	A	Georgian	S C
Botlikh	N C	Gilyak	P
Budug, see Budukh	N C	Godoberi	N C
Budukh	N C	Gold	A
Buinak, see Kumyk	A	Gurian, see Georgian	S C
Buryat	A	Imeretian, see Imerian	S C
Bzyb, see Abkhaz	N C	Imerian, see Georgian	S C
Caraite, see Karaim	A	Ingilo, see Georgian	S C
Carelian	U	Ingrian	U
Chamalal	N C	Ingush	N C
Chan, see Laz	S C	Inkagir	A
Chapogir	A	Ir, see Ossetic	I-E
Chavchuven, see Koryak	P	Irtysh Tartar	A

INDEX OF LANGUAGES AND DIALECTS

Language	Language Group	Language	Language Group
Isurian, see Ingrian	U	Kumanda, see Oirot	A
Itel'men, see Kamchadal	P	Kumyk	A
		Kyakar	A
Jek	N C	Kyakh, see Circassian	N C
Kabardin, see Adyge	N C	Kyuri, see Lezgin	N C
Kakhetin, see Georgian	S C	Lak	N C
		Lalegir	A
Kalmez, see Votyak	U	Lamut	A
Kalmyk	A	Lappish, Kola	U
Kamass	A	Latgalian, see Latvian	I-E
Kamchadal	P		
Kangalass	A	Latvian	I-E
Kapuchi	N C	Laz	S C
Karacha	A	Lezgin	N C
Karagass	A	Lithuanian	I-E
Karagin, see Koryak	P	Livonian	U
Karaim	A	Luoravetlan, see Chukcha	P
Karakalpak	A		
Karata	N C	Ludian	U
Kartvelian, see Georgian	S C	Madur, see Motor	A
		Manegir	A
Kazakh	A	Mangun, see Olcha	A
Kazikumukh, see Lak	N C	Mansi, see Vogul	U
Ket, see Yenisei Ostyak	P	Mari, see Cheremiss	U
		Maya	A
Khaidak, see Kumyk	A	Megrel, see Mingrelian	S C
Khakass	A		
Khanty, see Ostyak	U	Meshcheryak, see Mishar	A
Khaputli, see Jek	N C		
Khar'yuz, see Kamchadal	P	Meskh, see Georgian	S C
		Mishar	A
Khasav-Yurt, see Kumyk	A	Misher, see Mishar	A
Khevzur, see Georgian	S C	Moksha, see Mordvin	U
Khinalugh	N C	Mordvin	U
Khorezmi	A	Mthiul, see Georgian	S C
Khwarshi	N C	Mykhad, see Rutul	N C
Khyurkili, see Dargwa	N C	Nanai, see Gold	A
		Negda	A
Kile	A	Negidal, see Negda	A
Kipchak	A	Nenets, see Yurak	U
Kirgiz	A	Nganasan, see Tavgi	U
Koibal, see Abakan	A	Nivkh, see Gilyak	P
Komi, see Zyryan	U	Nogay	A
Koryak	P	Nymylan, see Koryak	P
Kot	P	Odul, see Yukagir	P
Krymchak, see South Crimean Tartar	A	Oirot	A
		Olcha	A
Kryz, see Jek	N C	Olonecian	U
Kubachi	N C	Onkor	A

157

LANGUAGES OF THE U.S.S.R.

Language	Language Group	Language	Language Group
Oroch	A	Tat	I-E
Orochel, see Orochon	A	Tavgi Samoyed	U
Orochon	A	Teleut, see Oirot	A
Orok	A	Tepter	A
Oroshori, see Pamiri	I-E	Thush, see Georgian	S C
Os, see Ossetic	I-E	Tindal	N C
Ossetic	I-E	Tindi, see Tindal	N C
Ostyak	U	Tobol Tartar, see Irtysh Tartar	A
Ostyak Samoyed	U	Torgout, see Kalmyk	A
Pamiri	I-E	Tsakhur	N C
Permyak, see Zyryan	U	Tsets, see Dido	N C
Pshav, see Georgian	S C	Tsova-Tush	N C
Rachin, see Georgian	S C	Tuba, see Oirot	A
Rushani, see Pamiri	I-E	Turkmen	A
Russian	I-E	Turuk	A
Ruthenian, see Ukrainian	I-E	Tuva	A
Rutul	N C	Tyumen Tartar, see Irtysh Tartar	A
Saam, see Kola Lappish	U	Ubykh	N C
Sagai, see Abakan	A	Uchur	A
Samagir	A	Ude	A
Samogitian, see Lithuanian	I-E	Udekhe, see Ude	A
Samur group	N C	Udi	N C
Samurzakan, see Abkhaz	N C	Udmurt, see Votyak	U
'Sart', see Uzbek	A	Ukrainian	I-E
Sedanka, see Kamchadal	P	Ulcha, see Olcha	A
		Uryankhai, see Tuva	A
Sel'kup, see Ostyak Samoyed	U	Uzbek	A
		Vatka, see Votyak	U
Setu, see Estonian	U	Vepsian	U
Shor	A	Viryal, see Chuvash	A
Shughnani, see Shughni	I-E	Vodian	U
		Volga Tartar	A
Shughni, see Pamiri	I-E	Votyak	U
Soyon, see Tuva	A	White Russian	I-E
Soyot, see Tuva	A	Yakut	A
Svan, see Svanetian	S C	Yazghulami, see Pamiri	I-E
Svanetian	S C		
Tabassaran	N C	Yenisei Ostyak	P
Tagaur, see Ossetic	I-E	Yenisei Samoyed	U
Tajiki	I-E	Yukagir	P
Talysh	I-E	Yurak	U
Taranchi	A	Zan, see Mingrelian and Laz	S C
Tartar, see Volga Tartar	A	Zyryan	U

APPENDIX V

SYMBOLS AND PHONETIC VALUES

NOTE. The various written characters used in the text of this book are interpreted here in terms of the International Phonetic Association (I.P.A.) alphabet. In several cases the individual language or language-group in which the character occurs is mentioned. This makes it possible to discriminate between the value of, say, Kamchadal (Itel′men) *cz* (i.e. [tʃz]), which is not a digraph, and Polish *cz* (i.e. [tʃ]), which is.

Alphabetic Symbol	Phonetic Symbol	Alphabetic Symbol	Phonetic Symbol
ä (Finnic)	[æ]	h (Ukrainian)	[ɦ]
å (Lappish, Tartar)	[ɔ]	ı (Turkish)	[ɨ]
ă (Chuvash)	[ɐ]	ı (Kola Lappish)	[ɩ]
B (Yurak)	[ḅ]	ï (Tartar)	[ɨ]
β (Cheremiss)	[β]	j	[j]
c (Hungarian, Latvian)	[ts]	ķ (Latvian)	[c]
		kh	[x]
c (Chukcha, Mongolian)	[tʃ]	ł	[ɫ]
		ng	[ŋ]
c (Turkish)	[dʒ]	ny (Hungarian)	[ɲ]
ç (Turkic)	[dʒ]	ŋ	[ŋ]
ç (Turkish)	[tʃ]	ö	[ø],[œ]
č	[tʃ]	ɵ (Turkic)	[œ]
ch	[x]	ɵ (Ostyak)	[o]
cs (Hungarian)	[tʃ]	õ (Estonian)	[ɣ], [ɨ]
cz (Polish)	[tʃ]	q	[q]
D	[d̥]	꙯	[ʁ]
đ (O.Norse)	[ð]	ρ	voiced bilabial vibrant
δ (Cheremiss)	[ð]		
dž	[dʒ]		
ě (ѣ)	[jɛ], [je]	s (Hungarian)	[ʃ]
ĕ (Chuvash)	[ə]	ş (Turkish)	[ʃ]
ę (Vodian, Livonian)	[ɣ]	š	[ʃ]
		sz (Hungarian)	[s]
ė (Lithuanian)	[e:]	sz (Polish)	[ʃ]
ë (Russian)	[jo], [jö]	τ	voiceless bilabial vibrant
ə	[ə]		
G	[g̊]		
ġ (Latvian)	[ɟ]	tš	[tʃ]
ğ (Turkish)	[ɣ]	þ (Runic)	[θ], [ð]
gh	[ɣ]	θ (Turkic)	[θ]
ɣ	[ɣ]	ü	[y]

LANGUAGES OF THE U.S.S.R.

Alphabetic Symbol	Phonetic Symbol	Alphabetic Symbol	Phonetic Symbol
u̯	[w]	ʒ (Kola Lappish)	[ʒ]
w	[w]	ӡ (Tungus)	[dʒ]
w (Tungus)	[v]	ъ	sign of velarisation
x (Kamchadal)	[x]		
y (Finnish)	[y]	ы (Russian)	[ɨ]
y (Lithuanian)	[iː]	ь (Kirgiz)	[ɨ]
y (vowel)	[ɨ]	b (Samoyedic)	[ʔ]
y (consonant)	[j]	b (Vogul)	[ɣ]
ẏ	[ω]	I (Adyge)	sign of glottalisation
ž	[ʒ]		
zs (Hungarian)	[ʒ]		

The phonetic values of the separable diacritics are as follows:
postliteral ' (e.g. kʻ) indicates aspiration,
postliteral ' (e.g. t') — glottalisation,
postconsonantal ' (e.g. l') — palatalisation,
postconsonantal ʷ (e.g. qʷ) — labialisation,
subconsonantal . (e.g. ṇ) — lingual retroflexion,
subconsonantal , (e.g. ț) — palatalisation,
subvocalic . (e.g. ẹ, ọ) — a close ('raised') pronunciation,
subvocalic ̮ (e.g. u̮) — consonantalisation,
subvocalic ̨ (e.g. ę, ǫ) — an open ('lowered') pronunciation, except in Slavonic, where it indicates nasalisation,
supraliteral, chiefly supravocalic ˜ in Lithuanian (e.g. ã) — the long rising tone,
supraliteral ' (e.g. k̇) — half length,
supravocalic ¯ (e.g. ā) — a long vowel,
supravocalic ´ (e.g. á) — stress, except in Hungarian, where it is the length mark, and in Lithuanian, where it indicates the long falling tone,
supravocalic ` in Lithuanian (e.g. à) — the short falling tone.

INDEX

The references here are to items which occur in the text of the book (pp. 1–120), not in the footnotes, maps, diagrams, and appendices. The scope of the Index has been further limited by the exclusion of linguistic illustrations.

Äänis, *see* Onega
Aavik, Johannes, 35
Abakan, 66, 73
abessive, *see* case
Abkhaz, 87, 93; *see also* literature; Republic
Abkhazo-Circassian, 87, 93
ablative, *see* case
Ablaut, *see* apophony
abruptive, *see* case, ejective
absolute, *see* case
abstract, *see* case
accent, *see* stress
accusative, *see* case
Achundov, M. F., 70, 84
Achvlediani, G. S., 99
active, *see* case
additive, *see* numeration
adessive, *see* case
adhesive, *see* case
adjective, 5, 6, 10, 11, 22, 32, 44, 60, 62, 75, 89, 90, 91, 95, 96, 99, 103, 104, 108, 112, 114, 116
adverb, 18, 53, 56, 63
Adyge, 87, 94, 95; *see also* Republic
Aestic, *see* Baltic
Aestii, 34
Afghanistan, 52, 58, 83, 104, 105
affirmative, *see* conjugation; mood
affix, 56, 74, 77, 95, 100, 114
affricate, *see* consonant
affrication, 60
Age, Stone, 19
Ages, Middle, 52, 115
agglutination, 31, 53, 66, 68
Agul, 86, 89, 91, 92
Agul, *see* River
Ahlquist, A., 38
Aimak, 58
Ainu, 3, 4, 9, 10
Ajar, *see* Republic
Akhti, *see* dialect

Alans, 102
Albani, 40
Albanian, 66, 101, 108
Alfred, King, 24, 25
Algonkin, 4
Alijev, U. D., 77
al-Kāšgharī, Maḥmūd, 65
Al'kor, Ja. P., 54
allative, *see* case
Alma-Ata, 74
alphabet, Arabic, 68, 69, 70, 83, 84, 93, 96
  Aramaic, 69, 79
  Armenian, 97
  Cyrillic, 22, 29, 31, 33, 49, 60, 61, 70, 71, 73, 76, 78, 82, 83, 84, 95, 96, 103
  Fijian, 31
  Gothic, 111
  I.P.A., 17
  khutsuri, 97
  Latin, 6, 17, 21, 22, 24, 70, 71, 72, 73, 75, 76, 77, 78, 83, 84, 93, 95, 96, 103
  Manchu, 68
  mkhedruli, 97
  Mongolian, 55, 59
  New Daghestan, 76
  runiform, 69
  Semitic, 79
  Tagalog, 71
  Uigur, 59, 61, 68, 69
  uncial, 107
Altai, *see* Oirot
Altaic, 1, 3, 12, 14, 52, 53, 55, 58, 63, 67; *see also* languages
alternation, consonantal, 14, 35, 62
  vocalic, 56
alveolar, *see* consonant
American, North, 3, 9, 32
Amerindian, North, *see* American, North
Ami, 64

ML 161 11

amorphism, 17, 31
Amur, *see* River
Anadyr', 3
Anatolia, 68, 83
Anatri, *see* dialect
Anderson, N., 49
Androphagi, 30
'Ανδροφάγοι, 30
animate, *see* gender
aorist, *see* tense
apophony, 18
approximative, *see* case
Arabic, 89, 99, 104; *see also* alphabet
Arabs, 104
Aral, *see* dialect
Aramaic, *see* alphabet
Archi, 86, 92
Arctic, *see* Ocean
Area, Chukcha National, 3
   Evenki National, 55
   Katong National, 57
   Khanty-Mansi National, 21
   Komi-Permyak National, 26
   Koryak National, 7
   Memel, 110
   Nenets National, 20
   Taimyr National, 20
   Yamal National, 20
   Yukagir National, 8
Arisu, 30
Armenia, 107
Armenian, 32, 98, 101, 102, 107, 119
   Classical, *see* Old
   Eastern, 108–9
   Middle, 107
   Old, 107
   see also alphabet; Republic
Arsaiju, 30
Arthani, 30
article, definite, 108
   postpositive, 94
articulate, *see* declension, definite
Arya, 102
Aryan, *see* Indo-European
Ashkhabad, 83
Asia, Central, 52, 63, 74, 126
   Minor, 87
aspect, 8, 75, 89, 94, 100
   durative, 77
   iterative, 45
   semelfactive, 45

aspective, *see* suffix
aspirated, *see* consonant
assimilation, 9, 18, 31, 66, 83
astevaihtelu, *see* alternation, consonantal
Astrakhan', 80
Asyka, Prince, 21
asyndetism, 74
asyndeton, 7
attribute, 5, 8
auditive, *see* mood
Aunus, *see* Olonecian
Austroasiatic, 1
Austronesian, 1
auxiliary, *see* verb
Avars, 52
Awar, 76, 88, 89
Awaro-Andian, 86
Äyrämöiset, 41
Azerbaijan, 70, 71, 76, 102, 104, 107;
   see also Republic
Azerbaijani, 64, 76, 83, 84, 86, 92;
   see also literature

Babur, 70
back, *see* vowel
Baikal, *see* Lake
Baku, 70, 84, 104
Balkan (languages), 32
Balkar, 64, 66, 76, 77, 86
Baltic (languages), 33, 36, 110; *see also*
   Sea
Bantu, 10, 66, 88
Baraba, 64
Bargut, *see* dialect
Bartangi, *see* dialect
base, 53, 60, 61, 62, 63, 66, 67, 81, 88,
   89, 99, 100, 114
   culture, 8, 24
Bashkir, 64, 70, 78, 79; *see also* literature, Republic
Bashkirs, 70, 79
Bašqort Ajmaǧy, 79
Basque, 108
Bats, *see* Tsova-Tush
Batum, *see* Batumi
Batumi, 98
Begloj, 29
Belo-ozero, 40
benedictive, *see* mood
Beormas, 24, 25
Bessarabia, 64, 80

INDEX

Beszéd és Könyörgés, A Halotti, 24
bilabial, *see* consonant
Birar, 54
Bital, 54
Bjarmar, 25, 38
Bjarmeland, 25
Bogoras, W., 4
Bogoraz-Tan, V. G., *see* Bogoras, W.
Bohais, 12
Böhtlingk, Otto, 72
Bolgar, 64, 81
Bolgar the Great, 27, 82
Bolgars, 27
Bolnis Sion, 97
Βουδῖνοι, 27
Bougainville, Southern, 88
Budenz, J., 48
Budini, 27
Bremen, Adam van, 39
Brière, M., 99
Brockelmann, C., 66
Brugmann, K., 65
Budug, *see* Budukh
Budukh, 86, 90
Buinak, *see* dialect
Bukhara, 70, 80, 83
Bulgarian, 108
  Macedonian, 116
  Old, 117
Bulgarians, 81
Buryat, 58, 59, 60, 62; *see also* literature
Buryat-Mongol, *see* Republic
Buryats, 70, 72
Bzyb, *see* dialect

Carelia, Eastern, 37, 38
Carelian, 25, 37, 38, 39, 40, 42, 101
Carelians, 25, 38
Carelo-Finnish, *see* Republic
caritive, *see* case
case, 5, 6, 9, 11, 32, 37, 47, 56, 60, 61, 62, 67, 89, 90, 93, 99, 100, 103, 108, 112, 113
  abessive, 44
  ablative, 9, 56, 62, 67, 73, 91, 99, 101
  absolute, 5, 6, 99
  abstract, 28, 31, 47, 90
  accusative, 9, 44, 56, 62, 67, 81, 99, 104, 108, 112
  active, 96
  adessive, 28

adhesive, 91, 99
allative, 28, 44, 90, 114
approximative, 26
caritive, 11
collative, 91
comitative, 5, 11, 35, 37, 43, 44, 46, 99
comparative, 26, 73, 75
conjunctive, 26
conversive, 93
dative, 44, 56, 62, 67, 81, 90, 91, 99, 104, 106, 108
definite, 56
destinative, 101
directive, 61, 99, 101
disjunctive, 26, 99
ergative, 90, 91, 99, 100
elative, 28, 44, 90, 93
epicene, 106
equative, 93
essive, 44
exablative, 91
finitive, 26
genitive, 26, 35, 44, 56, 62, 67, 91, 100, 104
genitive-accusative, 108
illative, 28, 56, 114
inceptive, 26
indefinite, 56
inessive, 28, 44, 99
instructive, 35
instrumental, 56, 62, 73, 96, 99, 112
lative, 18
limitative, 26, 62, 99
local (spatial), 28, 31, 47, 90, 99, 103
locative, 7, 44, 67, 73, 90, 99, 103
motive, 93
nominative, 28, 44, 56, 81, 99, 100
obessive, 91
oblique, 28, 56, 99, 119
passive, 96
possessive, 26, 96
privative, 26
prolative, 56
prosecutive, 11
sociative, 61, 99, 103
superallative, 91
superessive, 99
terminative, 99
translative, 26
vocative, 118
see also suffix

Caspian, *see* Sea
Castrén, M. A., 11, 12, 14, 72
casus agens, 88, 89
casus obliquus, 103
casus patiens, 88, 89
casus rectus, 103
category, grammatical, 5, 88
　notional, 28
　phonetic, 5
Catherine II, 74
Caucasia, 76
Caucasian, *see* North Caucasian
Caucasian, Central, 87
　East, 87
　North, 1, 66, 77, 86, 88, 94, 103
　North-East, 86, 87, 91, 92, 93, 103
　North-West, 89, 92, 93, 98
　South, 1, 86, 87, 94, 97
Caucasus, 2, 63, 76, 84, 86, 87, 93, 95, 109
causative, *see* verb
Cawcuven, *see* Chauchuven
central, *see* vowel
centralised, *see* vowel
Černecov, V. N., 22, 24
Chagatai, 70, 80, 83, 84
Chahar, 58
Chan, *see* Laz
Chapogir, 54
character, *see* alphabet
Chauchuven, *see* dialect
Cheboksary, 81
Chechen, 86, 92, 93
Chechen-Ingush, *see* Republic
Chechenia, Great, 93
Chelkan, 73
Cheremiss, 29, 30, 31, 32, 33, 46, 48, 81, 82
Cherkess, *see* Circassian
Cherkessk, 87
China, 12, 52, 59, 64
Chinese (language), 12, 56
　(people), 71
Chishima, *see* Kuriles
Chronicle, First Novgorod, 25
　Primary, 36
Chukcha, 3, 4, 5, 6, 8; *see also* literature
　Fishing, *see* dialect
　Reindeer, *see* dialect
　see also Area
Chukotka, 3

Chuvash, 27, 30, 32, 53, 63, 64, 68, 70, 75, 80, 82; *see also* literature
Čikobava, A., 88, 99
Cimmerian, 97
Circassia, 77
Circassian, 71, 87, 88, 94, 95; *see also* Republic
class, noun, 88, 89, 90, 96
classification, 54, 61, 63, 64, 65
classifier, 90, 92
clause, subordinate, 101
Codex Cumanicus, 65, 72, 77
Colchians, 101
collative, *see* case
comitative, *see* case
comparative, *see* case
comparison, 6, 91
complement, 61, 62
compound, *see* tense
concessive, *see* mood
conditional, *see* mood
confirmative, *see* mood
conjugation, 6, 9, 31, 32, 48, 62, 73, 100, 108
　affirmative, 27
　flexional, 27
　intransitive, 6
　negative, 27
　objective, 22
　subjective, 100
　transitive, 6
　uninflected, 9
conjunction, 5, 37, 41, 42, 74, 92, 100, 101, 110, 114
conjunctive, *see* case; mood
consonant, 35, 44, 66, 69, 75, 78, 79, 81, 88, 90, 91, 93, 95, 98, 113, 116, 118, 119
　affricate, 37, 65, 89, 91, 94, 98, 105, 111, 113, 116, 118
　alveolar, 17, 26, 39
　aspirated, 9, 97
　bilabial, 98, 105
　constrictive, 53
　dental, 17, 26, 67, 98
　ejective, 89
　fricative, 31, 88, 98, 106, 116, 118
　geminated, 53
　glottal, 19, 37, 79, 91, 111
　glottalised, 88
　interdental, 66

INDEX

consonant, labial, 60
  labialised, 22
  lateral, 89
  liquid, 67, 88
  nasal, 22, 57, 69, 73
  palatalised, 32, 43, 116
  pharyngal, 91
  plosive, 5, 10, 17, 22, 28, 37, 39, 53, 57, 60, 61, 65, 66, 73, 84, 88, 89, 91, 98, 101, 108, 111, 115
  postvelar, 105
  uvular, 91, 103, 105
  velar, 5, 9, 22, 39, 60, 98, 104, 106, 116, 117, 119
  velarised, 7
  vibrant, 66, 93, 94
  voiced, 4, 17, 26, 28
  voiceless, 4, 9, 26, 28
consonantal, *see* system
constrictive, *see* consonant
construction, ergative, 8, 77, 84
  nominative, 9
  objective, 95
  subjective, 95
continuant, *see* constrictive
converba, 61, 62
conversive, *see* case
cooperative, *see* case, sociative
Crimea, 14, 64, 76, 79, 80
Crimean, North, *see* Tartar
  South, *see* Tartar
Čuchari, 39
Čud', 39, 41
culture, Bronze Age, 21
  Iron Age, 25
  Uralian, 19
  Volga Tartar, 80
  West European, 117
  West Finnic, 42
Cumanic, 77
Cumans, 52
Curian, 109
Curonia, 33
  Western, 110
Curonians, 110
Cyrillic, *see* alphabet
Czech, 111

Daghestan, New, *see* alphabet
  Northern, 76, 86
  see also Republic

Dagö, *see* Hiiumaa
Dahurs, 54
Dargwa, 86, 89, 91
Daugava, *see* Dvina, Western
Daurs, *see* Dahurs
De administrando imperio, 30
De origine actibusque Getarum, 30
decimal, *see* numeration
declension, 6, 22, 28, 31, 32, 60, 61, 73, 74, 77, 81, 89, 90, 91, 92, 94, 100, 101, 103, 105, 113
  definite, 32
  indefinite, 32
  possessive, 31
definite, *see* article; declension; mood
degree, comparative, 113
  superlative, 36, 113
demonstrative, *see* pronoun
dental, *see* consonant
Derbet, *see* dialect
derivation, 31, 33
Desert, Gobi, 52
desiderative, *see* mood
destinative, *see* case
dialect, Akhti, 86, 90
  Anatri, 82
  Aral, 74
  Bargut, 59
  Bartangi, 105
  Buinak, 76
  Bzyb, 93
  Chauchuven, 6
  Chukcha, Fishing, 6
    Reindeer, 6
  Derbet, 60
  Digor, 103
  Erzya, 32
  Gilaki, 103
  Gurian, 98, 101
  Imerian, 97, 98, 101
  Ingilo, 98
  Ingrian, 37, 38, 39
  Ishkashmi, 105
  Kakhetin, 98
  Kalmez, 28
  Kama, 26
  Karagin, 6
  Khaidak, 76
  Khar'yuz, 7
  Khasav-Yurt, 76
  Khevzur, 98

dialect, Kyuri, 86, 90
   Latgalian, 111
   Ludian, 39, 40
   Mazandarani, 103
   Meskh, 98
   Minjani, 105
   Moksha, 32
   Mthiul, 89
   Olonecian, 37, 38
   Oroshori, 105
   Pshav, 98
   Rachin, 98
   Rushani, 105
   Samnani, 103
   Sargilami, 105
   Sarikoli, 105, 106
   Savo, 38
   Sedanka, 7
   Shughni, 105
   Tagaur, 103
   Taiga (Yurak), 17
   Tallinn, 34
   Tartu-Setu, 34
   Thush, 98
   Torgout, 60
   Tundra (Yukagir), 8
   (Yurak), 17
   Upper Kolyma, 8
   Vatka, 28
   Viru, 111
   Viryal, 82
   Vychegda-Pechora, 26
   Wakhi, 105, 106
   Wanchi, 105
   Yaghnobi, 102, 105
   Yazghulami, 105
Digor, *see* dialect
diminutive, 41
diphthong, 8, 35, 37, 60, 79, 92, 103
direct, *see* object
directive, *see* case
Dirr, A., 86
disjunctive, *see* case
Dnieper, *see* River
Dolgans, 19
Donelaitis, K., 113
Donner, Kai, 19
   Otto, 14
Dravidian, 1
Dregoviči, 117
dual, *see* number

dubitativus abhorrens, 61
   optans, 61
Dudinka, 20
Duléby, 118
Dumézil, G., 87
Düna, *see* Dvina, Western
durative, *see* aspect
Dvina, Northern, *see* River
   Western, *see* River
Dyrenkova, N. M., 73
Dyushambe, 102
Džabajev, Džambul, 75
Dzaujikau, 102
Dzungaria, 58

ejective, *see* consonant
elative, *see* case
Elista, 58
Elkenbeye, *see* Negidal
Ema, *see* River
Embach, *see* Ema
Enciclopedia Italiana, 63
Encyclopedia, Brockhaus-Efron, 64
   Minor Soviet, 80
Enets, *see* Yenisei Samoyed
English, 108, 116, 117
epicene, *see* case
equative, *see* case
Erckert, R. von, 86
Erevan, 102, 119
ergative, *see* case; construction
Ermanaric, 30, 39
Erthani, 30
Erz'ä, *see* Erzya
Erzya, *see* dialect
Eskimo, 4, 8
essive, *see* case
Estonia, 38
Estonian, 21, 33, 35, 36, 38, 39, 40, 41, 42, 44, 47, 109, 110, 111, 112, 113; *see also* Republic
Ethiopian, 108
Eurasia, 52
Europe, 20, 52
Even, *see* Lamut
Evenki, *see* Area; Tungus
exablative, *see* case
exclusive, *see* conjugation, objective

Fellin, *see* Viljandi
Fenni, 2

INDEX

Fergana, 64
Fifth, Vodian, 41
Fijian, *see* alphabet
final, *see* syllable; vowel
Finck, F. N., 99
finite, *see* verb
finitive, *see* case
Finland, 37, 42, 43; *see also* Gulf of
Finlandia irredenta, 37
Finnar, 25
Finnic, 16, 19, 20, 24, 40, 45, 46, 47
  East, 24, 29, 47
  West, 11, 24, 25, 26, 27, 30, 31, 33, 35, 36, 37, 39, 43, 44, 45, 47, 48, 111
Finnisch-Ugrische Forschungen, 48
Finnish, 21, 31, 35, 36, 37, 38, 40, 41, 42, 43, 46, 47, 48, 68, 101
Finno-Ugrian, 20, 22
Finns, 34, 37
flexion, 17, 31, 53, 60, 62, 99, 117
flexional, *see* conjugation
fokváltakozás, *see* alternation, consonantal
formant, 106
French, 117
frequentative, *see* verb
fricative, *see* consonant
front, *see* vowel
Frunze, 74, 76
future, *see* tense

Gagauzi, 64, 70, 80, 83
Galicia, 118
Γαλίνδαι, 110
Garðaríki, 38
Garuḍa, 56
Gasprinskij, Izmail, 80
Ge'ez, *see* Ethiopian
Geiger, W., 105
geminated, *see* consonant
gender, 9, 10, 11, 22, 53, 57, 88, 90, 96, 99, 103, 108, 111, 112, 113, 116
  animate, 28
  inanimate, 28
Genetz, A., 43, 48
genitive, *see* case
genitive-accusative, *see* case
Georgia, 87, 102, 107
Georgian, 87, 97, 98, 99, 101, 102, 108, 109, 119
  Old, 98, 99
  see also Republic

Georgians, 88
German, 112, 115, 117
  Low, 36, 110
Germania, 34, 43
Germanic, 36, 108
gerund, 60, 74, 75, 104
Ghalchah, 106, 109
Gilaki, *see* dialect
Gilyak, 3, 4, 9, 10, 13
glottal, *see* consonant
glottalised, *see* consonant
Gold, 54
Golds, 58
Gothic, *see* alphabet
Gothic, 107, 114
Goths, 30
Greek, 99, 101, 116
  Old, 97, 113
Greeks, 97
Grierson, G. A., 105
Grozny, *see* province
Gulf, Khatanga, 17
  of Finland, 34
Gunsteinn, 25
Gurian, *see* dialect
Gypsies, 104, 106

Hálogaland, 25, 38
Hämäläinen, 43
Hanti-hə, *see* Khanty
Hanty, *see* Khanty
harmony, vowel, 4, 5, 6, 14, 16, 18, 28, 31, 35, 40, 42, 45, 53, 55, 57, 60, 61, 65, 66, 67, 69, 72, 75, 76, 78, 81, 83, 84, 111
Hazara, 58
Heimskringla, 25
Herat, 70
Herodotus, 27, 30
Hevesy, W., 1
Hiiumaa, 34
Hindu Kush, 104
Hindustani, 116
Hirt, H., 66
hiss-sibilant, *see* sibilant, hiss
Historiae adversus paganos, 25
Hólmgarðr, 40
holophrase, 4
Horde, Golden, 79
Hübschmann, H., 108
Hunfalvy, 14

Hungarian, 21, 22, 23, 24, 46, 47, 62, 68, 82, 102, 111, 112
Hungarians, 102
Hungary, 21
Huns, 52
hush-sibilant, *see* sibilant, hush
hypothesis, Uralo-Altaic, 14
hypothetical, *see* mood

I-chia, 12
I.P.A., *see* alphabet
Iberi, 97
Ibero-Cucasian, *see* Iverian
῎Ιβηρες, *see* Iberi
ideograms, 59
Igaunians, 34
Ili, *see* Taranchi
Ilian, 54
Il'ja Muromec, 30
illative, *see* case
Imeretian, *see* Imerian
Imerian, *see* dialect
Imniscaris, 30
imperative, *see* mood; suffix
imperfect, *see* tense
inanimate, *see* gender
inceptive, *see* case
inclusive, *see* conjugation, subjective
incorporation, 4, 6, 33
indefinite, *see* case; mood
index, 11, 35, 37, 45, 47, 78, 88, 90, 95
India, 1, 52
Indic, 110
indicative, *see* mood
indirect, *see* object
Indo-European, 1, 12, 66, 67, 86, 99, 102, 104, 107, 108; *see also* languages
inessive, *see* case
infinitive, *see* mood
infix, 9, 114
Ingilo, *see* dialect
initial, *see* syllable
Ingermannland, *see* Ingria
Ingilo, *see* dialect
Ingria, 37, 41, 42
Ingrian, *see* dialect
Ingush, 86, 92, 93
Inkagir, 54
inscriptions, Orkhon, 65, 68, 69, 73
    Yenisei, 68

Institute, Chuvash Research, 82
    Leningrad Oriental, 24
    Northern Peoples', 9
instructive, *see* case
instrumental, *see* case
interdental, *see* consonant
interrogative, *see* mood; particle; pronoun
intransitive, *see* conjugation; verb
Ir, *see* Ossetic
Iran, *see* Persia
Iranians, 27
Iranic, 2, 27, 30, 102, 103, 108, 110
Irtysh, *see* River
Ishim, *see* Tartar
Ishkashmi, *see* dialect
Istanbul, 107
Isurian, *see* Ingrian
Itä-Karjala, *see* Carelia, Eastern
Italian, 39
Itel'men, *see* Kamchadal
iterative, *see* aspect
Ivan IV, 80
Ívar Vídfamne, King, 38
Iverian, *see* Caucasian, South
Izhevsk, 27

Jakovlev, I. J., 82
Jakovlev, N. F., 89
Jakstere Tešte, 33
Japan, 3, 10
Japanese, 3, 10, 12, 14
Japanese (people), 55
Japhetic, 108
Jek, 86, 90
Jelgava, 111
Jenghiz Khan, 59
Jevsev'jev, M. E., 32
Jews, 74, 104
Jochelson, V. M., 7
Jomala, 25, 38
Jordanes, 30, 102
Jornandes, *see* Jordanes
Juslajev, Salavat, 79

Kabardin, 87, 92, 94, 95
Kabardins, 71
Kacha, 17
Kajvany, 39
Kakhetin, *see* dialect
Kalevala, 37

INDEX

Kalinin, *see* province
Kaliningrad, *see* province
Kalmez, *see* dialect
Kalmyk, 58, 59, 60, 62, 81; *see also* literature; Republic
Kalmyks, 58, 59, 70, 72
Kama, *see* dialect; River
Kamass, 17
Kamasses, 19
Kamchadal, 3, 7
Kamchadals, 7
Kamchatka, 3, 54
Kangalass, 54
Kanin, *see* peninsula
Kara, *see* River
Kara-Kirgiz, *see* Kirgiz
Karachay, 64, 66, 73, 76, 77, 86; *see also* province
Karachays, 70
Karafuto, *see* Sakhalin, Southern
Karagass, 17, 72
Karagasses, 19
Karagin, *see* dialect
Karaim, 64, 66
Karakalpak, 64, 74, 76, 77; *see also* Republic
Karela, *see* Carelia
Karl, 25
Kartvelian, *see* Caucasian, South
Kashgar, 64, 65
Katong, *see* Area
Kaunas, 113; *see also* province
Kazak, 19
Kazak-Kirgiz, *see* Kazakh
Kazakh, 64, 74, 75, 76, 77, 78; *see also* literature
Kazakhs, 70, 75
Kazakhstan, 74
Kazan', 27, 79, 80, 81
Kazikumukh, *see* Lak
Keleti Szemle, 48
Kemal, Mustafa, 71
Ket, *see* Ostyak, Yenisei
Kets, *see* Ostyaks, Yenisei
Kettunen, L., 37
Khabarovsk, *see* Region
Khaidak, *see* dialect
Khakass, 64
Khanty, 22
Khanty-Mansi, *see* Area
Khar'yuz, *see* dialect

Khasav-Yurt, *see* dialect
Khatanga, *see* Gulf; River
Khazars, 53, 80
Khevzur, *see* dialect
Khinalugh, 86, 92
Khiva, 64
Khorezmi, 64, 65
Khotan, 64
Khutsuri, *see* alphabet
Kiev, 118
Kile, 54
Kipchak, 64, 65
Kipchaks, 52
Kireng, *see* Katong
Kirgiz, 53, 70, 74, 76
Kirgizia, 74
Kirgiz-Kaisak, *see* Kazakh
Kislovodsk, 96
Klaipėda, *see* Memel
Koibal, 17, 65, 72
Koibals, 19
Kola, *see* peninsula
Kolarian, 1
Kolyma, *see* River
Komi, *see* Republic; Zyryan
Komi-Permyak, *see* Area
Komia, 21
Königsberg, *see* Kaliningrad
Korea, 3
Korean, 3, 4, 10, 12, 14, 61
Korela, *see* Carelia
Korš, F. E., 64
Koryak, 3, 4, 5, 6, 7, 8; *see also* Area
Koškin, *see* Al'kor, Ja. P.
Kostroma, *see* province
Kot, 11
Kots, 12
Kovno, *see* Kaunas
kraj, see Region
Krasnoyarsk, *see* Region
Krivičí, 115
Krymchak, *see* Tartar, South Crimean
Kubachi, 86
Kublai Khan, 59
Kudatku Bilik, 70
kul'tbaza, *see* base, culture
Kunos, I., 48
Küri, *see* Kyuri
Kuriles, 10
Kurzeme, *see* Curonia
Kyakar, 54

169

Kyakh, *see* Circassian
Kyrjalabotn, 38
Kyuri, *see* dialect
Kьzьl Kьrgьzstan, 76

Laatokka, *see* Ladoga
labial, *see* consonant
labialised, *see* consonant
Ladoga, *see* Lake
Lak, 86, 89
Lake Baikal, 19
  Ladoga, 37
  Onega, 39
  Peipsi, 35
Lalegir, 54
Lamut, 8, 14, 54
Lamuts, 55, 58
languages, Altaic, 52–84
  Indo-European, 102–20
  North Caucasian, 86–96
  Palaeoasiatic, 3–13
  South Caucasian, 97–101
  Uralian, 14–50
Lapp, 43
Lappish, 17, 39, 42, 43, 44, 45, 46
  Kola, 43, 44, 45, 46, 48
  see also literature
Lapps, 22, 25, 42, 43
  Kola, 42
Laptev, *see* Sea
Latgalian, *see* dialect
Latin, 117; *see also* alphabet
lative, *see* case
Latvian, 17, 34, 35, 37, 109, 110, 111, 112, 113, 114, 115; *see also* Republic
Laz, 87, 98
Lazistan, 98
Lemberg, 118
Lenin, 71
Leningrad, 9, 38
Lentz, W., 106, 107
letters, *see* alphabet
Lezgin, 89, 90, 91, 92
limitative, *see* case
lingua franca, 1, 92, 115, 120
liquid, *see* consonant
literature, Abkhaz, 84
  Azerbaijani, 84
  Bashkir, 79
  Buryat, 59
  Chukcha, 6

Chuvash, 82
Kalmyk, 59
Kazakh, 75
Koryak, 6
Lappish, Kola, 42
Livonian, 37
Mordvin, 33
Ostyak, 22
Tartar, 80
Tungus, 58
Votyak, 29
Zyryan, 26
Lithuania, 117
Lithuanian, 34, 109, 110, 111, 112, 113, 114, 115
  High, 112
  Low, 112
  see also Republic
Livonian, 33, 36, 39, 40, 41, 42, 115; *see also* literature
Livonians, 34, 36
loan, *see* loan-word
loan-words, 13, 19, 20, 36, 39, 42, 43, 48, 52, 56, 58, 73, 82, 92, 101, 110, 115
Lobnor, 64
local, *see* case
locative, *see* case
Loorits, O., 37
Ludian, *see* dialect
Ludians, 41
Luga, *see* River
Luoravetlan, *see* Chukcha
Lūtsa, 19
Luuga, *see* Luga
Lytkin, 49
L'viv, *see* Lemberg
Lwów, *see* Lemberg

Madur, *see* Motor
Magyar, 22
Maikop, 87
Maišev, I. I., 26
Makhachkala, 77, 90
Manchu, 12, 54; *see also* alphabet
Manchukuo, *see* Manchuria
Manchuria, 12, 54, 59
Manchurian, 52, 53, 54, 55, 61, 62, 66
Manchus, 55, 56, 62
Mandarin, *see* Chinese
Manegir, 54

INDEX

Mangun, *see* Olcha
Manja Keln, 59
Mansi, *see* Vogul
Mari, *see* Cheremiss; Republic
Marr, N. J., 86, 87, 97, 99, 107
matriarchate, 13
Maya, 54
Mazandarani, *see* dialect
Mažvydas, M., 113
Mediterranean, *see* Sea
Megrel, *see* Mingrelian
Meillet, A., 119, 120
Melanchlaeni, 30
Μελάγχλαινοι, 30
Melanesian, 10, 66
Melioranskij, P. M., 64
Memel, *see* Area; River
Merens, 30
Merja, 30
Meskh, *see* dialect
Mesrop, St, 97, 107
Meščera, 30
metathesis, 77
Miller, V., 104
Mingrelian, 87, 98, 101
Mingrelians, 101
Minjani, *see* dialect
Minsk, 117
Mishar, 73
Mitau, *see* Jelgava
mkhedruli, *see* alphabet
modality, 8, 56
Mokša, *see* dialect
Mongolia, 52, 56, 67
   Outer, 72
Mongolian, 52, 53, 56, 60, 61, 62, 66, 81
   Khalkha, 13, 58, 59, 62
   proper (Literary), 58, 59, 62
   see also alphabet; Republic
Mongols, 59
mood, 22, 45, 47, 48, 57, 60, 75, 78, 89, 92, 95, 100
   affirmative, 96
   auditive, 18
   benedictive, 62
   concessive, 10, 47
   conditional, 6, 28, 32, 82, 95, 112, 114
   confirmative, 96
   conjunctive, 47
   definite, 8
   desiderative, 32
   hypothetical, 10, 18, 57
   imperative, 8, 16, 26, 28, 53, 62, 90, 96, 109
   indefinite, 8
   indicative, 6, 26, 47, 90, 103
   infinitive, 39, 48, 104, 105, 115
   interrogative, 96
   necessitative, 57, 90
   negative, 96
   optative, 6, 28, 47, 90, 96, 100, 114
   potential, 8, 10, 47
   precative, 62
   prescriptive, 62
   relative, 36, 112
   subjunctive, 6, 16, 32, 101, 103
Mordia, 30
Μορδία, 30
Mordens, 30
Mordva, *see* Republic
Mordvin, 30, 31, 32, 33, 45, 46, 47, 48, 81, 82, 108; *see also* literature
Mordvins, 29
morpheme, 10, 23, 36, 47, 84, 91
morphology, 32, 44, 73, 77, 79, 90
Moscow, 26, 115
motive, *see* case
Motor, 17
Motors, 19
Možgin, M., 29
Mthiul, *see* dialect
Müller, F., 69
multiplicative, *see* numeration
Munḍa, *see* Kolarian
Munji, *see* Minjani
Munkácsi, B., 24, 28, 48
Muroma, 30
Mykhad, *see* Rutul

Nal'chik, 77, 87
Nanai, *see* Gold
Naryan-Mar, 20
nasal, *see* consonant
necessitative, *see* mood
negation, 48, 67
negative, *see* conjugation; mood; particle; suffix; verb
Negda, *see* Negidal
Negidal, 54
Németh, Gyula, 63
Nehrung, Kurische, 109

Neman, *see* River
Nemunas, *see* Neman
Nenecia, 20
Nenets, *see* Area; Samoyed, Yurak
Nganasan, *see* Samoyed, Tavgi
Nivkh, *see* Gilyak
Nogay, 75, 76, 77, 78, 80
Nogays, 77
nomina verbalia, 62
nominative, *see* case; construction
North Caucasian, *see* languages
North Ossete, *see* Republic
Norwegian, 43
noun, 5, 6, 8, 18, 22, 26, 32, 47, 60, 61, 62, 67, 89, 91, 92, 95, 96, 100, 104, 108, 119
Novaya Zemlya, 17
Novgorod, *see* province
Novgorod the Great, 26, 27, 40, 41, 115
Novgorodov, S. P., 73
Nukus, 74
number, 6, 10, 18, 28, 56, 62, 88, 91, 92, 106, 112
 dual, 5, 22, 23, 45, 53, 113, 114
 singular, 5, 28, 99
 plural, 5, 6, 9, 10, 28, 88, 99, 106
numeral, 5, 16; *see also* system
numeration, 4, 22, 44, 47, 48, 68, 73, 77, 89, 100, 108, 112, 114
 additive, 10
 decimal, 5, 8, 18, 112
 multiplicative, 10
 quintal, 7
 subtractive, 10, 11, 44
 trial, 8
 vigesimal, 10, 91, 100
Nymylan, *see* Koryak

Oandi, *see* Ugandi
Ob′, *see* River
Obdorsk, *see* Salekhard
obessive, *see* case
object, 8, 32, 45, 61, 62
 direct, 76, 94, 101
 indirect, 100
objective, *see* conjugation; construction
oblique, *see* case
Ocean, Arctic, 3, 55
 Pacific, 12, 14, 55
Od Vele, 33

'Ode to Felica', 74
Odul, *see* Yukagir
Odulok, Teki, *see* Spiridonov, N.
Oguz, 65
Ohthere, *see* Óttarr
Oirot, 64, 65, 73, 76; *see also* province
Oirottura, 73
Oka, *see* River
Okhotsk, *see* Sea
okrug, *see* Area, National
Óláfr Haraldsson, King, 25
Óláfr Tryggvason, King, 30
Olav, St, *see* Óláfr Haraldsson, King
Olcha, 54
Olonecia, 43
Olonecian, *see* dialect
Omsk, *see* province
Onega, *see* Lake
Onkor, 54
open, *see* syllable
optative, *see* mood; suffix
Ordoss, 58
Orkhon, *see* inscriptions; River
Oroch, 54
Orochel, 54
Oroches, 54
Orochon, 54, 55
Orok, 54
Oroshori, *see* dialect
Orosius, Paulus, 25
Os, *see* Ossetic
Ösel, *see* Saaremaa
Osmanli, *see* Turkish
Ossetes, 70
Ossetic, 77, 102, 103
Ostyak, 20, 21, 23, 45, 46, 48; *see also* literature; Samoyed
Ostyak, Yenisei, 4, 11, 12
Ostyaks, 19, 22
Ostyaks, Yenisei, 3
Óttarr, 25, 38
Oyat′, *see* River

Paasonen, H., 48
Pacific, *see* Ocean
Palaeoasiatic, 1, 4, 32, 67; *see also* languages
Palaeoasiatics, 12
palaeontology, linguistic, 108
Pamiri, 105
Pamirs, 2, 105

INDEX

palatalisation, 104, 119
palatalised, *see* consonant
Pallas, P. S., 17
Pannonia, 102
Papuan, 88
paradigm, adjectival, 44, 102
  nominal, 8, 22, 28, 44, 61, 74, 104, 106
  pronominal, 61, 94
  verbal, 6, 106
Parnavaz, King, 97
participle, 47, 60, 61, 74, 77, 84, 90, 93, 112, 114
particle, 10
  interrogative, 101
  negative, 36, 37, 42, 47, 100, 108, 114, 115
  syndetic, 53, 81, 92
passive, *see* case; voice
past, *see* tense
Πατзινακία, 30
Pecheneg, 65
Pechenegia, 30
Pechenegs, 52
Pechora, *see* River
Peipsi, *see* Lake
Peipus, *see* Peipsi
Pekarskij, E. K., 72
peninsula, Kanin, 17, 20
  Kola, 42
  Taimyr, 17, 55
Penza, 33
perfect, *see* tense
Perm′, 24, 25
Permian, 24, 26, 28, 30, 47
Permians, 27, 38
Permyak, 26, 27
Permyaks, 25
Persia, 83
Persian, 84, 101, 102, 103, 104, 105, 106, 108, 109
person, 6, 18, 56, 62, 67, 82, 91, 92, 96, 100
personal, *see* pronoun
Peter the Great, 21
Petermann, 108
Petrozavodsk, 37
'Phagspa, 59
phoneme, 22, 44, 60, 72, 78, 81, 87, 88, 89, 93, 94, 101, 103, 104
phonetic, *see* system

phonetics, 44, 79
Pillai, T. R., 1
Pishpek, *see* Frunze
plain, Major Danubian, 102
pleophony, 119
plosive, *see* consonant
plural, *see* number; suffix
Poland, 117
Polish, 110, 117, 118
Polovecian, *see* Cumanic
Pombak, 19
Portuguese, 117
possessive, *see* adjective; case; pronoun; suffix
postposition, 10, 22, 26, 56, 78, 91, 99, 100, 103, 104, 106
postpositive, *see* article
potential, *see* mood
Poti, 101
Povĕst' vremennych lĕt, 36
precative, *see* mood
predicate, 5, 32, 45, 53, 89
predicative, *see* suffix
prefix, 5, 7, 37, 99, 100, 112
preposition, 103, 104, 108
prescriptive, *see* mood
preterite, *see* tense
privative, *see* case
Procopius, 43
progressive, *see* tense; verb
prolative, *see* case
pronominal, *see* system
pronoun, 5, 6, 9, 22, 26, 92
  demonstrative, 36, 41, 89, 112
  interrogative, 16, 28
  personal, 10, 16, 28, 36, 44, 45, 60, 61, 66, 75, 89, 90, 95, 106, 108
  possessive, 16, 60, 78, 96
  reflexive, 28
prosecutive, *see* case
Province, Grozny, 86
  Kalinin, 38
  Kaliningrad, 110
  Karachay Autonomous, 77
  Kaunas, 112
  Kostroma, 116
  Leningrad, 41
  Novgorod, 38
  Oirot Autonomous, 73
  Omsk, 21
  Petseri, 35

Province, South Ossete Autonomous, 102
Suvalkai, 112
Sverdlovsk, 26
Tartu, 35
Valga, 35
Viljandi, 35
Vilnius, 112
Vladimir, 116
Vodian, 41
Võru, 35
Yaroslavl', 116
Prussia, East, 109, 112
Prussian, Old, 111
Prussians, 110
Pshav, see dialect
Pskov, 116
Ptolemy, 110
Pugačov, Jemel'ka, 79
Pustozersk, see Naryan-Mar

qualified, 18, 32, 33, 61
qualifier, 18, 32, 33, 61
quintal, see numeration
Qutadgu Bilig, see Kudatku Bilik

Rachin, see dialect
radical, see base
Radloff, W., 72
Ramstedt, G. J., 62
reflexive, see pronoun; verb
Region, Khabarovsk, 3
Krasnoyarsk, 55
Stavropol', 77
Reguly, 22, 24
Reichelt, H., 105
relative, see mood
Republic, Abkhaz Autonomous, 87
Adyge Autonomous, 87
Ajar Autonomous, 98
Armenian Federal, 102, 107
Azerbaijan Federal, 84
Bashkir Autonomous, 78
Buryat-Mongol Autonomous, 58
Carelo-Finnish, S.S., 37
Chechen-Ingush Autonomous, 86
Circassian Autonomous, 87
Daghestan Autonomous, 77, 90
Estonian, 33
Estonian S.S., 34
Georgian Federal, 87

Kalmyk Autonomous, 58
Karakalpak Autonomous, 72
Komi Autonomous, 26
Latvian S.S., 109
Lithuanian S.S., 109, 112
Mari Autonomous, 29
Mongolian People's, 58
Mordva Autonomous, 29, 32
North Ossete Autonomous, 102
of Tajikistan, 102, 106
of Turkmenistan, 83
Russian Federal, 117
Udmurt Autonomous, 27
Ukrainian Federal, 118
White Russian Federal, 117
Yakut Autonomous, 72
Revolution (October), 6, 8, 31, 33, 42, 58, 76, 82, 103, 117, 119, 120
(1905), 29
Riga, 36, 109
Rion, see River
River, Agul, 12
Amur, 3, 9, 54, 55, 58
Dnieper, 117
Kama, 26, 27
Khatanga, 20, 55
Kolyma, 63
Neman, 110, 112
Ob', 17, 20, 21, 22, 53
Orkhon, 69
Rion, 101
Selenga, 69
Shilka, 55
Sungari, 55
Sura, 115
Svir', 39
Tunguska, 55
Tyl, 71
Ussuri, 55
Volga, 29, 31, 58, 76, 115
Vyatka, 27
Western Dvina, 36, 117
Yana, 55
Yenisei, 12, 17, 53, 55
Rogov, 49
Romance (languages), 116
Rome, 41
root, 26
Roþs, 19
Rudenko, B. T., 99
Rudnev, A. D., 58

INDEX

Rumanian, 108
runiform, *see* alphabet
Rus, 19
Rus′, 41
Rushani, *see* dialect
Russia, 38, 41, 109
Russian, 1, 3, 7, 8, 23, 32, 39, 40, 78, 79, 80, 84, 110, 115, 116, 117, 118, 119, 120; *see also* Republic
Russians, 21, 25, 27, 29, 31
Ruthenia, Subcarpathian, 118
Ruthenian, 118
Rutul, 86, 90
Ryurik, 40

Saam, *see* Lappish, Kola
Saams, *see* Lapps, Kola
Saaremaa, 34
Sabme(laš), *see* Lappish
Sagai, 17
Sakha, *see* Yakut
Sakhalin, 1, 3, 9, 10, 54
Salekhard, 20
Samagir, 54
Samarkand, 70, 83
Same, *see* Lappish
Samnani, *see* dialect
Samojlovič, A. N., 64, 77, 78
Samoyed, Ostyak, 17, 19
   Tavgi, 17, 18
   Yenisei, 17
   Yurak, 17, 18
Samoyedic, 16, 17, 19, 47
Samoyeds, 19, 20, 22, 24, 55
Saransk, 79
Sargilami, *see* dialect
Sarikoli, *see* dialect
Sary-Yugur, 64
Šaumjan, R., 91
Sauvageot, A., 14, 63
Savakot, 41
Savo, *see* dialect
Scandinavia, 42
Scandinavian, 32
Schmidt, P., *see* Šmits, P.
Schrenck, L. von, 4, 54
script, *see* alphabet
Σκριθίφινοι, 43
Scritovinni, 43
Scythian, 1
Sea, Baltic, 14

Black, 87
Caspian, 76
East Siberian, 63
Laptev, 55
Mediterranean, 63
of Okhotsk, 10, 14, 55
White, 17
Sedanka, *see* dialect
Selenga, *see* River
Sel′kup, *see* Samoyed, Ostyak
semelfactive, *see* aspect
semipalatalised, *see* consonant
Semitic, 49, 66, 99; *see also* alphabet
sentence, 7, 23, 53, 57
Serbian, 113
series, possessive, 57
   apophonic, 65
Setälä, E. N., 16, 22, 43, 48, 49, 50
Shaw, R. B., 106
Shibos, 54
Shikotan, *see* Kuriles
Shilka, *see* River
Shor, 64
Shore, Carelian, 38
Shors, 70
Shughnani, *see* Shughni
Shughni, *see* dialect
Shumshu, 7
Siberia, 3, 11, 12, 19, 20, 21, 63, 72, 79, 115, 117
Siberian, East, *see* Sea
sibilant, hiss, 39, 65, 101, 113, 116
   hush, 39, 65, 93, 101, 113, 116
Sievers, E., 108
Sineus, 40
singular, *see* number
Sinitic, 11
Sjögren, J. A., 38, 43
Slavonic, 1, 36, 81, 108, 110, 112, 114
   Church, 116
   East, 115, 119
   Old Church, 117
Slověne, 115
Šmits, P., 3, 12, 54, 63
sociative, *see* case
Society, Bashkir Learned, 79
Sogdian, 59, 69, 112
Solon, 54
Somali, 90
Somian, *see* Finnic
Šorcy, *see* Shors

175

South Caucasian, *see* languages
South Ossete, *see* province
Soyot, *see* Tuva
Soyots, 19
Spanish, 108, 117
spatial, *see* local
Spiridonov, N., 74
Sremniscans, 30
Stalinabad, 102
Stalingrad, 115
Stalinir, 102
State, construct, 56
Stavropol', *see* province
Stebnickij, S. N., 7
Stefan, St (of Perm'), 24, 25, 49
stem, *see* base
Sternberg, L. G., 9
Stolbovo, Treaty of, 41
Strahlenberg, P. J. von, 17
Strait, Bering, 3
stress, 10, 11, 22, 31, 35, 60, 111, 113
stroj, *see* construction
Stufenwechsel, *see* alternation, consonantal
Sturluson, Snorri, 25, 34
subject, 5, 6, 7, 10, 18, 23, 45, 53, 60, 100
subjective, *see* conjugation; construction
subjunctive, *see* mood
subtractive, *see* numeration
suffix, 18, 57, 62, 66, 67, 68, 89, 95, 99, 100, 104, 114, 115
   aspective, 27
   case, 28, 66
   imperative, 48
   negative, 74
   optative, 46
   plural, 11, 47, 56, 57, 78, 81
   possessive, 18, 22, 26, 28, 44, 47, 53, 60, 62, 75, 81
   predicative, 56, 82
Sukhumi, 87
Sungari, *see* River
superallative, *see* case
superessive, *see* case
Sura, *see* River
Suvalkai, *see* province
Svan, *see* Svanetian
Svanetian, 87, 98, 100
Svanetians, 101
Sverdlovsk, *see* province
Svir', *see* River
Sweden, 41

Syktyvkar, 26
syllable, final, 60
   initial, 26, 32, 60
   open, 53
syndetic, *see* particle
synharmonism, *see* harmony, vowel
syntagma, 28
syntax, 7, 8, 32, 61, 75, 77, 79, 91, 93, 101, 104, 117
Syriac, Estrangelo, 69
system, consonantal, 17, 31, 60, 66, 75, 89, 94, 103, 104, 105, 111
   numeral, 9
   phonetic, 7, 26, 28, 42, 76, 91
   pronominal, 96
   verbal, 5, 94, 95, 104, 111, 115
   vowel, 94, 104, 108
Syväri, *see* Svir'

Tabassaran, 86, 89, 90, 93
Tacitus, 34, 43
Tagalog, *see* alphabet
Tagaur, *see* dialect
Tagliavini, C., 63
Taiga (Yurak), *see* dialect
Taimyr, *see* peninsula; Area
Tajiki, 102, 104, 105, 106
Tajikistan, *see* Republic
Tallinn, 34; *see also* dialect
Talysh, 102, 103, 104
Tannu Tuva, 72
Taranchi, 64, 66
Tardžiman, 80
Tartar, 23, 28, 32, 33; *see also* literature
   Ishim, 79
   North Crimean, 64, 80
   South Crimean, 64, 77, 80
   Tobol, 64, 79
   Tyumen', 79
   Volga, 64, 70, 77, 78, 79, 80, 81
Tartars, 27, 53, 80
   Crimean, 70
   Volga, 70
Tartary, 11
Tartu, *see* province
Tartu-Setu, *see* dialect
Tashkent, 83
Tat, 102, 103, 104, 105
Tatars, *see* Tartars
Tavgi, *see* Samoyed
Tbilisi, 87, 119

INDEX

Teleut, 73
tense, 9, 22, 32, 45, 47, 56, 57, 60, 61, 67, 75, 78, 89, 90, 92, 94, 95, 100, 103, 104, 114, 115
  aorist, 18, 100
  compound, 29
  future, 11, 26, 28, 36, 57, 62, 96, 100, 106, 112, 114
  imperfect, 8, 114
  past, 6, 17, 26, 36, 45, 47, 61, 95
  perfect, 6, 8, 9, 47, 100
  present, 6, 36, 45, 61, 100, 105, 114, 118
  preterite, 16, 18, 62, 106, 112, 114
  progressive, 47
Tepter, 64
terminative, *see* case
Tesnière, L., 63
theory, Austric, 11
Thomsen, V., 65, 69, 72
Þórir Hundr, 25, 38
Thush, *see* dialect
Tibet, 58
Tibetan, 59
Tiflis, *see* Tbilisi
time, *see* tense
Tobol, *see* Tartar
Tobol'sk, 21
Tomaschek, W., 27, 30
tone, 9, 10, 111, 112, 113
Torgout, *see* dialect
Transbaikalia, 58
Transcaucasia, 92
transcription, 29, 48, 73
transitive, *see* conjugation; verb
translative, *see* case
trial, *see* numeration
Trombetti, 11
Trubetzkoy, Prince N., 86, 93
Trubeckoj, *see* Trubetzkoy
Truvor, 40
Tsakhur, 86, 90
Tsarevokokshaisk, *see* Yoshkar Ola
Tsinkhval, *see* Stalinir
Tśin' Stjamo, 33
Tsova-Tush, 86, 92, 98
Tuba, 73
Tundra (Yukagir), *see* dialect
  (Yurak), *see* dialect
Tungus, 3; *see also* literature
  (people), 19, 55
  proper, 54

Tungusic, 52, 54, 55, 56, 57, 58
Tunguska, *see* River
Turania, 80
Turanian, *see* Turkic
Turcoman, *see* Turkmen
Turfan, 64
Turkestan, Chinese, 83, 105
Turkey, 71, 72, 95, 107
Turkic, 17, 19, 20, 30, 48, 52, 53, 56, 61, 62, 63, 66, 67, 68, 78, 80, 83, 84, 104
Turkish, 21, 62, 64, 65, 67, 68, 80, 83, 84
Turkmen, 64, 73, 76, 83, 84
Turkmeni, *see* Turkmen
Turkmenistan, *see* Republic
Turkmens, 70
Turuk, 64
Tuva, 17
Tver', *see* Kalinin
Tyl, *see* River
Tyumen', *see* Tartar

U.S.S.R., 1, 10, 16, 21, 24, 33, 34, 38, 39, 57, 58, 63, 71, 74, 80, 109, 115, 119
Ubykh, 87
Ubykhs, 95
Uchur, 54
Ude, 54
Udekhe, *see* Ude
Udi, 86, 89, 92
Udmurt, *see* Votyak; Republic
Ufa, 78
Ugandi, 34
Uigur, 55, 59, 65; *see also* alphabet
Ugrian, 16, 19, 20, 21, 23, 24, 25, 26, 32, 45, 46, 47, 48, 49
  East, 21, 48
Ugrians, 20, 21, 22
Ukrainian, 78, 115, 117, 118, 119; *see also* Republic
Ulan-Bator, 58
Ulan-Ude, 58
Ul'yanovsk, 33
uncial, *see* alphabet
uninflected, *see* conjugation
Union, Soviet, 29, 47
Upper Kolyma, *see* dialect
Uralian, 1, 11, 14, 16, 19, 21, 22, 27, 49, 52, 63, 66, 67, 68; *see also* languages

Uralians, 19, 21, 24
Uralo-Altaic, 14
Urals, 21, 34
Urga, *see* Ulan-Bator
Uryankhai, *see* Tuva
Uslar, Baron P. K., 86, 93
Ussuri, *see* River
Ustav o mostěch, 41
Ust'sysol'sk, 26
uvular, *see* consonant
Uyghur, *see* Uigur
Uzbek, 64, 76, 81, 83, 104
Uzbeki, *see* Uzbek
  Old, *see* Chagatai
Uzbekistan, 75, 83, 104

Vadja, *see* Vodian
Väina, *see* Dvina, Western
Vakh, *see* River
Valga, *see* province
Varnefrid, Paul, 43
Vasilevič, G. M., 57
Vasina-broncas, 39
Vasyugan, *see* River
Vatka, *see* dialect
velar, *see* consonant
Velynjane, 118
Ventspils, 36
Vepsian, 36, 39, 40, 41, 42
verbal, *see* system
verb, 5, 8, 9, 10, 11, 18, 26, 28, 36, 45, 47, 53, 56, 60, 61, 62, 63, 67, 68, 75, 82, 89, 91, 92, 93, 96, 103, 104, 108, 109, 112, 114, 117
  auxiliary, 29
  causative, 56
  finite, 49, 57, 60, 67, 105
  frequentative, 48
  intransitive, 5, 18, 23, 88, 91, 100
  negative, 36, 48
  progressive, 108
  reflexive, 56, 112
  transitive, 88, 91, 100
verbum finitum, 27
  infinitum, 27
Verkhneudinsk, 58
Verny, *see* Alma-Ata
Ves', 40
vigesimal, *see* numeration
Viljandi, 35; *see also* province
Vil'na, *see* Vilnius

Vilnius, 110; *see also* province
Virk', 97
Vironians, 34
Viru, 34; *see also* dialect
Viryal, *see* dialect
Visu, 39
Vladikavkaz, *see* Dzaujikau
Vladimir, *see* province
vocabulary, 16, 17, 36, 39, 40, 43, 47, 61, 66, 73, 75, 79, 84, 88, 93, 96, 101, 102, 104, 109, 118
vocative, *see* case
Vod', 27
Vodia, 41
Vodian, 27, 36, 39, 41, 42; *see also* province
Vodians, 41, 42
Vogul, 20, 21, 22, 23, 24
voice (diathesis), 10, 67, 100
  middle, 112, 114
  passive, 84
voiced, *see* consonant
voiceless, *see* consonant
Vojna ys' Ivor, 29
Volga, *see* River; Tartar
volost', *see* province
Volynia, 118
Võru, *see* province
Votish, *see* Vodian
Votud, 27
Votyak, 24, 27, 28, 29, 46, 48, 82; *see also* literature
Votyaks, 27, 28
vowel, 4, 5, 9, 26, 31, 35, 37, 53, 55, 57, 61, 65, 66, 69, 73, 75, 78, 79, 81, 84, 91, 95, 98, 100, 103, 104, 105, 111, 119
  back, 28, 35, 42, 100
  central, 57, 81, 101
  centralised, 18, 81
  final, 42, 62
  front, 16, 42, 100, 103, 118
  see also system
Vyatka, 27; *see also* River
Vychegda-Pechora, *see* dialect

Wakhi, *see* dialect
Wanchi, *see* dialect
Watland, 41
Weil, G., 79
Welsh, 56

INDEX

White Russian, 115, 117, 118, 119; *see also* Republic
Wiedemann, F. J., 35
Windau, *see* Ventspils
Windischmann, 108
Winkler, H., 14
Wizzi, 40
word-formation, 28, 33
word-order, 6, 10, 33, 61
writing, picture, 6, 8
Wulfstan, 34
Wyatt, J. L., 1

Xa Ošir, 59

Yaghnobi, *see* dialect
Yakut, 38, 53, 63, 64, 67, 68, 70, 72; *see also* Republic
Yakutia, 1, 14, 55, 68
Yakutsk, 72
Yakutskay, *see* Yakutsk
Yamal, *see* Area; peninsula
Yana, *see* River
yanalif, 70
Yaroslavl', *see* province
Yatvingians, 110
Yazghulami, *see* dialect
Yenisei, *see* Ostyak; River; Samoyed
Yeniseian, 54
Yoshkar-Ola, 29
Yugra, 21
Yukagir, 3, 4, 7, 8, 9, 10, 11; *see also* Area
Yura, 21
Yurak, *see* Samoyed
Yuraks, 19, 20

Zan, 87, 98
Zaya Paṇḍita, 59
Zebaki, *see* Ishkashmi
Zyryan, 20, 23, 24, 25, 26, 27, 28, 46, 47, 48, 49; *see also* literature
Zyryans, 24, 25